D0893416

Entertainment, Propaganda, Education

REGIONAL THEATRE IN GERMANY
AND BRITAIN
BETWEEN 1918 AND 1945

THE SOCIETY FOR THEATRE RESEARCH

Entertainment, Propaganda, Education

REGIONAL THEATRE IN GERMANY

AND BRITAIN

BETWEEN 1918 AND 1945

———

ANSELM HEINRICH

VOLUME EDITOR: TONY MEECH

UNIVERSITY OF HERTFORDSHIRE PRESS

THE SOCIETY FOR THEATRE RESEARCH

STR

First published in Great Britain in 2007 by
University of Hertfordshire Press
Learning and Information Services
University of Hertfordshire
College Lane
Hatfield
Hertfordshire AL10 9AB

British Library Cataloguing in Publication Data
A catalogue record for this book is available from the British Library

ISBN 978–1–902806–74–7 hardback
ISBN 978–1–902806–75–4 paperback

Design by Geoff Green Book Design, CB4 5RA
Cover design by John Robertshaw, Harpenden, AL5 2JB
Printed in Great Britain by Cromwell Press Ltd, BA14 0XB

For my parents,
Gerlinde and Carl-Joachim Heinrich

Contents

List of Figures

Cover Illustrations

German air force map, October 1939: aerial view of York's city centre. The German Luftwaffe took this image as a reconnaissance picture on 4th October 1939. The areas around the railway station, goods sidings and railway yards are clearly marked as a target for later bombing raids (City of York Council, local studies collection)

Theatre Royal York, c.1910, photographer I. J. Hodgson from Cleckheaton, showing the theatre's frontage as rebuilt in the 1870s (City of York Council, York Central Library)

Theatre Münster, c.1900, photographer unknown, showing the *Lortzing-Theater*, which opened in the Romberger Hof in 1895 (Münster City Archives, photographic collection no. 320)

Every effort has been made to contact copyright holders in order to seek permission to reproduce images. Where it has been impossible to trace copyright holders, the publishers would be pleased to hear from them.

Acknowledgements

It is a great pleasure to thank all those who have helped, encouraged and supported me in the course of writing this book. The study developed out of my doctoral dissertation at the Drama Department of the University of Hull. First of all, therefore, I would like to thank my supervisors Tony Meech and Terry Hale for their unfailing support, critical comments and friendship over the years. Equally I am obliged to my PhD examiners Alan Best (Hull) and in particular Viv Gardner (Manchester).

I am extremely grateful for the financial support I received from different organisations over the years. Awards and grants from the German Historical Institute London, the Society for Theatre Research, the German History Society, the Conference of University Teachers of German, the Drama Department and the Faculty of Arts at the University of Hull, St Deiniol's Library, Hawarden, and in particular two generous PhD scholarships from the University of Hull and the Stiftung für Bildung und Wissenschaft (im Stifterverband für die deutsche Wissenschaft) in Germany have made the research for this study possible. Crucial, too, was the support I enjoyed at various archives. Staff on many occasions went far beyond what I could have expected to retrieve some hidden document or provide help at short notice. In particular I would like to thank Rita Freedman and Letitia Lawson at York and Bradford city archives, Günther Högl and Bernd Wagner at Dortmund and Bielefeld city archives, as well as Wolfgang Türk from Münster's municipal theatre.

From the first unfocused attempts to define where I wanted to go with my research through to the last corrections to the manuscript I received much moral support and scholarly advice, suggestions and encouragement. Just being able to share where I was in the project often proved invaluable. My special thanks go to the following friends and colleagues: Christoph Müller (Dublin/Bremen), Fiona Wright (Hull), Katja Krebs (Glamorgan), Caro Miranda (Hull), Wolfgang Jacobmeyer (Münster), Konrad Dussel (Mannheim), Gerwin Strobl (Cardiff), Edward Royle (York), Angus Winchester, Keith Hanley, Andy Tate and Rachel Dickinson (all Lancaster), Alan Deighton, Michelle Delaney and Pauline Chambers (Hull), Richard Schoch (London), and Stephan Wackwitz (Goethe-Institut). I am also indebted to Alexander Hirt (Tübingen) for information on ENSA and Stefan Hüpping for letting me share his research on Osnabrück's theatre.

Thanks, too, go to my friends on 'home turf', who shared the pain (and a beer) on sometimes intense research trips. In particular I would like to thank Kai Hense and Bernd Göckmann, Klaus Klockenhoff, Thomas Kässens and Heiner Frankholz, Tanja and Andreas Schwarze, Wolfram van Well, Marina Bourgeois and Birgit Steffens, Anke Börsel, and Karsten Loer.

My special thanks are due to Jeffrey Richards (Lancaster) and Kate Newey (Birmingham) for opening my mind to the nineteenth century, for productive work on the *Ruskinian Theatre* project and enthusiasm for new approaches to theatre history, and for their endless support as the book proposal and the book itself took shape; to Benedikt Stuchtey and Hagen Schulze (London) for the opportunity to present my research at the German Historical Institute London and for much helpful feedback; to my friends at *Thalia Germanica*, in particular Bronwyn Tweddle (Wellington, New Zealand), Ieva Viluma (Riga), and Gunilla Dahlberg (Lund); to the Society for Theatre Research and in particular Eileen Cottis; to my colleagues in the Department of Theatre, Film and Television Studies at the University of Glasgow; to Jane Housham at the University of Hertfordshire Press and Richard Foulkes of the Society for Theatre Research, for publishing this book together, and for being so supportive and understanding in every phase of this project; to my sister Caroline for constantly challenging my way of thinking and broadening my perspective, and generally for being such a passionate, honest and intelligent scholar; and to my wife Anne and our daughter Lili who had to put up with a stressed husband and father for a long time, but supported me beyond words with their love.

Last, but not least, I want to thank my parents, Gerlinde and

Carl-Joachim Heinrich. Without their moral and financial support, their unfailing interest and curiosity, and their enduring love and friendship over the years, this book would not have been possible. I dedicate it to them.

Introduction

In January 1933 the *Theatre World*'s Central European correspondent published an article suggesting some reasons for the scant interest shown by the German theatre in contemporary British drama:

> Let us take an obvious example, *The Barretts of Wimpole Street*. This certainly ranks among the finest plays of recent years. It is not because the *Barretts* are less known in Germany than in England ... but the play as such would not appeal to a German audience. The first demands for a play in Germany are plot, action, drama and conflict, and not one of these is sufficiently developed in this play to make it attractive to the German public. In the *Barretts* there is just a flavour of incest and sadism without allowing it to mould into real conflict, problem or drama, as the Germans would have it. There is not a single manager in Germany who could be persuaded to stage the play.

The same correspondent then goes on to explain in some detail one of the main characteristics of the British play:

> If a certain scene is unrolled before the eyes of the spectator, it is difficult to conceive the necessity of repeating the contents of the scene and specially referring to it in another. Such repetitions are merely for the benefit of late-comers and members of the audience who stay for an act in the bar and wish to return to the play without having missed anything. ...
>
> Max Reinhardt, after reading a translation of a popular English play, remarked to me: 'Here goes another Derby-play.' Asking him what he meant by this expression he explained: 'That's a typical English play. Everything is repeated so often that play-goers can safely go to the races and be an hour late for the theatre without missing anything!'[1]

These remarks already seem to sum up the fundamental differences between the British and the German theatre. Plays which proved highly successful in Britain were 'more or less useless' in Germany, where large state subsidies, the seriousness with which the Germans regarded their theatre, and their 'odd' taste for monumental Schiller productions and the radical avant-garde amused British commentators. Max Reinhardt's comments on the 'Derby-play' likewise seem equally typical of German attitudes towards the British theatre system. They expressed their astonishment at the long prevailing influence of melodrama, farce and musical comedy. They commented on the thinness of productions on the commercial West End stage and looked askance at an audience, which seemed to lack both political consciousness and any kind of critical interest in aesthetics.[2]

Although it was not only remarked at the time, the claim coming from both sides of the Channel that the theatre in Britain and Germany is fundamentally different and incompatible has never been challenged. Scholars both then and now have systematically failed to address the possibility of similarities, and one looks in vain for detailed comparative studies. Hitherto, research has not only assumed that theatre in Britain and Germany developed along entirely different lines, but also that any points of contact, even the reciprocal interest in each other's theatrical system, simply did not exist. This study represents the first attempt to draw some new conclusions. In fact, on the basis of extensive primary research in British and German archives documented here, the detailed comparison of repertoires in both countries indicates that their theatres became increasingly similar during the Second World War. This finding in turn suggests that there is renewed scope for research into all aspects of Anglo-German cultural relations during the period and, indeed, the function of entertainment in general. In addition to a general awareness of the fundamental differences between theatre as a whole and the repertoire in particular, commentators in both countries had a lively interest in what was going on across the Channel. However, contemporary British commentators were not only concerned with spotting differences, they also wanted to adapt certain elements to their own advantage. During the late nineteenth century German music and drama were regularly performed in London, the debates for a National Theatre constantly referred to the German example and commentators were fascinated by the German theatre system. Ashley Dukes, for example, praised Munich's theatres for producing 'almost the entire list of controversial plays of the period' and added that all 'the works that our Stage Society had presented on experimental Sunday evenings were played here nightly as matter of course, before a regular and appreciative public'.[3] And from the mid-1950s onwards German interest in British drama has increased significantly.[4] In light of this it is astonishing, therefore, that a comparative study between theatre in Britain and Germany has not so far been undertaken.[5]

SOURCES, LITERATURE AND RESEARCH SITUATION

Research for this study has been carried out in local, regional and national archives, libraries and collections in Britain and Germany. One of the outcomes of this research has been the setting up of a database comprising complete lists of the repertoires at Yorkshire and Westphalian theatres. This primary material together with other archival sources, some of which have not previously been examined, forms the basis for this comparative study. Differences in archiving, however, have also become obvious. Whereas Westphalian authorities meticulously collected files relating to civic theatres, neither Yorkshire's city councils nor the theatres themselves tended to do so. Useful information, however, could be gathered from an increasing number of local history studies, which often use interviews with contemporary witnesses as a source.[6] Methodological issues, however, such as those concerning selective memory and reliability cannot be entirely ignored.[7]

Regarding the literature, although there are numerous studies of Britain and Germany during the twentieth century and especially the Second World War, there is an absence of comparative analyses.[8] With regard to theatre history, there are relatively few studies on British theatre history between the wars, and although theatre during the Third Reich has received increased scholarly attention during the last twenty years, the detailed examination of regional theatres represents a new field of study.[9] This desideratum has recently been addressed by scholars and has resulted in the AHRC project *An alternative history of the Victorian Theatre* and the corresponding conference *Shifting scenes: theatre histories beyond London*. Similarly, the *Theatre and Performance*

Research Association at their latest conference organised a session on *Does size matter? – micro-histories, macro-histories and grand narratives in theatre history*. This renewed interest in the relationship between the local/regional and the national/global was equally mirrored by the 2006 conference of the *International Federation for Theatre Research*.[10] This study relates to these themes and puts particular emphasis on regional repertoires within the context of national cultural landscapes. It will not simply discuss the histories of individual theatres in isolation but will relate them both to their local social, political and economic contexts and to one another. Such a focus might also help to question established notions of dichotomies between the popular versus the literary as well as national versus local. Ultimately, it will be interesting to investigate whether these networks of independent and influential regional playhouses increasingly constituted the national theatre.

Regarding the history of state funding of the arts in Britain, Minihan's *Nationalization of Culture* (1977) was helpful even though it is not solely concerned with theatre and hardly mentions the provinces. Weingärtner's recently published study on CEMA (*The Arts as a Weapon of War*) has proved invaluable although the author concentrates on policymaking and the history of the organisation rather than the performing arts themselves. Useful regional and local history studies included Holdsworth's *Domes of Delight* (1989), Hillerby's *Lost Theatres of Sheffield* (1999), Joy and Lennon's *Grand Memories* (2006), Wilkinson's *Grand Theatre and Opera House Leeds* (1977), and Rosenfeld's *The York Theatre* (1948/2001). More analytical studies such as Linda Fitzsimmons' articles (1981, 2004), however, are still thin on the ground. Similarly, in Westphalia research has largely concentrated on general city histories resulting in some well-documented multi-volume studies of Münster (Jakobi 1994), Dortmund (Högl 1994) and Bielefeld (Vogelsang 1988, 2005). More recently, some exciting work on particular theatres has been undertaken, of which Ketelsen's book on Bochum's theatre (1999) and collections on the centenaries of Bielefeld's and Dortmund's theatres (both 2004) have provided much insight. Additionally, regional history studies have contextualised findings especially with regard to the Nazi years, Möller (1996), and, with an emphasis on Westphalia, Ditt (1988) and Schmidt (2006). This attention has also led to numerous BA and MA dissertations at German universities. Additional information was gathered from contemporary publications, newspaper reviews, collections, biographies and memoirs, government directives, legal documents and memoranda, as well as private correspondence. Contemporary theatre periodicals have proved a particularly valuable source. Interestingly, the change in government perception of the arts in Britain during the war was accompanied by numerous publications on opera, ballet, individual theatres and actors, the sheer volume of which is astonishing.

Although it is almost impossible to avoid comparison, scholars have been nearly unanimous in stressing the alleged fundamental differences between theatre in Britain and Germany and the futility of comparative approaches. In his 1963 article, which is still regarded by many as seminal, Martin Esslin claimed that 'organisation and goals of the English theatre system are so fundamentally different from the German theatre world that it is very difficult to offer a description of the current situation to a German readership'.[11] According to Esslin it was not only the present situation which differed from the German experience but the entire tradition and history of British theatre.[12] Employing terms such as commercialism, repertoire and organisation, Esslin made it clear that, in contrast to Germany, 'artistic concepts *naturally* did not play any role in this kind of theatre'.[13] The foreign repertoire is another area often quoted to illustrate the differences. Commentators claim that whereas interest in playwriting from abroad has always been considerable in German-speaking countries British theatres have kept their 'splendid isolation'.[14] British observers, too, have concentrated on the differences when attempting a comparative perspective. They mention the diversified German theatre system, the extraordinary subsidies and the seriousness with which the Germans take their theatre.[15] Mark Ravenhill summarises the differences by asserting that in contrast to British theatregoers a 'German audience is used to having no points of empathy with the characters' and 'naturalism is frowned upon as intellectually unjustifiable'.[16] At the same time, the fact that so many contemporary plays from Britain and America are being produced in Germany is a cause for special congratulation on the part of Anglo-American commentators. The playwright Charles Marowitz even asserts 'that without the generosity of German cultural interests there might be no experimental theatre in England'.[17]

*

SCOPE

The aim of this study is not only to present the histories of regional theatres in Britain and Germany but also to study them in relation to each other in order to examine their function in society. The focus throughout will be on the fundamental principles on which repertoires were based and, regarding the comparative approach, whether we can find similar concepts.

The choice of topic, however, also needs some justification. In terms of both public interest and propaganda, cinema rather than theatre is often considered to have been the artistic medium of the day. Apart from that, why concentrate on the provinces when everything seems to have happened in London and Berlin? And finally: how can one compare theatrical activity in two totally different political systems? Although it is undeniable that cinema had become increasingly popular during the 1920s and even threatened the very existence of live theatre in Britain, the performing arts gradually recovered from the mid-1930s. Many playhouses became repertory theatres with their own companies and a strong local identity. The closure of all places of entertainment in September 1939 met with a wave of protest and could not be sustained. Drama was hugely popular during the war and according to Basil Dean, head of the Entertainments National Service Association (ENSA), theatre was even better equipped to boost morale for the war effort than 'mechanised entertainment'.[18] Regional theatres are especially interesting to look at, not only because they have not been at the centre of scholarly attention so far, but also because of their sheer number. In Germany regional theatres made up 90 per cent of all theatres, and in Britain the 'repertory movement' in particular put the provinces back on the theatrical map. Regional theatres with their high dependence on attendance figures can also provide us with information about audience taste. Even in Germany where subsidies resulted in some security, attendances had to be substantial and were closely monitored by the public and the civic authorities.[19] In this respect a differentiation between production and performance figures can reveal how far managers were successful in pursuing a certain repertoire. During the first season under Nazi rule, for example, many managers put the demands concerning the new 'national' theatre into practice and produced a high number of *völkisch* plays.[20] These plays, however, clearly had a negative effect on attendances. The choice of programme was, therefore, crucial and the claim by Nazi critics that 'the character of the repertoire determines the nature of theatre' was not only true for Germany but was also being subscribed to in wartime Britain.[21]

The reason for the choice of Yorkshire and Westphalia is not only that they feature strong theatrical traditions but also that they are typical regions, which exemplify some fundamental issues in the history of regional theatres. They are regions of comparable size, social structure, geography, as well as political, economic and cultural importance. Also, there are significant connections between them. Cultural exchanges can be traced back to early modern times, playing an important role in the first half of the twentieth century and continuing to be strong today.[22] Interesting parallels are particularly apparent in the two regional centres, York and Münster, which have been twinned since 1957.[23] Both cities have enjoyed a role of major importance since the Middle Ages and have been regional, even national, centres of commerce, administration and education. Until today York and Münster have been home to military garrisons, have attracted tourists from all over the world and have profited from a similar geographic location as urban centres in regions largely dominated by agriculture. Despite their role being challenged by the growing importance of the rising industrial towns of Leeds and Sheffield as well as Dortmund and Bochum, both cities have retained their image as important and proud provincial centres. Their role as ecclesiastical centres especially has been a characteristic feature over the centuries as both cities are dominated by large episcopal churches dating back to the eighth century.[24] The church's crucial importance only diminished with the decline in religious belief, which York experienced earlier than Münster.[25] This does not mean that York's clerics did not try to influence the theatre. On Good Friday 1931, for example, the Bishop of Whitby and the Archbishop of York held a service in the Theatre Royal.[26] Both theatres were founded at about the same time, and during the first years of their existence enjoyed national importance.[27] Both playhouses struggled during the nineteenth century, and both took on a new lease of life after the First World War. Although there are also some differences, which mainly concern their size and questions of employment, the clear parallels in the development of the two cities serve as a fruitful ground for comparison.[28]

TERMS AND METHODOLOGY

Comparison should not be taken as a synonym for similarity. Comparative history is interested in difference as well as similitude.[29] To compare theatrical activity in democratic Britain with theatre under the Nazi dictatorship, therefore, does not mean equating the two political systems. Concerning this particular project, however, one might expect that a comparison was a one-sided affair. Considering the different political circumstances and theatrical traditions, the comparison would only stress the many differences between Britain and Germany and, perhaps, add even more to the known list. Indeed, research so far suggests that, in view of the differences in organisation, tradition, social, educational and cultural role, similarities are unlikely to be found. The differences start already with terms and definitions. In Germany *Theater* tends to include its management, company and other staff as well as a historical tradition and the repertoire. In Britain, by contrast, the term is likely to incorporate not much more than the building itself, an object in the property market rather than a haven for the arts.[30] Equally different is the conception of the theatre's chief aim, which in Britain has predominantly been commercial. Politics are a matter for Parliament, religious questions are discussed in church, and art is exhibited in museums and galleries. The most important quality for a popular playwright is usually to be funny.[31] To make things even more complicated, however, it is important to understand that the term 'entertainment' itself has different connotations in both countries. Not only do the British have a broader concept of entertainment, which tends to include plays Germans are reluctant to describe as entertaining, but also the whole concept of theatre in general is different. Schiller's dictum of theatre as a moral institution means that in Germany *Unterhaltung* tends to be regarded as something inferior to 'proper' drama, which is morally instructive and educational.[32] The British, by contrast, have an ultimately positive attitude to any forms of entertainment.[33] Closely linked to this idea of entertaining audiences rather than uplifting them is the concept of theatre being regarded primarily as a commercial enterprise. Every theatre has to make money, and if it becomes a financial liability it has to close.

Until the outbreak of the Second World War the government did not want to get involved in theatrical matters, and state subsidies for the theatre were unimaginable. Interestingly, many managers did not want to receive subsidies either. They cherished their independence and rejected subsidies as a means of political control.[34] Being controlled by economic constraints seemed an altogether lighter burden.[35] West End theatres, for example, traditionally raised their curtains at 8pm to allow patrons to dine beforehand, and shows ended in time for a late supper. Such considerations were highly unlikely in Germany where dramatic art was to fulfil a role beyond the worldly needs of the well-heeled. There, the theatre's function was not only seen as a means of preserving the cultural heritage but also as part of an active engagement in political discourse, as food for thought and a 'Temple of the Muses'.[36] The aims of education and enlightenment have always been central to German theatre – as has control by the authorities in particular with regard to the repertoire. Although theatres had been freed from feudal patronage after the First World War, the new democratic authorities stepped in, funded theatre with taxpayers' money and had a keen interest in its repertoire. The different aim of theatre in Germany also meant that popular culture has found it extremely difficult to enter the established canon. Even today, bourgeois audiences tend to regard musicals and farces as inferior to Goethe and Beethoven and not worthy of representation in a subsidised theatre. The theatres in Yorkshire and Westphalia seem to have reflected these different concepts. Whereas Yorkshire's theatres concentrated almost entirely on purely entertaining fare, Westphalian playhouses relied not only on Shakespeare and Schiller, but also on modern classics like Ibsen, Hauptmann and Shaw. What British patrons would have rejected as 'high-brow' seems to have been the accepted canon in Germany.[37]

Apart from the differences concerning programmes and organisation, the theatres in Yorkshire and Westphalia also seem to have differed regarding the way they were patronised. Looking at the 'topography of entertainment' the first obvious difference is the existence of variety theatres and music halls, which had no equivalent in Westphalia. This is linked to another factor, which is, however, difficult to substantiate: the audiences' social composition. Although the management of York's Theatre Royal, for example, gave away 600 free tickets to the unemployed each week, it was, apparently even more so than Westphalian stages, a theatre for the middle class. In Germany the foundation of the 'People's Theatre' movement in 1890 succeeded

– at least in part – in bringing working-class patrons into the bourgeois theatre, especially because of the cheap tickets, which the free People's Theatre movement offered.[38] Detailed contemporary information regarding audiences, however, is not available and it only rarely appears between the lines. In 1923 York Theatre Royal's acting manager, Follett Pennell, for example, on praising his acquisition of a painting of Tate Wilkinson auctioned at Christie's, stated that the 'theatre was then, as now, patronised by the best classes of society, including the Church, the county families, and the military'.[39] Although this statement seems questionable concerning its exclusiveness, York's working classes definitely preferred the Empire to the Theatre Royal, and interviews with contemporary witnesses support this view.[40] Apart from the cheaper ticket prices at the Empire, the different locations of the venues played a significant role, too.[41] The Empire was close to the river Ouse with its utilitarian warehouses, whereas the upmarket Theatre Royal stood on prestigious St Leonard's Place in the shadow of the Minster. The Empire's main appeal, however, was its music hall variety programme, which differed fundamentally from the Theatre Royal. Apart from famous acts such as Gracie Fields, Harry Lauder, Vera Lynn, Charlie Chaplin and the Tiller Girls, the bill consisted of songs, acrobatics, juggling and dancing.[42] Because of these differences patrons referred to the Empire as 'comic' and to the Theatre Royal as 'classic'.[43] Interestingly, these terms would never have been used by German commentators as the Theatre Royal's repertoire, in their eyes, was far from classic. This discrepancy in definitions also relates to other dramatic genres. Terms such as 'legitimate drama' or 'pantomime' were not known in Germany.[44] Equally confusing for German observers were the many different kinds of comedy. Whereas in Germany every play aiming primarily at amusement tended to be called a comedy, British commentators distinguished, for example, between 'serious' comedies and those 'musically equipped'.[45]

Research so far has largely ignored the fact that despite all these differences the outbreak of the Second World War prompted a similar reaction in Germany and Britain with the realisation on the part of government that theatre could play a decisive role in the war effort. This is certainly not a new finding with regard to Nazi Germany but it may come as a surprise in a country that constantly stressed the commercial and political independence of its entertainment industry.

STRUCTURE

The book is divided into four main chapters, the first two of which will concentrate on historical aspects, placing the respective theatres in their national cultural landscapes. The underlying argument concerns the extent to which we can substantiate similarities in their development, especially with regard to their wartime role. My research shows that although the approaches to the exploitation of theatre as a propaganda tool were different, the basic motivation was the same. Research so far, however, suggests that, whereas Britain's Ministry of Information largely relied on voluntary support of people such as newspaper editors and theatre managers, Goebbels' Propaganda Ministry exerted direct control. But does the fact that German theatre managers mainly conducted their business in a way which pleased Goebbels mean that the regime exerted complete control? What about the concept of 'rushed-ahead obedience' (*vorauseilender Gehorsam*)? And, relating to Britain, does the obvious absence of clear political guidelines for theatres, which makes it difficult to find proof of direct state influence, mean that theatre managers were left to decide entirely on their own what they wanted to produce? What about the foundation of ENSA, the Council for Encouragement of Music and the Arts (CEMA) and the introduction of state subsidies? Plus, what about possible laws of which research so far have failed to take due cognisance?

The first chapter on the history of theatres in Yorkshire briefly illustrates the development from stock companies and regional circuits in the eighteenth century to the change of most theatres into receiving playhouses in the nineteenth century. Against this background the study will then devote particular attention to the repertory movement and the transformation of some theatres into non-profit-making ventures in the early twentieth century, not least because this development offers scope for comparison with Germany. Changes to the attitude towards the arts culminating in the Local Government Act in 1948 conclude the chapter. The second chapter on the history of theatres in Westphalia gives a similar introduction to historical developments and socio-political conditions at German playhouses. Starting with the times and conditions of their foundation the chapter details how theatres developed from business enterprises to places of municipal arts provision. Special attention is given to the Nazi seizure of power and its implications for regional theatres, challenging the view taken by many scholars, that it represented a clear break with the past. Emphasis is equally put on the attempts by the Nazis to lay claim to the theatre and use it for propaganda purposes, especially during the Second World War.

In chapters three and four we then turn our attention to the repertoires and examine not only how politics encroached on regional stages but also how far these findings support our previous results. Are we right to assume that the dramatic vehicles used to communicate propaganda were different in both countries as a consequence of their different approach to entertainment? Did British theatres employ only comedies, musicals and variety shows to put ideological points across? And, by contrast, did German playhouses concentrate entirely on straight propaganda plays, heroic drama and nationalistic opera to fulfil its *völkisch* mission?[46]

Chapter three investigates the repertoires of Yorkshire's theatres and examines how far they mirrored not only changes in management but also political, cultural and socio-economic developments in society at large. A substantial part of this chapter concerns the changes, which the outbreak of the war and the subsequent government interest in the performing arts instigated, and shows that this interest, epitomised in the introduction of state subsidies, resulted in a repertoire similar to the one presented at German regional theatres. This repertoire is characterised by a growing emphasis on national identity and education, and finds expression in productions of Shakespeare, contemporary drama, opera and dance. In chapter four, on the programmes of Westphalian theatres, the emphasis is on the development of a repertoire, which on the one hand mirrored the central European approach to theatre but on the other remained dominated by audience demand for entertainment. Although there are obvious differences regarding, for example, the amount of public funding, production procedures and quality of equipment, the repertoires were not too different from British regional playhouses. It is particularly interesting to realise that this did not substantially change during the Nazi dictatorship and remained intact throughout the Second World War. The conclusion eventually pulls the different threads together, sums up the book's major findings and points out scope for further research.

THEORETICAL UNDERPINNINGS

One of the most important aspects of theatre programmes is their role within a wider framework of cultural history. Like anthologies of poetry or art galleries, theatre repertoires claim to present a comprehensive overview of the essential dramatic works of the time to their audience – from ancient Greek drama to the latest comedies. Although the intentions of managers in Britain and Germany clearly differed – corresponding to the particular role of theatre in society – and Greek drama might have been less of an issue in Britain than in Germany, the basic idea was the same. The repertoire of every single regional theatre can, therefore, be seen as a closed entity.[47] Interestingly, contemporary commentators were well aware of this role. Dortmund's manager Richard Gsell distinguished between Berlin theatres with their different agendas and audiences and municipal playhouses, which, as the sole provider of music and drama, 'have to meet the expectations of all potential visitors'.[48] The importance of this exclusiveness does not only lie in the fact that it is based on deliberate decisions concerning the works which make it into the repertoire but also regarding those which do not. The arrangement of theatre repertoires, therefore, creates a certain meaning as they become 'configurated corpora'. They stabilise, at least for a while, the sense among their respective audiences of what constitutes the relevant drama of the world.[49] This in turn opens up the question of the purpose of a particular selection, and this book will seek to establish the nature of this purpose, why a particular repertoire was chosen and how changes can be accounted for. The concentration on programmes as the main source for this study can, therefore, not only offer interesting insights into the tastes of audiences and managers, but also reflect the manner in which repertoires mirrored social, cultural and political developments. In other words, to what extent is the selection of a particular repertoire governed by concepts such as censorship and canon?[50] Relating to its mission, theatre in Germany, at least in part, presented what was commonly accepted as the established dramatic canon. This canon, although subject to change, aimed to preserve a certain cultural heritage, a fact which, especially during times of war, became a focal point for those in power who wished to influence the theatre. The question within the context of this study is whether British theatres subscribed to a certain canon, too, and whether its development was subject to change.

The differences mentioned above seem to suggest that the concepts of canon and censorship were more relevant for German regional stages and less so for Britain where theatre programmes seem to have been governed solely by economic constraints. In what seems to be one of the crucial differences to German repertoires, British managers presented the latest London successes and spectacular novelties in opulent productions. It seems only logical to expect that repertoires in Yorkshire would fundamentally differ from those in Westphalia where the programme surely must have been entirely based on the theatre's mission of education and moral improvement. Shallow amusement on British, serious education on German stages?

REPERTOIRE

The comparison between theatre programmes in Yorkshire and Westphalia is based on the different dramatic genres established by contemporary as well as modern theatre criticism. The first genre is classical drama. This group of plays incorporates the established dramatic 'masterpieces' of the past, plays which theatres and audiences turned to to foster their cultural awareness. These works traditionally played a central role in Germany where the concept of education represented a core task of theatre. It seems logical, therefore, to expect some of the major differences between Yorkshire's and Westphalia's theatre programmes in this genre.[51] The second group are the modern classics ranging from Naturalism to near-contemporary playwrights, who tackled issues of a more lasting nature and were not primarily written with long West End runs in mind.[52] Instead, many of these plays experiment with new approaches to drama, especially in reaction to melodrama. Whereas the classics were often regarded as 'dated' in Britain and, therefore, not produced as frequently as in Germany, modern classics seem to have aroused a similar interest in both countries.

It is within the large group of contemporary plays that the differences between British and German regional theatres become most obvious. The group of political plays, for example, seems mainly confined to the German stage. Corresponding to the highly charged situation during the Weimar Republic, both contemporary left- as well as right-wing dramatists played an increasingly important role.[53] Despite some interest in Sherriff's *Journey's End* in Britain, it seems as if left-wing drama was mainly confined to groups such as the Workers' Theatre Movement.[54] The group of right-wing and nationalistic drama is perhaps the most problematic in this context – given the comparative approach of this study – as there would appear to be almost no common features here between Britain and Germany. The *völkisch* plays of the 1920s and 1930s had no equivalent in Britain, and the anti-German spy comedies, which became increasingly popular from 1941, have no German counterpart. At the same time, however, plays like *Bull-Dog Drummond*, with its anti-Bolshevik and anti-Semitic undertones,[55] do indeed have something in common with some of the nationalistic fare produced in Germany. Another group of more or less serious plays are the contemporary dramas, which often deal with problems such as social injustice, domestic violence and human conflict without being radically political.[56]

Last, but by no means least, come the contemporary comedies. This group includes comedies, farces, musical comedies, dialect plays, thrillers, and other pieces, which were primarily designed to entertain rather than to uplift audiences.[57] In a contemporary conclusion, the plays of this genre were written by 'an army of clever craftsmen doing capable, efficient work. But if the truth be told, our Ackneys, Armstrongs, Cowards, Levys, Milnes and Novellos are all rather small-beer. Largely their concern is with polishing the small-change of society chatter in Mayfair and Bayswater, with [*sic*] giving a clever twist to the obvious situation'.[58] The assumption is, of course, that the share of this category was much bigger in Britain than in Germany, where the importance of Schiller's dictum of theatre as a moral institution seems to make it unlikely that the repertoire should be dominated by purely amusing plays. The educative aspect of the German repertoire appears to stand in clear contrast to a British programme determined by economic demands.

In a framework of research, which has largely ignored comparative aspects between stages in Britain and Germany, this study will show that the concentration on regional theatres in two typical regions leads to remarkable results. It also proves that similar projects deserve scholarly attention, too. In this context the mutual experience of the Second World War in particular serves as a valuable model against which the similarities and differences can be articulated – always bearing in mind the most important difference after 1933: Britain being a democracy and Germany a dictatorship.

NOTES

1   'Flashlights from Central Europe.' *Theatre World*, January 1935: p. 35.

2   Leopold von Hoesch, the German ambassador in London, explained why Werner Krauß, the eminent German actor, did not enjoy any success in Britain with Hauptmann's play *Before Sunrise*. According to von Hoesch the main reason was the character of the drama which stood in contrast to audiences' desire for entertainment and 'nice impressions' (quoted in Wulf, Joseph. *Theater und Film im Dritten Reich. Eine Dokumentation*. Berlin: Ullstein, 1983. pp. 208–9). Similar considerations were voiced by German theatre émigrés in the 1930s who found it difficult to establish themselves on British stages. They blamed the British insularity and the gap between the two theatre systems (see Berghaus, Günter. 'The Emigrés from Nazi Germany and their Contribution to the British Theatrical Scene.' Mosse, Werner E., et. al., eds. *Second Chance. Two Centuries of German-Speaking Jews in the United Kingdom*. Tübingen: Mohr, 1991. pp. 297–9). Many émigrés called the West End a 'cultural desert' regarding scene design, acting and production methods long overcome on continental stages (see Berghaus, Günter. 'Producing Art in Exile: Perspectives on the German Refugees' Creative Activities in Great Britain.' Berghaus, Günter, ed. *Theatre and Film in Exile. German Artists in Britain, 1933–1945*. Oxford: Berg, 1989. pp. 39–40). Julius Berstl summed up the typical English play of the period as 'Act 1 – tea is served. Act 2 – cocktails are served. Act 3 – whisky is served' (quoted in Clarke, Alan. 'They came to a Country': German Theatre Practitioners in Exile in Great Britain, 1938–45.' Berghaus, *Theatre and Film*, p. 101).

3   Dukes, Ashley. 'Journey Through Theatre. Chapter II: Old Germany. And home Again via Zurich.' and 'Journey Through Theatre. Chapter IV: Germany 1919.' *Theatre Arts* 25 (1941): pp. 22 and 312.

4   German interest in theatre in Britain had been significant before but had been almost entirely related to Shakespeare. The *Shakespeare-Jahrbuch* reported annually on Shakespearean productions in London.

5   Some interesting work on opera productions under European perspective is currently being carried out by a research project at the *Europa Universität Viadrina* in Frankfurt (Oder). In the context of this project Sven Oliver Müller looks at the social influence, cultural practice and political significance of opera performances in Berlin, London and Vienna during the nineteenth century (see special issue of *Journal of Modern European History* 1 (2007)). See also Ther, Philipp. *In der Mitte der Gesellschaft. Operntheater in Zentraleuropa 1815–1914*. Munich: Oldenbourg, 2006.

6   Regarding their scholarly value, some of these studies have to be handled with care. Studies like *X at War*, for example, suggest that every place has its original war history and focus on the positive experiences of the home front, subscribing to an overall trend of nostalgia. They tend to overemphasise the importance of people as individuals, whereas key players, such as councils, become marginalised (see Sokoloff, Sally. 'The Home Front in the Second World War and Local History.' *The Local Historian* 32 (2002): pp. 22–40).

7   See, for example, York Oral History Project. *Through the Storm: York Memories of the Second World War 1939–1945.* York: York Oral History Project, 1993; York Oral History Project. *York Memories of Stage and Screen. Personal Accounts of York's Theatres and Cinemas 1900–1960.* York: York Oral History Project, 1988.

8   See, for example, A.J.P. Taylor (1976 and 1987), Calder (1999), T.O. Lloyd (1993), P. Johnson (1994), Clarke (1996), Smart (1999) on Britain, as well as Burleigh (2001), Hildebrand (2003), Thamer (1994), Bracher, Funke and Jacobsen (1993), Kolb (1998), Schulze (1994) and Peukert (1997) for Germany.

An additional problem with German research has been that for a long time it was written in an apologetic fashion. Commentators claimed that the productions of the classics during the Third Reich were of a high standard – and anyway, the year 1933 provided a 'cleansing' which the theatrical scene had long been waiting for (see Stahl, Ernst Ludwig. *Shakespeare und das deutsche Theater. Wanderung und Wandelung seines Werkes in dreieinhalb Jahrhunderten.* Stuttgart: Kohlhammer, 1947. pp. 669 and 701–5).

9   There are a few notable exceptions, such as Barker and Gale's excellent study on British theatre between 1918 and 1939 (2000), Collins' book on theatre during the First World War (1998) and, especially, Rowell and Jackson's seminal book on the repertory movement (1984). The situation regarding theatre under the Nazis has improved with London's volume (2000), the first book in English on the topic. The most important German studies are Fischli (1976), Drewniak (1983), Wardetzky (1983), Dussel (1988) and Rischbieter (2000). One of the problems in the literature has been either the tendency to assume that theatrical life survived largely untouched by the Nazis, or the supposition that every single theatre was supportive of the regime. An example of the latter position is Peter Adam who claimed that the 'cultural infiltration of every sphere of life never ... stopped until it brainwashed almost the whole nation' (Adam, Peter. *The Arts of the Third Reich.* London: Thames & Hudson, 1992. p. 21. Similarly, Ketelsen (1970), Drewniak (1983), Gadberry (1995) and, more recently, Rühle, Günther. 'Eine deutsche Karriere. "Schlageter" von Hanns Johst – eine Uraufführung zu Hitlers Geburtstag.' *Theater heute* August-September 2002: pp. 56–63). Another problem has arisen from the respective methodological approaches. Scholars like Ketelsen concentrate on the literary quality and on special characteristics

of the drama much more than questions regarding its success. Dussel, on the other hand, has left aesthetics aside and concentrates on the question of how far single theatres were drawn into the political system. As a result, questions of performance tend to be overlooked. Dussel's approach, however, seems much more appropriate to deal with one of the crucial aspects concerning cultural life in Nazi Germany in general: the discrepancy between high demands and actual artistic output. One of the central questions of this study, therefore, will be in how far the Nazis were able to transform Westphalian theatres according to their ideology.

10   See, for example, Gale, Maggie and Vivien Gardner, eds. *Women, Theatre and Performance: New Histories, New Historiographies.* Manchester: Manchester University Press, 2000; Bratton, Jacky. *New Readings in Theatre History.* Cambridge: Cambridge University Press, 2004. See also Fitzsimmons, Linda. 'The Theatre Royal York, in the 1840s.' *Nineteenth Century Theatre and Film* 31/1 (2004): pp. 18–25.

11   Esslin, Martin. 'Wohin geht das englische Theater? Eine Bilanz – gezogen im Sommer 1963.' *Theater heute* August 1963: p. 27. In April 2002 Henning Rischbieter returned to Esslin's article and praised it as the 'fundamental' introduction to the topic (see *Theater heute* April 2002: p. 76).

12   Esslin stressed the importance of the Puritan influence which accounted for a general anti-theatrical atmosphere. It was out of the question for Parliament to spend public money on 'frivolous' theatre (see Esslin, *Bilanz*, pp. 28 and 33).

13   Ibid., 28. One of the common points in stressing the differences has been the claim that British theatres concentrated entirely on amusement (see Martin, Richard. 'Hinter den Kulissen. Einige erfolgsbedingende Faktoren des englischen Theaters: Geld, Macht und Subvention.' *Das zeitgenössische englische Drama. Einführung, Interpretation, Dokumentation.* Fehse, Klaus-Dieter and Platz, Norbert, eds. Frankfurt: Athenäum Fischer, 1975. p. 11).

14   It is sometimes even claimed that if you want to see the latest British play performed you will probably have to turn to Bochum, Hamburg or Berlin. In 2002 alone *Theater heute* reviewed the productions of eight plays by contemporary British playwrights at leading theatres in Germany, Switzerland and Austria. Apart from these, there were many more contemporary British plays on regional stages. Another interesting feature of the journal are regular reports of London productions.

15   See, for example, Fischer, Peter. 'Doing Princely Sums – Structure and Subsidy.' *The German Theatre. A Symposium.* Hayman, Ronald, ed. London: Oswald Wolff, 1975. pp. 215–17; similarly, Ardagh, John. *Germany and the Germans.* 3rd ed. London: Penguin, 1995. pp. 314–24; Innes, C.D. *Modern German Drama. A Study in Form.* Cambridge: Cambridge University Press, 1979. pp. 1–2.

16   Quoted in Sierz, Aleks. *In-Yer-Face Theatre: British Drama Today.* London: Faber, 2001. p. 133.

17 Quoted in Fischer, *Structure and Subsidy*, p. 216. Similarly from an US perspective see Dace, Wallace. *Subsidies for the Theatre. A Study of the Central European System of Financing Drama, Opera and Ballet, 1968–1970.* Manhattan: AG Press, 1972.

18   See Dean, Basil. *The Theatre at War*. London: Harrap, 1956. p. 51.

19 Dukes stressed that German theatres 'were quite commercial in their study of the public taste, and never gave more performances of a play than the audiences were willing to pay for' (Dukes, Ashley. 'Journey Through Theatre. Chapter II: Old Germany.' *Theatre Arts* 25 (1941): p. 23).

20 The term *völkisch* derives from the German word *Volk* (people). It has strong romantic, folkloric and 'organic' undertones, which, in its emphasising of the 'Blood and Soil' idea, combine with an anti-urban populism. The *völkisch* movement was also characterized by anti-communist, anti-immigration, anti-capitalist, anti-parliamentarian and strong anti-Semitic undercurrents.

21 Mettin, Hermann Christian. *Die Situation Des Theaters*. Wien: Sexl, 1942. p. 29.

22 In early modern times English strolling players visited Westphalia on a regular basis, and during the twentieth century adaptations of plays originally written in English became increasingly popular. The Händel revival in the 1920s in particular highlights this continuing interest, for example when Edward Dent, prominent representative of the British Händel movement, visited Münster and claimed – to the delight of his audience – that the English theatre owed its success to the German influence (*Westfälische Landeszeitung* [*WL*], 15 August 1933). Around 1900 sizeable German communities existed in Sheffield, Hull and Bradford, which even had its own *Schiller-Verein*.

23 Other twin-city links between the two regions are Leeds and Dortmund, and Sheffield and Bochum. Bielefeld is twinned with Rochdale.

24 There is an interesting direct link between Münster and York as early as 767 when Bishop Liudger studied with the famous Alcuin (see Freise, Eckhard. 'Vom vorchristlichen Mimigernaford zum honestum monasterium Liudgers.' *Geschichte der Stadt Münster*. Jakobi, Franz-Josef, ed. 3rd ed. vol. 1. Münster: Aschendorff, 1994. pp. 20–1).

25 See Royle, Edward. 'Religion in York, 1831–1981.' *York 1831–1981. 150 Years of Scientific Endeavour and Social Change*. Feinstein, Charles, ed. York: Sessions, 1981. pp. 225–9. In Münster the Catholic influence declined only in the 1960s (see Teppe, Karl. 'Politisches System, gesellschaftliche Strukturen und kulturelles Leben seit dem Zweiten Weltkrieg.' *Geschichte der Stadt Münster*, vol. 3, p. 70).

26 Residents were aware of this. They claimed that 'there was very little that was risqué or obscene or over the top. Of course York being the headquarters of the northern church and a heavy Quaker influence, it was always a moderate kind of place in terms of entertainment' (York Oral History Project, *Memories of Stage and Screen*, p. 30).

27 York's theatre dates back to 1744 and still stands on the same site. Münster's playhouse was founded in 1775. From the late nineteenth century both

theatres have enjoyed substantial popular support. During the 1930s the Theatre Royal featured the successful *Playgoers Club* and in Münster the visitors' organisations, *Volksbühne* and *Bühnenvolksbund*, were the backbone of the theatre's financial planning because of the number of season tickets they guaranteed.

28   Münster's 1940 population of 145,000 was considerably higher than York's 98,000 a year earlier. Also Münster had grown more rapidly in size. In 1933 the city had only had 123,000 inhabitants (see Kuropka, Joachim. 'Münster in der Nationalsozialistischen Zeit.' *Geschichte der Stadt Münster*, vol. 2, p. 317. For the York figure see *York City Year Book and Business Directory*. vol. XX. Watson, A.G., comp. and ed. York: Yorkshire Gazette, 1939. p. 7). York was a manufacturing city whereas Münster was dominated by its role as an administrative centre. In 1939 31 per cent of the jobs in Münster were in industry, farming and commerce, but 41 per cent were in administration and the civil service. In 1936 in York the London North Eastern Railways (LNER) employed 7,800 men and boys, and in 1939 the other main activity of the city, the cocoa, chocolate and confectionery industry, employed 12,000 workers (see *Survey of the effects of the air raid on York, 28/29 April 1942*, dated 31 December 1942. PRO. Home Office. HO 192 Air Raids. HO 192/1656 Air Raid Assessment Reports York-General (1942/43). p. 1. See also Feinstein, Charles. 'Population, Occupations and Economic Development, 1831–1981.' *York 1831–1981*, pp. 109–59).

29   The merits of comparative historical analysis are currently widely discussed. See, for example, Möller, Horst. 'Diktatur-und Demokratieforschung im 20. Jahrhundert. Wo liegen neue Zugänge zur Zeitgeschichte?' *Vierteljahreshefte für Zeitgeschichte* 51 (2003): pp. 29–50. Classic studies include Haupt, Heinz-Gerhart and Kocka, Jürgen, eds. *Geschichte und Vergleich: Ansätze und Ergebnisse international vergleichender Geschichtsschreibung*. Frankfurt: Campus, 1996; and Kocka, Jürgen, ed. *Arbeiter und Bürger im 19. Jahrhundert. Varianten ihres Verhältnisses im europäischen Vergleich*. München: Oldenbourg, 1986. See also Rieger, Bernhard. *Technology and the Culture of Modernity in Britain and Germany, 1890–1945*. Cambridge: Cambridge University Press, 2005.

30   This study uses a more inclusive understanding of the term, based on the German concept.

31   In W.S. Maugham's novel *Theatre* the protagonist, Julia Lambert, contemplates a career for her son Roger. Every job seems fine but he 'can't be a playwright, he hasn't a sense of humour' (Maugham, William Somerset. *Theatre. A Novel*. London: Heinemann, 1937. p. 272). Interestingly, Maugham's novel was quickly translated into German (Maugham, William Somerset: *Theater*. Transl. Renate Seiller. Leipzig: Bastei, 1937).

32   Schiller's 1785 treatise was entitled 'The Stage Considered as a Moral Institution' (see English translation in Brandt, George W. and Wiebe Hogendoorn, comp. *German and Dutch Theatre 1600–1848*. Cambridge:

Cambridge University Press, 1993. pp. 217–21).

33 This study makes use of a concept of entertainment which is as broad as possible (and thereby more closely corresponds to the British idea), to include all performances put on stage.

34 At the turn of the twentieth century Charles Wyndham and Henry Irving, for example, opposed the 'fostering of a State nurse' (see letter by Wyndham to the *Daily Telegraph*, 26 March 1908).

35 Even today cuts in subsidies are reported with a sense of satisfaction in the British media. Whereas cuts in the budget of a Berlin opera house or even a 'minor' municipal theatre cause storms of protest in Germany (see, for example, *Westfalenspiegel* 53 (2004): pp. 36 and 50–1), there is a general feeling in Britain that if a company or an orchestra 'underperforms' it serves them right if they lose out on subsidies. A recent example is the English National Opera (ENO), which was reported to face job losses. Rather than lamenting the possible threat to this flagship institution, the press pointed instead to ENO's repeated calls for public money without changing its structure (see *The Daily Telegraph*, 18 January 2003) and have appeared relieved that the Arts Council has denied ENO the chance to approach them 'cap in hand' again (see *The Guardian*, 24 February 2007).

36 Bochum's theatre manager Saladin Schmitt claimed to sum up the ultimate goal of a German theatre visit as following 'the wish for ethical enrichment'. The typical German wanted to be 'seized and gripped by the stage performance, he … wants to leave the theatre uplifted and strengthened in his self-confidence'. German sentiment towards theatre was characterised by a desire to experience something 'which stuck in one's mind, something more deeply rooted than the wish for diversion'. Grudgingly, Schmitt admitted though that 'sometimes our audiences also delight in pieces of entertainment' (*Bochumer Anzeiger*, 26 July 1933).

37 It is interesting to note that if foreign plays were produced in Britain they only tended to be successful as adaptations. Ashley Dukes, for example, acquired the rights for Alfred Neumann's *Der Patriot*, which had been a Berlin hit in 1926. Approached by the actor Matheson Lang, who was interested in the play as a vehicle for himself, Dukes was aware that a simple translation would not work in Britain. He was also sure that 'a less banal title could be found for the English version' and came up with *Such Men are Dangerous*. The production became a huge success (see Dukes, Ashley. 'Journey Through Theatre. Chapter IX: More Europe.' *Theatre Arts* 25 (1941): p. 757). Regarding the importance of adaptations of foreign plays for English-speaking countries, see Anderman, Gunilla. 'Drama Translation.' *Routledge Encyclopaedia of Translation Studies*. Baker, Mona, ed. Routledge: London, 1998. pp. 73–74.

38 It may be claimed with justification, however, that the social outlook of the audiences did not change fundamentally. Dukes may not be far wrong when observing that it probably 'never occurred to any workmen to go to the

Schauspielhaus or the *Residenz*' in Munich (Dukes, Ashley. 'Journey Through Theatre. Chapter II: Old Germany. And Home Again via Zurich.' *Theatre Arts* 25 (1941): p. 24).

39   *Yorkshire Herald [YH]*, 20 April 1923.

40   See York Oral History Project, *Memories of Stage and Screen*. p. 72). Mrs May Passmore, who had been in variety for years, stressed the division between the people in the 'straight theatre' and those in the 'variety theatre' (ibid., p. 35). Other theatres in the region made an equally clear distinction regarding the scope of the different places of entertainment. In Wakefield, for example, 'the Empire offered light live entertainment, the Picture House was dedicated to films and the Opera House offered live entertainment of a somewhat higher cultural tone' (Taylor, Coral. *Right Royal. Wakefield Theatre 1776–1994*. Wakefield: Wakefield Historical Publications, 1995. p. 209).

41   In the mid-1930s the Empire charged 1/6d for the Dress Circle and Stalls, 1/- for the Upper Circle, 9d for the Pit, and 5d for the Gallery. The Empire had a seating capacity of about 1,200 and a weekly attendance figure of 10,000, which corresponded to the Theatre Royal's attendance as estimated by Rowntree (see Borthwick Institute. Rowntree Papers [PP/21]. Folder *Social Survey of York. Leisure-time Activities. Interim Report for the Trustees of the J.R.V.T. May 1st 1936*. p. 32).

42   Mr and Mrs Allen summed the Empire's fare up as 'mostly comedians and dancing and all the glitter really' (York Oral History Project, *Memories of Stage and Screen*, p. 72).

43   See ibid., p. 60.

44   Perhaps the closest performances in Germany came to Pantomime were the large-scale shows mounted in the leading stationary circuses, such as *Busch* in Berlin at the turn of the nineteenth century (see Otte, Marline. *Jewish Identities in German Popular Entertainment, 1890–1933*. Cambridge: Cambridge University Press, 2006. pp. 38–41).

45   See *Yorkshire Evening Press [YEP]*, 14 September 1929.

46   As claimed, for example, by Gadberry, Glen W. 'The Year of Power – 1933.' Gadberry, Glen W., ed. *Theatre in the Third Reich, the Prewar Years. Essays on Theatre in Nazi Germany*. Westport: Greenwood, 1995. pp. 1–2. Similarly, Adam (1992) and Eicher (2000).

47   The idea of a closed entity, however, only works for theatres which were the sole provider of dramatic entertainment in a given community (the music hall is not considered here because it concentrated on a different fare). The theory is difficult to apply to bigger cities with several theatres because then the idea of exclusiveness is lost.

48   See Gsell, Richard. 'Der Kassenreport.' Ritter, Wilhelm, ed. *Das Theater. Festschrift zum 25 jährigen Bestehen der Städtischen Bühnen Dortmund*. Berlin: Verlag Das Theater, n.d. [1929].

49   See Frank, Armin Paul. 'Anthologies of Translation'. *Routledge Encyclopaedia of Translation Studies*, p. 13.

50 See Aleida and Jan Assmann. 'Kanon und Zensur.' *Kanon und Zensur. Beiträge zur Archälologie der literarischen Kommunikation II.* Assman, Aleida and Jan, eds. Munich: Fink, 1987. pp. 7–15 and 19–23.

51 This group of plays comprises of over two thousand years of playwriting and includes the ancient Greek drama by Sophocles, Aristophanes and Euripides as well as the classics of Italian, Spanish, French and Russian drama (Calderón, Lope de Vega, Goldoni, Molière, Scribe, Gogol, etc.). Lessing, Goethe, Schiller, Kleist and Grabbe feature alongside Marlowe, Shakespeare and Sheridan in this category. The classical genre has always been subject to change. Although today it may also include Brecht, Ibsen and Shaw, this study uses a contemporary understanding of the 'classical canon'. Even today, however, two key preconditions to feature in this group have remained the fact that a dramatist has to be dead and the play has to concentrate on some idea or concept of (supposed) timeless importance.

52 Some of the most important representatives of this group are Shaw, Wilde, Pinero, Zola, Claudel, Ibsen, Strindberg, Hamsun, Björnson, Hauptmann, Sudermann, Halbe, Hofmannsthal, the Schönthan brothers, Schnitzler, Pirandello, Chekhov, Tolstoy and Gorky.

53 To the group of left-wing drama belong playwrights such as Brecht, Toller, Piscator, Sternheim, Werfel, R.C. Sherriff, Synge, Elmer Rice, Upton Sinclair and Sergei Tretjakov. Influential nationalistic and *völkisch* playwrights are Bacmeister, Bethge, Cremers, Eckart, Ernst, Forster, Graff, Hymnen, Johst, Kolbenheyer, Lerbs, Möller and Reinecker. There are problems, however, concerning the classification (as in other genres, too) as some *völkisch* playwrights had had a connection with Naturalism and Expressionism before turning to nationalistic drama. Halbe and Johst are good examples.

54 See Samuel, Raphael, Ewan MacColl and Stuart Cosgrove. *Theatres of the Left 1880–1935. Workers' Theatre Movements in Britain and America.* London: Routledge & Kegan Paul, 1985.

55 For a discussion of *Bull-Dog Drummond* by 'Sapper' (Herman Cyril McNeile) see Watson, Colin. *Snobbery with Violence. Crime Stories and their Audience.* London: Eyre, 1971. pp. 63–71.

56 In contrast to the purely amusing plays, contemporary drama tries to go beyond the superficiality of most of the comedies and deals with some sort of anthropological, socio-economic or political issue. To this group belong the plays by Galsworthy, Bruckner, Fleißer, and some plays by Coward, Maugham and Priestley. Again, there are problems of classification. Perhaps here more than anywhere else we have to look at each single play to judge whether it corresponds to the concept set out above.

57 Among the most successful representatives of this group are Barrie, Novello, Milne, Drinkwater, Lonsdale, Hoffe, B. Thomas, Ridley, Wallace and St John Ervine. Most of the plays by Coward, Maugham and Priestley also belong here. In Germany the most successful comedy writers were Bernauer, Österreicher, Arnold, Bach, Molnar, Götz, L. Fulda, Hinrichs, Lenz, Lippl,

P. Schurek, W. Kollo, the late plays by Kaiser and some of the works by Zuckmayer.

58 Chisholm, Cecil. *Repertory. An Outline of the Modern Theatre Movement. Production, Plays, Management.* London: Davies, 1934. pp. 93–6. Chisholm went on to assert that 'they are commercial confectioners, one and all, occupied with the box-office formulae rather than with writing the enduring play' (ibid. p. 96).

CHAPTER ONE

History of Theatre in Yorkshire

In Britain theatre 'is regarded as a commercial affair, part of the entertainment business, and playgoing, like smoking and drinking wine and spirits, is severely taxed.'

J.B. Priestley[1]

Successful theatre means not only good art but also good business.

Edith J.R. Isaacs[2]

Modern history of regional theatre in Britain can roughly be divided into three different periods. During the eighteenth and first half of the nineteenth centuries stock companies ran (sometimes substantial) touring circuits in the provinces. The following period not only saw a general rise in the number of theatres, an increased social acceptance and a greater variety of entertainments, but also witnessed a qualitative change with the demise of many of the regional stock companies. Instead the scene became increasingly dominated by influential, mostly London-based, managers who sent their West End companies on provincial tours and often also owned a string of regional theatres. During the first half of the twentieth century the rising repertory movement reclaimed some of the territory lost to these chains. Many repertory companies deliberately stressed a particular local identity, established close links to communities and challenged the big receiving playhouses.

Yorkshire's theatres mirror these developments. Tate Wilkinson's Yorkshire circuit in the late eighteenth century was one of the most important in the country, but the stock companies declined in the course of the nineteenth century, at the end of which many playhouses became part of large business empires. Countless new theatres and music halls had opened by the outbreak of the First World War and, together with the phenomenal rise of cinema after the war, testified to a vibrant entertainment industry in Yorkshire. During the 1920s and 1930s many 'reps' sprang up proving a revived interest in theatre presented by resident companies. More than any other playhouse in the region, the Theatre Royal in the county's old capital York exemplified these different periods.

In view of the comparative approach of this study it is interesting to note that the differences in the respective theatre histories seem to become particularly obvious during theatre's heyday in Victorian and Edwardian Britain. Most towns and cities experienced a surge in theatrical entertainment and a growing variety with music halls, circuses and 'proper' playhouses springing up. This means that, in contrast to Germany, most places featured more than one theatre. For the sake of comparability, however, I will not deal with every venue offering theatrical entertainment in each place, but instead concentrate on what commentators have identified as the leading theatre in each locality. I will also restrict myself to the theatres in Yorkshire's biggest cities, and have, therefore, chosen York (Theatre Royal), Hull (Little/New Theatre), Leeds (Grand Theatre and Opera House), Bradford (Prince's Theatre and Alhambra) and Sheffield (Sheffield Repertory Company).

EARLY HISTORY

The first permanent theatres in Yorkshire were built in the course of the eighteenth century. In 1734 Thomas Keregan opened York's first playhouse, the Theatre in Sheffield was launched in 1762, Hull opened in 1768 and Leeds in 1771. Many of these early theatres thrived and quickly established themselves both within their communities and further afield. In the 1740s Joseph Baker established a successful circuit, which included York, Newcastle, Beverley and Hull.[3] An indication of these early successes is the official recognition some of them received in the form of royal patents. Tate Wilkinson became the first truly countywide theatre 'phenomenon' in the second half of the eighteenth century. He was impresario in York and Hull, and enlarged Baker's circuit to perform in York, Leeds, Pontefract, Wakefield, Doncaster and Hull. Wilkinson presided over a company that was praised as the best outside of London, and it was his management of which 'every actor was talking'.[4] As far as the repertoire was concerned Wilkinson staged most Shakespearean plays, although profits were more likely to be made with spectacles involving extensive use of stage machinery. As a matter of fact, Wilkinson only managed to make Shakespeare pay when he was able to secure the services of well-known London stars such as Sarah Siddons or John Philip Kemble.[5]

In the first half of the nineteenth century many theatres experienced increasing uncertainty with managers following each other in rapid succession, financial problems and declining audiences.[6] This was in part due to increasing competition, which was made possible by the 1843 Theatres Act. Additionally, places like York deteriorated as fashionable social centres with events like the Race and Assize Weeks declining in prestige.[7] Attempts to revive Wilkinson's Yorkshire circuit of theatres failed and it gradually disintegrated. The repertoire, too, seemed to become an increasingly one-sided affair with extravaganzas, sensational novelties and travesties being produced to meet the demand for the spectacular.[8] Criticism grew within communities, in particular within religious circles. Sheffield's Reverend Thomas Best claimed that theatre audiences were by their very nature 'already inclined to evil', and in 1853 York's City Corporation could only with some difficulty be prevented from closing 'Satan's synagogue'.[9] At the same time, however, Yorkshire's theatres became integral parts of urban social life.[10] York's Theatre Royal, for example, was very much part of a development which saw the foundation of the Yorkshire Philosophical Society, the Yorkshire Museum, the Subscription Library, the grand De Grey Rooms, and numerous music societies and festivals.[11] It comes as no surprise, therefore, that the theatre – sandwiched between the museum, the library and the Minster – was constantly renovated, updated and redecorated during the nineteenth century to keep up with changing tastes and expectations. Robert Mansel, for example, entirely remodelled its interior and fitted it with gas lighting. To fund the renovation Mansel organised a public subscription, and he also managed to persuade the City Corporation to offer financial assistance.[12] At the end of the nineteenth century most theatres had not only been updated internally but also externally with grand neo-Gothic façades (Leeds, York), domes and turrets (Bradford's Alhambra and Sheffield's Lyceum) and elaborate glass and steel canopies.[13]

Figure 1.1 Bradford Alhambra Theatre in the 1930s

REGIONAL THEATRE PROVISION IN LATE VICTORIAN
AND EDWARDIAN BRITAIN

Yorkshire's cities boomed during the second half of the nineteenth century, in particular its coal, steel and other manufacturing industries (Leeds, Sheffield, Hull), mills (Leeds, Bradford), railways (York, Hull), ports and docks (Hull). This economic surge, however, did not necessarily benefit the arts, as hardly any of these industrial centres offered their rising populations sufficient opportunities for recreation and entertainment. Bradford had no permanent playhouse until 1864, and on the occasion of a royal visit to Leeds in 1858 Prince Albert remarked that Leeds was in desperate need of a good theatre.[14] By the end of the century, however, the situation had changed. Leeds' magnificent Grand Theatre and Opera House on Briggate opened in 1878 and has been the city's main theatrical venue ever since,[15] Sheffield's spectacular Lyceum was built in 1897 by the famous architect W.G.R. Sprague, and Bradford's sumptuous Alhambra (opened just before the outbreak of the First World War) too, belongs in this group of proud statements of civic pride and artistic ambitions.[16]

Figure 1.2 Leeds Grand Theatre and Opera House, 1936

Figure 1.3 Theatre Royal York, c.1910, showing the theatre's frontage as rebuilt in the 1870s

Yorkshire's theatres thrived, especially around the turn of the century. Many profited from improved facilities and long-serving managers. At the same time this period was denoted by radical changes in the final dissolution of regional circuits, the concentration on touring companies and the competition from music halls and cinemas. Acknowledging the changing circumstances new circuits developed with managers like Francis Laidler who ran theatres in Leeds, Bradford and Keighley or John Beaumont who managed Leeds' Grand and Sheffield's Lyceum. In terms of repertoire, the 'straight' theatres tried to counteract the appeal of the new variety palaces. York's Theatre Royal put on twice-nightly variety from 1906 in a move aimed at attracting the big audiences drawn by the newly opened Grand Opera House. Novelties included *Fred Karno's Troupe of Pantomimists*, with 'over ten tons of scenery' in 1908, and an international wrestling match in 1909. The first films were also shown in theatres at this time, without managements realising that it was precisely this medium that soon proved the greatest danger to their existence.

Comparative perspectives

Put into context it is interesting to note that these glorious Victorian theatres in size, splendour and metropolitan stature resembled continental state theatres more than what might commonly be expected of a playhouse in England's industrial north. Here, however, the similarities seem to end. In contrast to Germany, these theatres were not supported by public subsidies and were regarded as private enterprises, which had to pay their way. The principal requirement for their managers was not to present a programme of artistic and educational value but to run their theatre as a sound business. A manager without financial success did not survive long, even if he was a gifted director and an outstanding actor. The famous actor-manager Wilson Barrett, who became the first manager of Leeds' Grand Theatre, did not survive at its helm for 15 years because he was one of the grandest and most successful actors of his time but because he was an acute businessman. Despite the different periods in regional theatre history identified above, the business character of British theatres is one of the major elements of continuity. Whereas German managers tried to distinguish themselves artistically from other playhouses in the region,[17] this was only a minor concern for British managers.[18] It seems that what made a theatre attractive was the question of how fast it could secure the latest London shows and how cheap its tickets were. Despite a growing interest in questions of repertoire and ensemble playing, especially in connection with the new repertory theatres, regional playhouses continued to present a programme which was mainly characterised by comedies, farces, musical plays and light operas – another aspect of continuity.

YORKSHIRE'S THEATRES DURING AND AFTER THE FIRST WORLD WAR

Entertainment Tax and competition from the cinema

Although Yorkshire's playhouses largely remained open during the war, theatre was not generally regarded as helping the war effort. The theatres themselves, however, tried to counteract these perceptions not only by presenting increasingly nationalistic programmes but also by offering voluntary contributions to war loans or collections for charities such as the 'Stranded Sailors and Soldiers' Fund'. Soldiers in uniform were admitted at reduced prices or had to pay nothing at all.[19] These measures, however, only contributed to the loss of revenue. Audiences generally declined because of residents being called up, darkened streets, travelling restrictions and patrons who believed it inappropriate to visit places of amusement in wartime. In addition, the bar receipts, until then a considerable proportion of the theatre's revenue, were drastically reduced by the 1915 Defence of the Realm Act, which regulated the drink trade.[20] Worse still was the financial duty imposed in 1916 on all theatres in the form of the Entertainment or Amusement Tax.[21] Together with the rising cost of materials, rents and rates, the duties became unbearable, and some regional theatres had to close.

Even more important was the increasingly fierce competition from the cinema. From the beginning of the 1920s, cinema enjoyed an ever-growing popularity. It became synonymous with a new cultural experience and a symbol of the fashionable American way of life, which had become so desirable after the First World War. Theatre, in contrast, seemed old-fashioned and outdated.[22] Apart from its attractiveness, cinema tickets were considerably cheaper, a great asset at a time of economic depression.[23] Ticket prices, therefore, became a crucial factor in the struggle for audiences. In 1931, for example, York's Theatre Royal boasted that prices were half those in Leeds and shortly afterwards entered into what seems to have been a local price war with the Empire.[24] Many theatres tried to face the challenge with a double strategy. York's Percy Hutchison, for example, on the one hand claimed that he 'would rather surrender my Lesseeship than be a party to turning York's historic Theatre into what would eventually mean an American Picture Theatre'.[25] On the other hand, he asked the City Corporation in 1931 to change his contract in order 'to be allowed to show Talkie films, if need be, for six months in each year, in place of the present terms of the Lease which provides for … the showing of cinema films for three months in each year'.[26] The public knew nothing of these plans, and theatre enthusiasts still held Hutchison in high regard. The local press even referred to him as 'the man who has saved the drama for York'.[27]

Amateur movement, resident companies and repertory theatres

This incident also shows that despite cinema's popularity, interest in live performances remained significant, a fact to which the growing amateur movement with its strong local links impressively testified. In addition many regional audiences grew tired of visiting companies and called for resident repertory companies. Instead of getting to know a new ensemble every week they preferred to see the same actors each time.[28] The chance to witness the development of certain actors and the feeling of a personal relationship to 'their' company seems to have been an important factor for the success of many 'reps'.[29] This close relationship occasionally resulted in friendships between actors and patrons, although it mainly remained a secret admiration.[30]

Sheffield's most famous theatre, the Lyceum, from the early 1920s faced competition from the Sheffield Repertory Company. The differences between the two theatres could hardly be more striking.[31] In comparison to the magnificent Lyceum the Repertory Company from 1928 performed in the rather less alluring Temperance Hall, later renamed The Playhouse. As regards importance and influence, however, it can be argued that the Repertory Company, growing out of a substantial amateur movement, had a much more profound impact on Sheffield's theatrical life – a fact mirrored in the foundation of the Crucible Theatre, which opened after the Sheffield Repertory

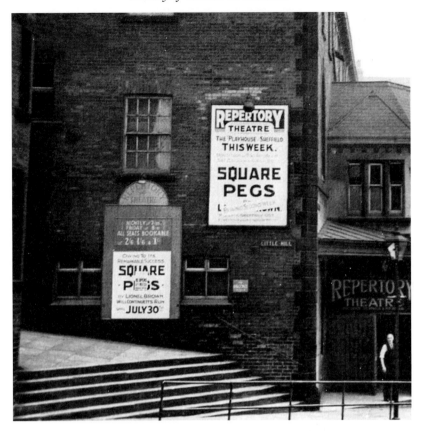

Figure 1.4 Sheffield Repertory Theatre

Company had been wound up in 1971 and quickly developed into one of Britain's leading regional theatres.[32] From the early 1930s the Repertory Company became increasingly established, ran successful public appeals to raise funds, employed a professional ensemble from 1935 and eventually made profits.[33]

Hull experienced a similar upsurge after the war. Until it was eventually closed in 1909, the Theatre Royal had been the city's first playhouse, but the 1920s were marked by a distinct rise in amateur theatricals with annual contests in the City Hall, and saw the opening and success of various 'Little Theatres'.[34] In its five years of existence the Playgoers Theatre, for example, produced 21 'full dress productions' and staged many unusual plays.[35] The Hull Repertory Theatre performed in an old lecture hall starting with four weeks in 1924, ten in 1925, twenty in 1926 and non-stop performances between

Figure 1.5 Aerial view of Hull Little Theatre and Assembly Rooms, 1937

August 1927 and April 1928. Similar to the situation in Sheffield, however, the company's home was far from glamorous, its stage was 'no larger than the dining-room of a semi-detached house',[36] and its artistic success did not translate into a financial one. After the 1932 and 1933 seasons had ended in financial loss, however, the company was eventually put on a professional footing, bought the lecture hall and founded Little Theatre Ltd. The new charismatic manager Peppino Santangelo introduced a strict business plan and turned things around.

Theatre life in Bradford, too, was influenced by changing attitudes and expectations. After the war the city's theatrical landscape was dominated by the Theatre Royal, the Prince's Theatre and the Alhambra.[37] Both the elegant Prince's Theatre and the lavish Alhambra with its variety bill were managed by Francis Laidler, who for decades controlled Bradford's theatrical life and whose pantomimes made him famous throughout the region. Whereas the Alhambra was entirely run as a receiving theatre, the older Prince's Theatre was home to repertory companies from 1932.[38] Terence Byron's company and the Harry Hanson Court Players, for example, became regular favourites. Another indication of the growing

Figure 1.6 Bradford Prince's Theatre, 1959

repertory movement was the opening of the Civic Playhouse in 1929/1937, with which J.B. Priestley was involved from the start.[39] And the staging of the Historical Pageant in 1931 further underlined a new-found civic identity and pride – and questioned the assertion that Bradford was less 'theatre-minded' than other towns in Yorkshire.[40]

Similar to Bradford, Leeds' theatrical life was for decades dominated by one person: John Beaumont, who became the Grand's resident manager in 1931 and from 1939 acted as general manager. Although also managing Sheffield's Lyceum, Beaumont increasingly acknowledged audience interest in a theatre with its own recognisably local characteristics – an acknowledgement no doubt influenced by the successful local amateur company, which performed in the Playhouse and later in the Little Theatre. The Theatre Royal (managed by Bradford's Francis Laidler), too, became home to resident repertory companies more frequently now. Despite their successes, however, Leeds audiences in the 1930s were criticised for not supporting 'intelligent theatre'.[41]

From 1911 York's Theatre Royal was managed by Percy Hutchison, a relatively well-known actor-manager, who, at least for

York, exemplified a new breed of impresario. He rarely stayed in town and directed the business from London, where he managed various theatres and companies, or from his extensive overseas tours. At first York audiences relished the metropolitan flair Hutchison seemed to bestow upon the city. Whenever he visited with special productions they offered him a grand welcome and made these shows major civic occasions, with the Lord Mayor and other dignitaries in attendance. Although the Theatre Royal was run entirely as a receiving theatre until the early 1920s, Hutchison realised earlier than many of his competitors the attraction of companies in residence. As early as 1922 he introduced annual 'Repertory Seasons', which from 1925 were presented by the Lena Ashwell Players.[42] In 1930, Hutchison founded his own repertory company, the 'Percy Hutchison Players' (PHP), who performed during the summer months.[43] They returned in 1931 and 1932 for extended seasons.[44] Hutchison's success, however, was in part due to cheap tickets. From the beginning repertory was offered at reduced prices.

Another remarkable factor for the later success of the non-profit-making 'Citizens' Theatre' seems to have been Hutchison's calling before the York Bankruptcy Court in 1933. In the following 'public examination' it transpired that Hutchison had liabilities of over £11,000. The fact that Hutchison, whom they had only just celebrated as 'the man who has saved the drama for York', had not only lived on credit but also enjoyed the high life of the 'man about town', while at the same time asking the public to support the theatre in difficult times, left many patrons with a feeling of having been betrayed.[45] It also led residents to think about alternative models of managing 'their' theatre. After another brief attempt to run the playhouse as before (as a receiving house run by managers from 'outside') had failed, a group of local businessmen took things in their own hands.[46] They formed a committee intending to preserve the theatre as a legitimate playhouse, approached the York Estates Committee and discussed the possibility of granting a lease to a company controlled by local residents. The driving force behind this group was Seebohm Rowntree, the proprietor of 'Rowntrees', one of the leading chocolate producers and a model of the socially conscious industrialist.[47] They rented the theatre as a limited company for two years at a rent of £800.[48] To finance the venture the committee raised a capital of £2,300 in £1 shares and founded the 'York Citizens' Theatre Ltd'.[49] Not only did York's residents show that they were prepared to accept responsibility for 'their' theatre and put it on a sound financial basis, they also acknowledged it as a community enterprise for the first time. The significance of this move can hardly be over-estimated and was widely acknowledged.[50]

Civic but *not* municipal theatres

Despite growing financial pressures regional theatre managers did not receive any regular subsidies from city councils. Even if theatre buildings were owned by the civic authorities, as in York, this did not translate into regular financial support (which would have been possible by way of, for example, waiving the rent, as happened increasingly in German cities) – quite the contrary. The lessees had to pay a rapidly increasing annual rent, which rose from £650[51] in 1921 and £900 in 1931[52] to £1,280 in 1933.[53] The assumption, however, that municipal authorities did not care at all about theatres needs to be re-examined. Apart from being interested in a 'decent' repertoire, many councillors from the turn of the nineteenth century started to appreciate the financial pressures theatres faced, for example in

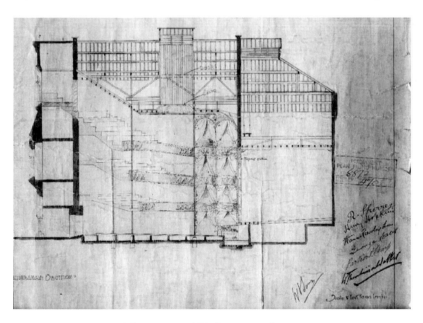

Figure 1.7 Theatre Royal York, proposed reconstruction, plan by Frank Tugwell, c.1888

connection with the challenge of the cinema. Two examples might suffice to illustrate these changing attitudes.

In 1901–02 the interior of York's Theatre Royal was completely rebuilt, its roof reconstructed and electric lighting installed. The scheme was both the most expensive and the most extensive building programme for the last 130 years.[54] The repairs went far beyond what could be expected to be carried out by the city as landlords and had, therefore, in large part to be paid for by the lessee.[55] However, although, practical necessity was the source of motivation rather than a deliberate plan to protect the theatre against the music hall's competition – as claimed by some commentators[56] – it is interesting to note that the city council scrapped the interest the management had to pay on the borrowed money four years later in view of the difficult financial situation of the theatre.[57] Hence, for the first time the council acknowledged its role in safeguarding the theatre – and so did York's residents.[58] Rumours that the theatre was to be converted into a music hall in 1905 caused a public protest. Citizens urged the city to safeguard their interests and even claimed that the city had a responsibility to protect the theatre as a 'potent educational force'.[59]

Two other incidents about thirty years later illustrate that – by then – municipal authorities not only appreciated the asset a flourishing theatre represented and were increasingly willing to make concessions, but show that they also started to voice their opinion as to how they wanted the theatre to fulfil its role – especially in relation to the cinema. For example, in 1933 York's city council made it clear that 'it be a condition in any new lease that the theatre be used for theatrical performances only', which the then new manager Crawshay duly accepted.[60] In return, councils were increasingly willing to help with rising expenses. In this instance, Crawshay produced a long list of repairs he wanted to have carried out, and although the Estates Committee had initially decided not to contribute a significant amount to the expenses, they eventually did[61] – despite the fact that they were not required to commit themselves to anything that went beyond basic repairs.[62] The take-over of the theatre by a group of York citizens (see above) also fits into this picture of changing attitudes. The council agreed to a considerably lower rent than previously demanded in view of the difficult economic situation and actively tried to preserve the Theatre Royal as a legitimate playhouse at a time when it would have been easy to find tenders for its conversion into a cinema. Not entirely unrelated to their popular and financial success city councils actually seemed increasingly keen to associate themselves with these new civic theatres – up to a degree, of course. Hull's Peppino Santangelo, for example, talked Hull City Council into exchanging the small Little Theatre site for the prestigious Assembly Rooms – at no extra cost to the repertory theatre.

Yorkshire's theatres in the late 1930s

The 1930s were a crucial period with resident companies not only fulfilling calls to present 'worthy' plays in repertory in many places but also thriving both financially and artistically. Regional repertory companies in Liverpool, Birmingham and Sheffield received national attention and praise, and their protagonists (like Barry Jackson) developed into near-celebrities. The repertory movement became the subject of serious study and developed into a viable alternative to the established commercial theatre.[63] Even theatres previously run entirely as receiving houses, like Bradford's Prince's and Leeds' Theatre Royal, deliberately used the pulling power of the new movement to attract new audiences as they played host to a number of different repertory companies. York's Citizens' Theatre was registered as a non-profit-making concern in 1935, which meant that it was now exempt from Entertainment Tax.[64] This decision together with changes introduced by the new managing director Redvers Leech (twice-nightly programme, block bookings and reduced prices) turned the project into a success and two years later the theatre underwent extensive structural alterations at a cost of £2,000.[65] Sheffield's Repertory Company became equally successful, and its management felt confident enough to embark on an extensive renovation programme.[66] Hull's Little Theatre company seemed to sum up the triumph of the new ventures. After having sustained losses in the early 1930s the company made increasing profits, reaching £4,500 in 1938. Not content with this, the management took the bold decision to acquire the grand Georgian Assembly Rooms next door, turn them into a theatre at a cost of £30,000 and double the available seating capacity.

Not surprisingly, Yorkshire's cities took pride in their repertory companies and the enthusiasm affected all spheres of life.[67] Public libraries registered increased demands for plays and for books on the theatre,[68] and playgoers' clubs sprang up all over the county. Interestingly, their aim was not only to support the local theatre but also to 'keep supporters of the repertory movement together'.[69] This eagerness also mirrored changing public perceptions of the function of theatre in society. The inaugural meeting of York's repertory company, for example, was attended by the Lord Mayor, Ben Iden Payne (director of the Shakespeare Festival Company at Stratford), the Archdeacon England and Major-General Jackson of the Northern Command. The Archdeacon assured the theatre of the Church's support as good theatre 'will educate, entertain and stimulate'. Rowntree urged the public 'to look upon the theatre as a civic institution and not as a money-making concern'.[70] And the public did. In Hull, Sheffield, York and Bradford (at least to some degree) resident repertory companies were eagerly supported despite (or perhaps because) they did not feature any London stars. A feeling of loyalty developed at many places and attendances rose. In Hull patrons had to be turned away regularly because of sold-out performances and in York 10,000 visitors per week became the norm as even Monday's performances were busy now.[71] At the end of the first season patrons caused a storm of protest because they did not want to see 'their' company depart – an enthusiasm never encountered before.[72]

This is particularly remarkable as the repertory system of performing a play for a whole week, while rehearsing the one for the following week and learning the lines for the one after that, proved a great strain for actors and regularly resulted in productions of poor quality.[73] On the other hand, the repertory experience was appreciated – largely in retrospect though – as an excellent training ground, and many actors became local celebrities. They were welcomed with applause on entering the stage – even if it was an inappropriate moment in the middle of a scene – they opened exhibitions and gave public talks. Local papers regularly carried out polls for the best productions and the most popular actors.[74] For some of them the 'rep' experience also proved a springboard on their way to the West End or to the film industry. York's stage was graced by Phyllis Calvert,[75] Imelda (later Anne) Crawford and Diana Morrison, one of the founding members of BBC's *ITMA*,[76] Sheffield was equally proud of its connection with Alec Guinness, Arthur Sinclair and Donald Wolfit and Hull claimed to have prepared the way for James Mason, Stewart

Figure 1.8 Theatre Royal York, theatre company, late 1930s

Figure 1.9 Theatre Royal York, theatre company, early 1940s

Granger and Maurice Denham. These examples also indicate the high level of turnover regional companies experienced. At the beginning of York's 1936 autumn season, for example, only five actors stayed on with nine new ones joining the company. Against this background the popularity of most of these regional companies is even more remarkable.

In their attempts to recruit loyal audiences, repertory managements cleverly pulled out all the stops. Stage properties, for example, were often borrowed from local businesses. This did not only prove the theatres' willingness to save money but it also offered businesses free advertising space in the programme notes and thereby strengthened relations with the community.[77] Earlier criticism of the emerging repertory theatres eventually shifted towards a positive assessment, which was in large measure due to their economic success – as in York, where the Theatre Royal made profits from 1936,[78] Sheffield and Hull, and even smaller towns like Wakefield and Harrogate.[79] By the late 1930s many regional theatres had developed from being liabilities into celebrated public assets. They stood on a sound financial basis, were firmly established within their communities and presented popular programmes.

Comparative aspects

Although the fact that some regional city councils offered assistance to theatres mirrored in some way the situation in Germany, it seems that the 1930s also highlighted the fundamental differences between theatres in the two countries. After the end of the First World War the performing arts in Germany experienced dramatic changes with most regional playhouses being turned into municipal theatres. Despite local initiatives, for example to save opera or ballet ensembles (a recurring feature at German regional theatres during the 1920s and early 1930s), the initiative of local businessmen saving *and* running a civic theatre would have been inconceivable there. By then, theatre had come to be recognised as a public concern, a cultural and educative institution undertaken and paid for with taxpayers' money. Additionally, there was, and still is, a deep mistrust towards private entrepreneurs 'interfering' in the arts – much the same as the fear in Britain of the state 'meddling' with the independence of the arts. Also, for the time being at least, British managers themselves did not show much interest in subsidies and cautious calls for some local subsidy to theatres were largely discarded as unrealistic and superfluous.[80]

WAR: CLOSURE, REOPENING AND NEW PERSPECTIVES

The outbreak of the Second World War did not only threaten the very existence of regional theatres, but had far-reaching implications for the performing arts in general. The government's first reaction, however, seemed in line with the prevailing understanding of theatre and its merits: all places of entertainment were closed down with immediate effect. The *Daily Express* seemed to sum up the general feeling when stating that 'there is no such thing as culture in wartime'.[81] The image of the newly acquired site for a future National Theatre opposite the Victoria and Albert Museum being excavated to fill sandbags, 'which is the most useful function it can now perform', as one commentator put it, seemed best suited to sum up the situation theatre found itself in at the outbreak of the war.[82] It seemed inconceivable that the public and government alike would focus their attention on the theatre in another devastating world war, which brought Britain to the brink of defeat. To the astonishment of most, however, this is exactly what happened.

The closure of theatres met with an immediate outburst of protest and proved impossible to uphold. A delegation of theatre managers presented themselves at Downing Street, and Bernard Shaw wrote a scathing and much-publicised attack on government policy.[83] After only one week most theatres were allowed to open again.[84] Although officially the U-turn was explained with the fact that theatres such as the ones in Yorkshire were considered to be in 'safe areas',[85] it is remarkable how quickly the government realised that the solution was not to prohibit theatrical performances but to make use of them.[86] Theatre continued to be regarded mainly as a business affair with no direct state control, but the government increasingly engaged in 'cultural policy', recognised the arts' propaganda potential and claimed that they were 'part of the system for which we are supposed to be fighting'.[87] For the first time in British history the government started to fund theatres, companies and other cultural institutions directly. The foundation of ENSA and CEMA together with the 'invention' of state subsidies was nothing short of a revolution and has to be seen in direct relation to Britain's war effort, with the arts expected to boost national morale in another devastating war.[88] Regional theatres during the war reflected these trends and quickly realised their new role of providing entertainment, education and propaganda – to great critical and popular acclaim.

Ensa and Cema

ENSA was founded in 1939 and headed by the well-known producer Basil Dean.[89] The importance the government attributed to the venture can be gathered not only from the fact that the Association had its headquarters at the Theatre Royal Drury Lane, in the heart of the West End, but also from its being fully funded through the Navy, Army and Air Force Institute (NAAFI). ENSA sent out concert parties and theatre companies to entertain troops and factory workers all over the world. In 1943 it received subsidies of £2 million; by the time it was wound up in 1946 this amount had risen to £5 million.[90] By that time ENSA had had thousands of members, had given hundreds of thousands of performances and entertained millions of people.[91] Dean claimed that the association had employed more than 80 per cent of the entertainment industry at one time or another.[92] Although stars like Gracie Fields or George Formby performed under its auspices, ENSA relied heavily on non-professional talent – and it was this group of artists who relished the security of ENSA contracts most of all.[93] This fact shows that, apart from its military image of the 'entertainment army', ENSA also fulfilled an important social function, which should not be underestimated. The jobs it provided for many hitherto unemployed actors had an additional effect on morale.[94]

Regarding its repertoire, ENSA was keen not to be seen to present purposeless entertainment, but to raise national morale.[95] This the association also attempted in selected showcase productions on large scales. Dean's production of his own *Cathedral Steps* in September 1942, for example, was announced as an 'Anthology in Praise of Britain', or even a 'service in praise of Britain'.[96] This massive nationalistic pageant was staged on the steps of St Paul's Cathedral, involved a cast of hundreds led by the cream of West End stars and presented Britain's 'glorious heritage'.[97] The propaganda value of this production was not only its immense size and the setting, which aimed to stress the close links between Church and nation, but also the aim to portray Britain's history as a success story from medieval times until today.[98] In 1942, when the war was far from won, the message that this country was indeed worth fighting for was an important propaganda stunt.

Whereas ENSA was mainly directed at the forces, CEMA's mission was different and directed at the home front.[99] The two organisations also differed in their political agenda as CEMA's aim to foster the arts through state support pointed beyond the end of military action.[100] CEMA was established in January 1940 as a result of a meeting held at the Board of Education.[101] The initial objective was to give financial assistance to artistic societies finding it difficult to maintain their activities during the war. The broader aim was to boost morale through the provision of art. At first CEMA was jointly financed by the Pilgrim Trust and the Treasury with the trust's grant of £25,000 being matched by a government subsidy of the same sum. Two years later the trust withdrew and the government accepted full financial responsibility for CEMA.[102] By 1945 the Treasury grant had risen to £235,000,[103] and the overall sum spent on CEMA and the Arts Council between 1940 and 1950 reached over £2 million.[104] This financial backing not only meant that the state for the first time in British history had become a patron of the performing arts, but also that CEMA's work was approved as being of national importance.

In diversified programmes CEMA brought classical music, visual art and drama of the highest standards to isolated rural areas and industrial towns, catered for the entertainment of evacuees and recognised the need to counterbalance the suspension of many customary entertainment facilities, long working hours and monotonous leisure time.[105] Soon after its foundation CEMA became associated with many stars and leading ensembles.[106] The Old Vic company was sent out to play classical drama in the provinces, the Pilgrim Players took serious plays to village halls, and Sybil Thorndike toured Shakespeare through Welsh mining villages for several consecutive seasons.[107] Ballet companies such as Sadler's Wells Ballet, Ballet Rambert and Ballet Jooss were sent out to tour factories, garrisons and hostels.[108] Kurt Jooss is especially interesting in this context because of his German past.[109] After having been seen as a rather un-English exercise with marginal audiences entirely concentrated in London for decades, ballet during the war took the provinces by storm and played to capacity houses.[110] Opera, too, took on a new lease of life thanks to the support of CEMA, and Sadler's Wells toured the industrial towns of the North.[111] Chamber music recitals were organised in factory canteens, symphony concerts were put on for war workers, and even the stars of the classical music scene were happy to 'do their bit'.[112] Pablo Casals played Elgar's Cello Concerto for the standard fee of three guineas, Yehudi Menuhin gave a series of recitals for factory workers and Myra Hess regularly performed in the National Gallery, which had been emptied of pictures.[113] In what appeared to contemporary commentators as a revolution in the arts, serious plays and classical music were brought to the remotest places and successfully found new audiences.[114] In fact the demand grew so strongly that it could never entirely be satisfied. CEMA's biggest and most influential undertakings, however, were the opening of the Theatre Royal, Bristol, as the first state theatre in British history and the establishment of the Old Vic as a true, i.e. continental, repertory company with a programme of classics.[115] Even the idea of a National Theatre, after decades of opposition and fruitless campaigning, from 1942 suddenly received official support.[116] In a generous gesture Parliament in 1949 agreed to pay £1 million to build a National Theatre on the South Bank. Only ten years earlier such a decision would have been virtually unthinkable.[117]

Propaganda

The new approach to the arts paid off and many commentators have since claimed that it was the provision of entertainment rather than the military successes that not only upheld the morale of newly recruited audiences for the arts but also made them rediscover a sense of Elizabethan magnificence.[118] Organisations such as the British Drama League were eager to establish this link from the early days of the war.[119] The attempts to concentrate on British plays and British composers, and the stress laid on the development of a typically British style of ballet dancing, painting and writing, only supported the feeling of national greatness.[120] The production of a classical repertoire in particular came to be seen as helping the war effort. Commentators claimed that the Old Vic classical repertory seasons were the best in British theatre for decades and that the company had developed into an 'emblem of national consciousness second only to Shakespeare'.[121] Further, it was asserted that through these performances audiences would regain their faith in the strength of their country. A nation which could mount *Peer Gynt* and *Richard III* concurrently with its forces' return to Europe, and mark 'Victory in Japan' day by the two parts of *Henry IV* gave real cause for hope. The 'years of genuine greatness in acting and production of the classics' were matched with Britain's greatness on the world's battlefields.[122] Ivor Brown noted that *Henry IV, Part One* gave 'one high pride in the English theatre, which, amid all the difficulties of our time, is offering … presentations of the classics worthy of a National Theatre'.[123] The new status of the Old Vic as a quasi National Theatre found expression in its European tour immediately after the war. The government sent the company abroad as cultural ambassadors and they performed in Hamburg and Paris.

In turn many leading artists were anxious to be seen supporting the war effort. Vaughan Williams, for example, composed music for several propaganda films, among them *Coastal Command*, *49th Parallel* and *The Flemish Farm*, and William Walton wrote a piece called *Spitfire Prelude and Fugue* based on his score for the film *First of the Few*.[124] Dramatists such as Clemence Dane produced scripts about national heroes, J.B. Priestley was eager to prove that he had not taken flight with his radio talks, and Noel Coward was desperate to show his patriotic credentials.[125] Shakespeare in particular turned into a perfect vehicle for the country's leading actors to show their national allegiance. Donald Wolfit's lunchtime Shakespeare performances in the Strand were celebrated achievements 'in a city of darkened playhouses [and] it was due to his courage that the lovely language of our greatest poet should be the first to break the silence'.[126] John Gielgud appeared on ENSA tours and in a series of Shakespearean lectures on *Shakespeare in War and Peace*, which earned £1,500 for war relief.[127]

Interestingly, with regard to propaganda the government followed a double strategy. On the one hand it was prepared to subsidise the performing arts on an unprecedented scale, while on the other it was keen to associate itself with artists who were supporting the war effort without obvious financial gain. The above-mentioned tour of the Old Vic through Welsh mining villages illustrates this strategy. It was extensively documented and widely publicised by the Ministry of Information. Although mentioning the government involvement, the Ministry stressed the personal touch and the basic working conditions of the ensemble – a far cry from the luxurious life style of the theatre stars of the 1930s.[128] Propaganda publications such as the *Bulletin from Britain* promoted this strategy worldwide.[129] They regularly featured articles about the theatre, about festivals and productions especially of Shakespearean drama. Ultimately, the government's apparent aim was to show that theatre had a clear political purpose in war.[130]

The importance attributed by the government to these contributions can be gathered by the way they were rewarded during and immediately after the war. The Ministry of Labour agreed to offer artists deferment when they offered to work for ENSA.[131] A special War Artists Advisory Committee was intended to establish closer links between the state and its artists.[132] In 1946 two of the most prestigious figures of wartime theatre, Ralph Richardson and Laurence Olivier, received knighthoods clearly to honour their war effort.[133]

Boost for regional theatre

In contrast to German cities Britons felt the reality of war from the early days of the conflict with food rationing, blackouts and gas masks becoming omnipresent and the production of peacetime goods quickly changing to suit wartime needs.[134] Theatres suffered from a shortage of paper and other raw materials, which made producing sets, properties and costumes increasingly difficult.[135] Actors were called up, and replacements were hard to find.[136] Makeshift solutions included producers and directors joining the players on stage, the hiring of amateurs and generally plays with small casts.

From the beginning of the war, however, one of the central aims within the framework of government support for the arts was a deliberate concentration on the provinces – and Yorkshire immediately profited from this policy.[137] At its heart was not only the idea to boost morale in places not necessarily catered for by organised entertainment but also a strong educational mission. Performances by the Old Vic or the London Symphony Orchestra were to offer audiences not just any kind of entertainment but 'better' entertainment to audiences who may have never seen a professional symphony orchestra or listened to Shakespearean verse before.[138] CEMA also supported performances of avant-garde ballet and pieces by contemporary composers – although no doubt many of these works must have been challenging for audiences.[139] And the policy worked: what would have been rejected as high-brow and patronising a few years earlier suddenly attracted large audiences and received enthusiastic reviews.[140]

CEMA's other main objective in the provinces concerned the establishment of independent repertory theatres, to raise production standards and the quality of programmes.[141] From its new base in Burnley the Old Vic sent out companies to tour the provinces and played seasons of ballet, opera and classical drama at Burnley's local theatre.[142] Additionally, CEMA supported regional companies, acted as an agency, drew up funding schemes and encouraged the establishment of non-profit-making companies all over the country, a lack of which had been lamented before the war.[143] For these companies the council further acted as sponsor with government departments and public bodies, 'testifying to the value of the work done in the interests of national service',[144] and offered support for companies to obtain exemption from Entertainment Tax for plays with educational value.[145] CEMA paid for the renovation of Bristol's Theatre Royal, established a permanent repertory company at the Liverpool Playhouse and was instrumental in the foundation of Glasgow's Citizens' Theatre. It also actively supported the foundation of the Council of Repertory Theatres.[146] These developments did not go unnoticed – on the contrary. The possibilities of changed governmental attitudes towards the arts were quickly realised by Yorkshire's theatres, in particular by the repertory theatres in Sheffield and York who quickly joined emerging schemes such as the Conference of Repertory Theatres.[147] The educational agenda behind these activities was no secret. CEMA openly stated that it hoped to create 'permanent, educated audiences all over the country'.[148]

Parallel to CEMA's activities the British Drama League submitted its Civic Theatres Scheme to Churchill in 1942.[149] This radical scheme proposed that cities should be able to run municipal theatres jointly financed by local and state subsidies.[150] As a matter of fact Ernest Bevin indicated government willingness to support regional theatres at the inaugural meeting of the Provincial Theatre Council. He hoped that the theatre would become 'one of our great national institutions to convey to the peoples of the world the real character of the ordinary British people'.[151]

At the heart of these initiatives was not only the belief that regional theatres could play an important role in the war effort in terms of entertainment, education and propaganda but also a concept of municipal arts provision which pointed at the long-term future – of which the 1948 Local Government Act was a direct outcome. Section 132 of the Act empowered local authorities to provide and maintain civic theatres. They were given the mandate to spend the sum of sixpence in the pound on entertainments, which made a possible total of £8 million available to subsidise the arts.[152] This concept was in fact not too different from the German system of municipal theatres. Although nobody would have admitted the country was to be a model for Britain and the amount of funding envisaged was admittedly on a much smaller scale, the basic idea of municipal responsibility for the arts was strikingly similar to Germany.

Touring companies

One of the effects of air raids and destroyed theatres in southern England was that an increasing number of London companies and stars toured the provinces while London's theatres remained closed.[153] In a reversal of the usual direction, West End stars now returned to the same provinces they had been so happy to leave behind.[154] In what came to be regarded as part of their war effort, John Gielgud, Emlyn Williams, Jack Hulbert, Michael Redgrave, Ivor Novello, Marie Tempest, Richard Tauber and many others all visited Yorkshire on their tours. More importantly, in the context of this study, Yorkshire's audiences immediately benefited from the introduction of state subsidies and experienced regular performances by renowned companies such as the Old Vic, D'Oyly Carte and Sadler's Wells opera and ballet ensembles, paid for by CEMA. Regional theatres quickly established certain patterns to accommodate both their own resident and/or visiting companies, local amateurs as well as the prestigious visits by London ensembles. For most regional theatres this mix proved highly lucrative.[155]

Air raids

More disturbing effects of the war, however, came to be felt quickly. With the threat from the *Luftwaffe* many theatres were forced to return to once-nightly shows, which had a negative effect on revenues, in order to allow patrons to return home before the blackout.[156] The opening of Hull's New Theatre was delayed and Sheffield's Repertory

Company even had to leave the city and move to Southport (although this proved a financially successful move and turned into a subsidiary venture as the company reopened, albeit briefly, the Playhouse in Sheffield). Also, from September 1939, Air Raid Precautions published in programme notes requested patrons to bring their gas masks, informed them about the nearest air raid shelters and reminded them that in the event of a raid they could feel safe in the theatre as the auditorium's walls 'are built of stone slabs of a thickness … that should prove extremely good cover'.[157] In fact audiences were almost encouraged to stay on as they were promised that 'immediately the exodus is complete the exit doors will be closed and the performance resumed'.[158] That the frontline had reached Yorkshire was apparent not only in the presence of foreign soldiers who were stationed on numerous air fields around the county,[159] but also when its cities came within the reach of German bombers.[160] At the same time, however, even war-torn Hull, whose New Theatre suffered a direct hit in 1941, after a brief period of dwindling audiences, made profits again from 1942.[161]

War effort

Yorkshire's theatres were keen to be seen playing an increasingly active role in the war effort.[162] They collected donations for the Comforts Fund of the Troops, National Air Raid Distress Fund or the RAF Benevolent Fund and admitted service personnel in uniform at reduced prices. Theatres in garrison cities gave special 'command performances' for the forces and some even went on their own ENSA tours.[163] Some of the former actors who had been called up returned for short visits when on leave and stressed not only their loyalty to their old playhouse but also their efforts to support wartime entertainment.[164] Theatre patrons were equally keen to contribute to the various local 'Spitfire Funds'[165] or 'Warship Weeks'.[166] After the German attack on the Soviet Union a huge wave of support ran through Britain – and again the theatre was at the forefront of events. In 1943 the Royal Albert Hall housed a celebration of Stalin's Red Army after the battle of Stalingrad, and theatre stars such as Gielgud, Richardson and Olivier were happy to lend their support.[167] In the previous year, a public meeting in York had already explained 'Why Russia Will Win'.[168]

Figure 1.10 Members of York's Theatre Royal company during a fire drill, early 1940s

The biggest organised home front entertainment event, however, was the 'Holidays-at-Home' scheme designed to persuade people to stay at home during the summer months in order to make public transport available for the armed forces. With these objectives in mind, local authorities co-ordinated the provision of entertainments to provide relaxation from the strain of war and long working hours, and to keep everyone fit for the tasks still to be undertaken.[169] It was clear from the outset that to most people this was a great limitation as holidays without a journey did not seem to be an appealing option. The cities were, therefore, required to present attractive programmes and to mix 'the gay with the grim'. In 1942 the Ministry of Labour requested local authorities to provide as much entertainment as possible, especially outside.[170] Theatre did not only play a vital part in the scheme, but also municipalities were explicitly encouraged to seek co-operation with CEMA.[171] Birmingham, Manchester and even Harrogate organised open-air theatre festivals of several weeks' duration, Durham held a Festival of Arts, and many of these initiatives received substantial state support.[172] Although the trains to the popular sea resorts kept running – in an obvious attempt not to appear to be forcing people to stay at home – officials stressed that travelling to Scarborough made no sense because 'it is a town of the dead'.[173] According to official reports the policy worked as, for example, 'only five per cent of Halifax people disregarded the advice to spend their Wakes holiday at home'.[174] For its first 'Holidays-at-Home' festival in 1942 York appointed an honorary secretary and mounted an extraordinary programme.[175] Theatrical performances formed a vital part and included amateur shows by the York Settlement Players who presented *Without the Prince* and the New Earswick Dramatic and Operatic Society with Priestley's *When We Are Married* as well as professional performances by members of the Theatre Royal company with scenes from Shakespeare. The actors played to packed houses and proved to everyone that they 'did their bit', too.[176] Although the organisers seem to have been anxious not to provide a programme too overtly propagandistic, York's Lord Mayor made it clear that the whole venture was regarded as 'a contribution to the national effort'[177] and Mr Neilson, president of the Free Church Council, added that residents should rest assured that 'this period of their holidays at home was quite in harmony with the will of God'.[178] Elsewhere the connection between entertainment and propaganda was equally stressed. In Leeds, residents voted for 'Miss Leeds, 1942', but the beauty competition was not in the 'lavish style' of pre-war days. Instead the girls 'wore simple, wartime evening gowns and the keynote was simplicity [as] *Miss Leeds, 1942* was to symbolise the hard-working, stay-at-home-holiday girl'.[179] In a similar event in Harrogate, the 'Holiday Queen' introduced her retinue of young women, 'Miss Saving', 'Miss Agriculture' and 'Miss Fuel Saving'.[180] It was even claimed that whether people had been spending their holidays at home or elsewhere 'they all realised that the purpose of their holiday was not only enjoyment but that they might be made more fit bodily, mentally and spiritually for the work that lay ahead'.[181]

Although it is doubtful whether the appeal of 'Holidays-at-Home' really was as attractive as officially claimed[182] – Home Intelligence Reports regularly featured public criticism on various aspects of the scheme[183] – for many towns the sudden governmental support for the leisure and entertainment sector came as a welcome relief in view of economic problems. More importantly in the context of this study, however, it came as a surprise after centuries of regarding these spheres as subjects of private enterprise. Until recently the 1925 Public

Health Act had restricted the powers of local authorities to support the arts. Sponsoring of museums and art galleries was possible, the support of theatres through public funds, however, illegal. Again, it was the war situation which changed circumstances. In 1942 the Ministry of Labour broke up the strict 1925 Act by encouraging local authorities to organise public entertainments as part of their 'Holidays-at-Home' programmes. The 1944 Education Act then legalised more permanent activities and enabled local education authorities to provide public entertainment. And the 1948 Local Government Act confirmed that local authorities were entitled to spend a certain amount of taxpayers' money on an extensive array of entertainment services – for example on municipal theatres.[184] But already during the war local councils quickly seized this opportunity to start planning for post-war civic arts provision in general and municipal theatres in particular.[185] In York, Seebohm Rowntree called for such an initiative as early as 1943.[186] It seemed clear to city councils that they were witnessing a fundamental change in government attitudes towards the arts and they were keen to make the most of it.

CONCLUDING REMARKS

As far as this study is concerned, it is interesting to note that the history of theatre in Yorkshire starts to become increasingly fascinating after the First World War when different city councils, although still regarding the theatre as a private commercial enterprise, started to accept some responsibility for their local playhouses on lines not too different from Westphalia. A 'civic spirit' began to influence both municipal authorities and residents, and this eventually led to the foundation of the repertory companies in York and Sheffield, the Little Theatre in Hull and had a clear effect on Bradford's Prince's Theatre with its increased focus on extensive repertory seasons.

The Second World War not only strengthened the 'civic spirit', it also had Yorkshire's theatres experiencing their 'golden years'. The big London stars came on provincial tours, resident companies were as popular as ever with many talented actors who later moved on to London or Hollywood, and the theatre increasingly stood on a sound financial basis with loyal followings. Apart from that, the special wartime demands were quickly realised with state-funded agencies and festivals clearly outlining the role the theatre was expected to play.

Yorkshire's playhouses successfully obliged with performances of escapist variety shows, farces, spy comedies and war plays, but especially with established classical theatre, opera, ballet and productions of the 'great national poet'.

NOTES

1   Priestley, John Boynton. *Theatre Outlook*. London: Nicholson & Watson, 1947. p. 17.

2   *Theatre Arts* 26 (1942): p. 3. Isaacs was editor of this leading American theatre journal.

3   Baker played in York from late December until May, in Newcastle from May until August, then he returned to York for the Summer Assizes and Race Week, went to Beverley to perform there between August and October and finally to Hull where the company stayed until December (see Fitzsimmons, Linda. 'The Theatre Royal, York.' *York History* 4 (1981): p. 170).

4   Bernard, John. *Retrospections of the Stage*. vol.1. London: Colburn & Bentley, 1830. p. 151.

5   See Tillott, P. M., ed. *A History of Yorkshire. The City of York*. Oxford: Oxford University Press, 1961. pp. 533–4. This development towards the spectacular intensified in the late nineteenth century when technical advances allowed for increasingly dramatic effects (see Rowell, George and Anthony Jackson. *The Repertory Movement. A History of Regional Theatre in Britain*. Cambridge: Cambridge University Press, 1984. pp. 10–11).

6   These problems were common at nineteenth century British theatres in general (see Crump, Jeremy. 'Patronage, Pleasure and Profit: A Study of the Theatre Royal, Leicester 1847–1900.' *Theatre Notebook* 38 (1984): pp. 77–88).

7   Again, similar problems were encountered by other regional playhouses (see Barker, Kathleen. 'Thirty Years of Struggle. Entertainment in Provincial Towns Between 1840 and 1870.' *Theatre Notebook* 39 (1985): pp. 25–9).

8   Examples include the different *Crazes* (Dickens, Scott etc.), 'Ching Lau Lauro, the Paganini of all Necromancers, Ventriloquists', 'Abel and his Dogs Hector and Wallace' in a series of canine dramas and 'Professor Cocker's 15 educated horses'.

9   Quoted in Dann, Frances. 'This Multiform Evil: The Annual Admonitions of the Revd Thomas Best of Sheffield.' Foulkes, Richard, ed. *Scenes from Provincial Stages. Essays in Honour of Kathleen Barker*. London: Society for Theatre Research, 1994. p. 90. For the York quote see Tillott, *History of Yorkshire* , p. 534.

10   With respect to York's case this has convincingly been argued for the 1840s by Linda Fitzsimmons (Fitzsimmons, Linda. 'The Theatre Royal, York, in the 1840s'. *Nineteenth Century Theatre and Film* 31/1 (2004): pp. 18–25).

11   See Royle, Edward. 'York in the Nineteenth Century'. Patrick Nuttgens, ed.

The History of York. From Earliest Times to the Year 2000. York: Blackthorn, 2001. pp. 295–301.

12 See Mansel's announcement in the *York Courant* on 22 November 1821. Mansel also managed Hull's Theatre Royal (see Mansel, Robert. *Free Thoughts upon Methodists, Actors and the Influence of the Stage.* Hull, 1814).

13 See Barker, *Thirty Years of Struggle*, pp. 140–2.

14 The need became all the more pressing after the old Theatre Royal was destroyed by fire in 1875 and one year later the Amphitheatre suffered the same fate.

15 Other late nineteenth-century additions to Leeds' theatre life included the Theatre Royal (1876), the Coliseum (1885), the Empire Palace Theatre (1898) and the City Varieties (1894).

16 See Holdsworth, Peter. *Domes of Delight. The History of Bradford Alhambra.* Bradford: Bradford Libraries and Information Service, 1989.

17 Festivals were a welcome means to achieve fame. Bochum, for example, was proud of its festivals honouring classical dramatists, and Münster tried to build a reputation through its Händel revival.

18 Kathleen Barker's observation for the second half of the nineteenth century that 'no [provincial A.H.] manager could afford to be too refined in his tastes: he had still to produce endless melodramas and "adaptations from the French", and to react quickly to contemporary events' certainly held true for the first half of the twentieth century just as well (Barker, *Thirty Years of Struggle*, p. 145).

19 In York Mrs Dawes recalled that the theatre 'was thrown open free of charge to wounded soldiers' (see *YEP*, 23 December 1932). Regular prices were reduced to Dress Circle 2/-, Orchestra Stalls 1/6, Upper Circle and Pit 9d, and Gallery 6d (see Rosenfeld, Sybil. *The York Theatre.* London: Society for Theatre Research, 2001. p. 318).

20 In some places this Act cut theatre bar receipts by 50 per cent (see Collins, L. J. *Theatre at War, 1914–18.* London: Macmillan, 1998. p. 46).

21 At the Theatre Royal the tax raised the 3d to 6d seats by 1d, the 6d to 1s/9d seats by 2d and the boxes by 1s/- (see Rosenfeld, *York Theatre*, p. 318).

22 In the mid-1930s Hull had thirty cinemas, Bradford had forty-two and Sheffield forty-five. York in 1934 hosted fourteen cinemas, five of which opened in 1934 alone. Leeds by the end of the decade had sixty-eight picture houses and commentators believed the city would not be able to cope with any more (see Preedy, Robert E. 'Variety Spells Entertainment: The Cinema Life of Claude H. Whincup.' Stevenson Tate, Lynne, ed. *Aspect of Leeds 2. Discovering Local History.* Barnsley: Wharncliffe, 1999. pp. 33–41).

23 It did not help that theatre managers still had to pay Entertainment Tax, which, instead of being scrapped, in 1931 was further increased. The tax was still in place after the Second World War although it had lost its original purpose.

24 See *YEP*, 5 November 1931. In March 1933 Percy Hutchison announced that

'on and after Monday, March 13th, ALL Stalls will be 2/6'. On the same day, the Empire declared that patrons were offered a 'Great Reduction in Prices of Admission' (*YEP*, 6 March 1933). Other examples of attempts to increase audiences include specially reduced prices for performances of the O'Mara Opera Company in January 1932 ('the cheapest prices that Grand Opera has ever been played to in York' – Theatre Royal advert in *YEP*, 18 January 1932) and reduced ticket prices for Monday performances, which were usually quiet, in February 1932.

25   Theatre Royal programme notes, 14 March 1932. Already in 1930 Hutchison had appealed for public support of the theatre, which was 'in danger of annihilation by the American talkies. Are you going to allow it to die, or will you back us up in our endeavour to save the theatre?', he asked (*Yorkshire Gazette* [*YG*], 10 May 1930).

26   Estates Committee meeting of 13 July 1931 (*York City Council, Estates Committee 1931–1940*. p. 18). The occasion was a letter from Hutchison in which he asked for a 'further term of seven years under the Lease', which the committee approved. The lease was renewed in February 1932.

27   The press devoted long articles to Hutchison's 'Grand Anniversary Week' claiming ' 'Twas "Percy's Night" at the Theatre Royal, York, yesterday. Surely on such an occasion the man who has saved the drama for York can be given the name he has earned in all the households of the city ... during the past 21 years. If it must be a "Mister", let us say it was "Mr. York's Night" (*YEP*, 9 February 1932). In his rather dire autobiography Hutchison quoted his uncle Charles Wyndham who had not approved of his taking over the lease at York as it 'is too little an affair for you to bother about' (Hutchison, Percy. *Masquerade*. London: Harrap, 1936. p. 160).

28   During the 1920s, York residents became increasingly enthusiastic about the idea of a repertory theatre with a permanent company (see *YG*, 17 August 1934).

29   Proof of the repertory's popularity in York, for example, is the success of block-bookings through the *Theatre Royal Playgoers Club*. Residents until today recall with appreciation their regular theatre visits. Mrs Willis, for instance, remembered that they 'had the same seat each week – you went and claimed your ticket during the afternoon the day before. Each week. We were upstairs. I can give you it to this day: D4 and D5, and we never missed. I mean it was the end of the world if you missed' (York Oral History Project, *Memories of Stage and Screen*, pp. 13–15).

30   The case of Nellie Woodhouse, whose theatre diaries were recently presented to York's City Archives on a permanent loan (and which have not been available for research before), is a good example of the appreciation which many actors enjoyed. Born in 1922, she was a regular theatregoer in the 1930s and 1940s and hardly missed a performance. In 15 books she collected theatre programmes, press cuttings, hand-written cast lists and photos. Her special appreciation concerned Diana Morrison and John Ellison, to whom she

dedicated a volume of her diaries as their 'friend and admirer' (see *Collection Nellie Woodhouse*. York City Archives. Acc 639).

31 Other similarly lavish Sheffield theatres included the Alexandra, which hosted grand opera and had a capacity of over 4,000, the Empire, which was built by Frank Matcham, the Hippodrome, its equally vast rival, and the Theatre Royal, which had opened in 1763 and burnt down in 1935. Today the Lyceum is the only surviving theatre (see Hillerby, Bryen. *The Lost Theatres of Sheffield*. Barnsley: Wharncliffe, 1999).

32 It is because of this importance that this study will concentrate on the Sheffield Repertory Company rather than the Lyceum. Another factor is that the Lyceum was managed by the same John Beaumont who was at the helm of Leeds' Grand Theatre and, therefore, produced a very similar fare.

33 See Seed, T. Alec. *The Sheffield Repertory Theatre. A History*. Sheffield: Sheffield Repertory Company, 1959. pp. 20–7.

34 For the 'Little Theatre Movement' see Jackson/Rowell, *Repertory Movement*, 70–2. In the mid-1930s there were also three variety theatres in Hull: Palace, Tivoli and Alexandra (see Gillett, Edward and Kenneth A. Mac Mahon. *A History of Hull*. 2nd ext. ed. Hull: Hull University Press, 1990. pp. 445–7).

35 The obscurity of some of its productions may have been a factor leading to the closure of the Playgoers Theatre in 1934. In any case attendances had been low.

36 Wareing, Alfred. 'The Little Theatre Movement. Its Genesis and its Goal.' Carson, L., ed. *The Stage Yearbook 1928*. London: The Stage, 1928. p. 13.

37 The historic Theatre Royal was turned into a cinema in 1921. The Prince's Theatre opened in 1876.

38 Bradford poses the difficult question on which theatre to concentrate as the Alhambra, as the more successful, famous and financially viable venue, could justifiably claim to be the city's first theatre whereas the Prince's, with its resident companies, resembled the rising repertory theatres in other Yorkshire cities to a greater degree. I have decided to look at both theatres, not least because CEMA used both playhouses to send touring productions to.

39 As the Playhouse did not stage plays on a regular basis it will not be looked at in greater detail.

40 See Yorkshire Observer, ed. *Bradford 1847–1947. The Centenary Book of Bradford*. Bradford: Yorkshire Observer, n.d. [1947]. See also *The Historical Pageant of Bradford. The Souvenir Book*. Bradford: Percy Lund, n.d. [1931].

41 See Chisholm, *Repertory*, p. 66. Chisholm might have alluded to the popularity of Leeds' City Varieties Music Hall (built in 1865).

42 Lena Ashwell was invited again in the following years and received official honours such as a Grand Civic Night in 1926. For more information on Ashwell, who had been organising tours of actors and musicians in the European war zones during the First World War, see Collins, *Theatre at War*, pp. 147–76.

43 Hutchison announced in 1930 that he proposed 'to establish my own
    Repertory Company in York presenting the masterpieces of our greatest
    authors living and dead. The company has been recruited entirely from the
    London stage' (*YEP*, 26 April 1930).

44 In 1930 the 'Percy Hutchison Players' played between March and July, in
    1931 between May to September, and in 1932 they even performed between
    February and September.

45 See *YEP*, 11 May 1933; *YG*, 13 April 1934. Hutchison claimed that there had
    been five main causes of failure: bad trade and general depression, the
    competition of the talkies, the debt of £4,000 'I incurred with Trans-Canada-
    Theatre, Limited, in the year 1921', the Entertainment Tax, the losses on
    productions and touring companies in general and his 1932 Canadian tour in
    particular. He asserted, however, that there had always been the probability
    'that one of his productions would prove a brilliant success, and he would
    then have been able to retrieve his position'. The judges accused Hutchison
    of 'reckless extravagance', and the Official Receiver stated that 'the amount
    of the bankrupt's personal expenditure has been unjustifiable under the
    circumstances and has been an additional cause' (*YG*, 13 April 1934).
    According to the report Hutchison took a lease on an additional house in
    1931 because he needed 'fresh air', he spent £1,100 a year on his wife and
    himself although he was losing money, the same sum he used annually for his
    London house, which was furnished with expensive antiques, and another
    £500 in 1932 alone on 'hospitality'. An additional problem was that
    Hutchison could not produce any accounts for his personal expenditure, it
    was only estimated. The trustees, however, were not satisfied with his claim
    'I gave her £1,000' – regarding the allowance he had made to his wife.
    Hutchison replied that not only had the public expected of him a lavish
    lifestyle but it had also been just for a man in his position. In April 1934
    Hutchison was eventually acquitted and granted discharge from bankruptcy
    (which was also the only way creditors could get some of their money back).
    After he had left York Hutchison remained in the business. In 1944 he was
    one of the co-opted members from the Touring Managers' Association on the
    board of the British Drama League (see British Drama League. *Twenty-Five
    Years of the British Drama League 1919–1944*. Oxford: Alden, 1944).

46 After Hutchison had left the theatre remained closed between April and
    September 1933, and its permanent closure seemed a realistic option.
    Eventually, the theatre reopened under the management of Stanley Weetham
    Crawshay of Scarborough who returned to visiting companies and did not
    pursue the repertory idea any further. He survived for only a few months, and
    in April 1934 the Corporation cancelled the contract after Crawshay had
    failed to pay the rent (see meeting of 16 April 1934. *York City Council, Estates
    Committee 1931–1940*. p. 197).

47 Rowntree's studies of poverty in York are regarded as seminal today, especially
    the first book on *Poverty: A Study of Town Life* (published in 1901). The sequel

of 1941 includes some remarks regarding the Theatre Royal and the foundation of the repertory company (see Rowntree, Seebohm B. *Poverty and Progress. A Second Social Survey of York*. London: Longman, 1942. pp. 413–15).

48   See *YEP*, 30 April 1934.

49   See Public Record Office [PRO]. BT 31/33529/290285 York Citizens Theatre Ltd. pp. 731–3. The company was formally incorporated and registered with the Board of Trade on 17 July 1934. One of the 'objects for which the Company is established' was 'to promote or aid in any way that may be deemed proper the interest of drama and theatrical entertainment' (ibid., p. 732). The PRO file also lists the 157 'persons holding shares in York Citizen Theatre Limited' (ibid., p. 113).

50   The Duke of York stated that 'as a Citizen of York I am glad to hear of this communal enterprise to maintain the Theatre Royal as a York Citizens' Theatre. I am glad to know of this endeavour to preserve drama and the best type of plays for the people of York' (*YEP*, 8 August 1934).

51   See *YEP*, 11 May 1933.

52   See Estates Committee meeting 13 July 1931 (*York City Council, Estates Committee 1931–1940*, p. 18).

53   See Theatre Royal Sub-Committee meeting 20 June 1933 (ibid., p. 132).

54   See Estates Committee Meeting 12 May 1902. *York City Council, Estates Committee 1894–1905*, p. 448.

55   'The Corporation are under a liability to maintain and keep the roofs, main walls, and main timbers in good repair, to paint the outside wood and iron work, to wire the Theatre for the purpose of a supply of electric light, and to provide modern sanitary conveniences' (*York City Council, Council Minutes 1900–1901*, p. 385).

56   Linda Fitzsimmons claims that 'the Corporation tried to counteract the Opera House's appeal by rebuilding the interior of the Theatre Royal', and Sybil Rosenfeld asserts that the Corporation was 'afraid that its property might suffer depreciation owing to the erection by a syndicate of the new Grand Opera House' and, therefore, 'proposed to rebuild the interior of the Theatre' (Fitzsimmons, *Theatre Royal*, p. 187; Rosenfeld, *York Theatre*, p. 311). The immediate reason for the building programme, however, was quite mundane: the theatre was in desperate need of repair. As the architect Frank Tugwell pointed out, the roof was 'in a very dangerous state, the nature having gone quite out of the wood, where it is not so worm-eaten, as to be positively unsafe' (*York City Council, Council Minutes 1900–1901*, pp. 445–7).

57   See *York City Council, Council Minutes 1905–1906*, pp. 965–8. It had been agreed that Waddington would have to pay interest 'on the balance of expenditure above £2,000 at the rate of 7.5% per annum' (see *York City Council, Estates Committee 1894–1905*, p. 376). Taking into account the eventual costs of nearly £7,000 the scrapping of the interest resulted in a reduction of rent by £351.

58   This also becomes obvious in the Council's negotiations with applicants for

the new lease in 1900. Although Waddington's offer was not better than that of his rival Milton Bode, the Council seemed to have had a strong interest to keep the theatre in the hands of a York resident, which Waddington was. Also they obviously disapproved of the idea that Bode only wanted to incorporate the Theatre Royal in his business portfolio. He was already running eight theatres and different companies and only intended to 'locate at York a first-class Manager' without himself being there – just as Hutchison later did (see *York City Council, Council Minutes 1900–1901*, pp. 9–10).

59 The full text of the 'Memorial' was read at the council meeting. The group noticed 'with extreme regret the proposal to convert the Theatre Royal in to a Variety House, thereby depriving a large number of the Inhabitants of the only opportunity of seeing the legitimate drama and opera in York. That this historic house, with its worthy past, should pass into a "twice nightly" variety place is deplorable on general grounds. There is already every facility in the City for those whose tastes desire a variety entertainment, and your petitioners most strongly urge that in any re-arrangement that may be necessary at the Theatre Royal the Corporation will duly safeguard the interest of the Citizens who look to a well-conducted Theatre as a potent educational force'. (*York City Council, Council Minutes 1905–1906*, pp. 965–6).

60 See *York City Council, Council Minutes, 1932–1933*, pp. 271 and 352.

61 The members of the Estates Committee had originally decided not to bear more than 50% of the cost of re-upholstering certain seats 'not exceeding £100' (see *York City Council, Estates Committee 1931–1940*, p. 142). Crawshay, however, also wanted new lamps, carpets and curtains, the whitewashing of walls and ceilings, a new electrical installation for the stage and a new switchboard. The estimated overall costs amounted to £730, but although this exceeded by far the sum agreed upon before, the Sub-Committee 'authorised the immediate carrying out of the work'.

62 See *York City Council, Estates Committee 1931–1940*, pp. 132–3. According to the lease most things on Crawshay's 'wish list' should have been paid by himself as one of the 'Lessee's Covenants' was to 're-decorate and re-upholster where necessary' (see *York City Council, Council Minutes 1923–1924*, p. 685).

63 See, for example, Chisholm, *Repertory*. The journal *Theatre World* ran a series of articles in which it introduced regional 'reps'.

64 See confirmation of the 'alteration in the memorandum of association' of 27 April 1935 (PRO. BT 31/33529/290285. York Citizens Theatre Ltd. p. 105).

65 Alterations included the installation of a roller stage and an extended canopy outside the theatre. Again the city authorities were prepared to cover the costs but in return asked for an increased rent. The 5 per cent increase, which resulted in a £900 rent, however, was still low in comparison to what the city had asked for in years previously (see *York City Council, Estates Committee 1931–1940*, pp. 316–18).

Prices new and old were as follows: Dress Circle first two rows 2/6 (3/6 old),

Dress Circle remainder 1/6 (3/6), Stalls 1/6 (3/6), Pit 9d (1/6), Upper Circle 7d (1/6), Gallery 4d (9d). The prices remained the same until 1943 when they were raised as twice-nightly performances discontinued and profits dropped. The management stressed, however, that the cheap prices were 'only available for repertory plays' (*YEP*, 7 September 1935). Tickets for other performances, especially at Christmas, were considerably dearer. Tickets for the 1936 Pantomime, for example, amounted to 12s for the Boxes, 3s for the Dress Circle, 2/5 for the Stalls, 2s for the Circle, 1s for the Pit, 9d for the Upper Circle, and 6d for the Gallery.

66 See Seed, *Sheffield Repertory Theatre*, pp. 28–9 and plates 51–4.

67 Commentators praised the 'astonishing change [which] has taken place' (*Yorkshire Post* [YP], 19 August 1936).

68 See *York Public Library Quarterly Bulletin*, 10 February 1936.

69 See *YH*, 12 November 1936.

70 See *YG*, 8 February 1935. In a prospectus the new directors stressed 'that if the best possible entertainment is to be given in a provincial theatre, it must be run, not from a profit-making point of view' (PRO. BT 31/33529/290285. York Citizens Theatre Ltd. p. 75).

71 See Rowntree, *Poverty and Progress*, pp. 414–15. The press, however, suggested that part of the success was 'the granting of permission to smoke in any part of the theatre' (*YEP*, 17 September 1935).

72 *YEP*, 18 December 1935.

73 Many commentators criticised the lack of quality of productions at regional repertory theatres, which they attributed to the limited rehearsal time. In contrast to an average of eighty hours spent on a West End production managers of weekly rep could only afford fifteen hours of rehearsal time for each production. As a way out of the misery St John Ervine proposed a regional touring system combining, for example, the theatres in York, Leeds and Bradford in some sort of Yorkshire circuit (see Marshall, Norman. *The Other Theatre*. London: Lehmann, 1947. pp. 190–3; Priestley, *Theatre Outlook*, p. 46).

74 See, for example, *YEP*, 10 March 1937.

75 'Miss Phyllis Calvert, formerly a York Repertory Company favourite and now a British film star' (*YEP*, 19 December 1944). See also the obituary on her death in *The Guardian* on 10 October 2002.

76 See *Collection Nellie Woodhouse*, vol. XII.

77 York's programme notes of 9 September 1940, for example, stated that for Bartlett Cormack's play *The Painted Veil* antique furniture was provided by Charles Thornton, Petergate, silverware by Hardcastle, Stonegate, China and glassware by Woollons and Harwood, Fossgate, flowers by Mrs Stork, Stonegate, the table lamp by York Corporation Electricity Department, telephones by G.P.O., baskets by the School for the Blind at the King's Manor, and so on.

78 The company had acquired an adequate reserve fund and did not require the

subscribed capital any longer. The limited company was wound up, the 400 shareholders were repaid, and the 'York Citizens' Theatre Trust' company was formed with a nominal capital of £1,000. From then on profits were devoted to the interests of drama entirely (see PRO. BT 31/33529/290285 York Citizens Theatre Ltd. p. 105).

79 See Chisholm, *Repertory*, 64–65; Taylor, Coral. *Right Royal. Wakefield Theatre 1776–1994*. Wakefield: Wakefield Historical Publications, 1995. p. 213.

80 See, for example, Chisholm, *Repertory*, 233–237.

81 Quoted in Gardiner, Juliet. *Wartime. Britain 1939–1945*. London: Headline, 2004. p. 122.

82 Dukes, Ashley. *Theatre Arts* 23 (1939): p. 784.

83 Shaw called the closure 'a masterstroke of unimaginative stupidity' and suggested that an 'agent of Chancellor Hitler' was responsible for the fact 'that we should all cower in darkness and terror "for the duration"' (*The Times*, 5 September 1939).

84 As in similar situations of national crisis, entertainments proved immensely popular. Between 1938 and 1944 the amount of money spent on entertainment rose by 120 per cent. The BBC noted an increase in serious drama, publishers found difficulty in responding to the public's thirst for classics, and new copies of novels by Trollope and Austen were eventually 'quite unobtainable' (see Calder, Angus. *The People's War. Britain 1939–1945*. London: Pimlico, 1999. pp. 357, 364 and 511). The output of popular literature, too, soared. Evacuation and *Blitz* novels, war diaries, spy thrillers and RAF romances headed the bill.

85 See PRO. Home Office. HO 186 Air Raid Precautions. HO 186/1036 Entertainment (1943). 'Entertainments Order' issued by the Home Secretary John Anderson, 8 September 1939. The term 'safe', however, was applied to theatres almost everywhere. Despite concerns regarding large congregations of people assembled under bombardment the government usually granted the night opening of theatres. In a reversal of official policy the government soon permitted shows even in densely populated Westminster (see Sanson, William. *Westminster in War*. London: Faber, n.d. [1947]. p. 170).

86 See Shellard, Dominic. *British Theatre Since the War*. London: Yale University Press. p. 6. In June 1940, while the war had disastrous effects on London theatres, the government 'clearly indicated that the theatres should carry on' (Fairweather, David. 'Over the Footlights.' *Theatre World* June 1940: p. 125). See also PRO. Ministry of Information. INF 1/260. Home Morale and Education During the Winter 1940–41.

87 Fairweather, David. 'Over the Footlights.' *Theatre World* July 1940: p. 5.

88 It is interesting to see, however, that the report on ENSA issued in March 1941 is the only official document concerned with the control of theatrical entertainments, to be circulated as a government paper during the war. The report made the provision of entertainments through the Association – and thereby state subsidies to the arts – an official policy (see PRO. T 161/1083.

Treasury Board Papers: Interdepartmental Entertainments Service Board. First Report).

89 For an account of ENSA's development during the war see Dean's own *Theatre at War*.

90 See ibid., pp. 249–50.

91 In 1943 alone ENSA provided an average of over 3,000 performances a week to the armed forces (see Minihan, Janet. *The Nationalization of Culture. The Development of State Subsidies to the Arts in Great Britain*. London: Hamish Hamilton, 1977. p. 226).

92 See Dean, *Theatre at War*, p. 541.

93 See Calder, *People's War*, p. 372.

94 See Shellard, Dominic. *Harold Hobson: Witness and Judge*. Keele: Keele University Press, 1995. p. 47.

95 Dean made it clear that the aim to 'work for national morale' was ENSA's 'most important objective' (Dean, *Theatre at War*, p. 18).

96 Ibid., p. 298.

97 The cathedral site was carefully chosen to establish a link to medieval Mystery Plays. The characters' names added to this impression as they were called 'Valour', 'Patience', as well as 'Any-Man', 'Any-Woman', who were – and this is interesting to note with respect to the aim of this performance not to be socially exclusive – 'just an ordinary working-class couple' (Dean, *Theatre at War*, p. 299). The list of artists involved reads like a wartime 'Who is Who' of the arts in Britain: the script had been prepared by Clemence Dane, the cast was headed by Leslie Howard, Sybil Thorndike, Edith Evans and the orchestra was conducted by Henry Wood. The War Office provided bands of the Brigade of Guards and the trumpets and drums of the Household Cavalry, the massed singers included members of the Royal Choral Society and the London Fire Service Choir. The event was performed under the patronage of the Lord Mayor and the Sheriffs of the City of London and they, together with all the Mayors and Aldermen of all the London Boroughs, witnessed the performance along with thousands (see ibid., pp. 294–303). A week after the London production the pageant was re-staged amid the ruins of Coventry Cathedral.

98 The pageant's scenes were accompanied by the words of Scott, Shakespeare, Shelley, Spenser, Milton, Kipling, Tennyson and Hardy and the music of Arne, Purcell, Elgar, Stanford, Sullivan, Parry and Walton.

99 For CEMA's development throughout the war see the 'EL' files in the Archive of Art and Design (AAD) in London (stored at Blythe House). See also Jörn Weingärtner. *The Arts as a Weapon of War. Britain and the Shaping of National Morale in the Second World War*. London: I B Tauris, 2006.

100 In the course of the war CEMA's chairman Lord Keynes increasingly worked towards its continuation in peacetime, and in 1946 CEMA became the Arts Council. CEMA, therefore, has to be seen in line with the Beveridge Report, plans for a National Health Service and the 1944 Education Act, although on

its foundation hardly anyone had in mind that CEMA could develop into a national agency offering subsidies to the arts (regarding the radical changes in the education system see Dent, H.C. *Education in Transition. A Sociological Study of the Impact of War on English Education 1939–1943*. London: Kegan Paul, 1944).

101 See 'Cultural Activities in War-Time. Notes of informal Conference held at the Board's Offices' (AAD, EL 1/1).

102 CEMA itself was a relatively small body at first with members appointed by the Minister of Education, who was also responsible to Parliament for its work (see Speaight, Robert. 'Drama Since 1939.' Hayward, John, Reed, Henry, Robert Speaight and Stephen Spender. *Since 1939*. London: Phoenix, 1949. p. 20). Soon, however, CEMA grew in size. In 1942 it had nine members with Lord Keynes as Chairman, an elaborated system of advisory panels of experts with executive power, committees in Scotland and Wales and ten regional offices in England. The six members of the Drama Advisory Panel were joined by the Drama Director Lewis Casson and Drama Assistant Charles Landstone. In line with rising government support the directors to CEMA for Music, Drama and Art became fully salaried in 1942 (see Minihan, *Nationalization of Culture*, 218; Landstone, Charles. *Off-Stage. A Personal Record of the First Twelve Years of State Sponsored Drama in Great Britain*. London: Elek, 1953. p. 66; CEMA. *The Arts in War Time. A Report on the Work of C.E.M.A. 1942 and 1943*. London: Council for the Encouragement of Music and the Arts, n.d. [1944]. p. 4).

103 See Taylor, Eric. *Showbiz Goes to War*. London: Robert Hale, 1992. p. 118. In 1943 the Treasury grant was £135,000, in 1944 it rose by almost 50 per cent to £175,000 (see CEMA. *The Fifth Year. The End of the Beginning. Report on the Work of CEMA for 1944*. London: Council for the Encouragement of Music and the Arts, 1945. p. 4).

104 See Whitworth, Geoffrey. *The Making of a National Theatre*. London. Faber & Faber, 1951.

105 In 1944 the Council organised fourteen tours, with 129 weeks' playing time. The actual costs for these 129 weeks were £16,000 – an average of £125 per playing week. The average gross costing per week was about £275, with takings of about £150 (see Landstone, *Off-Stage*, pp. 55 and 59).

106 The relations between CEMA and theatre companies and music ensembles varied from full financial responsibility to no financial connection at all. In between there were block grants, loans and limited guarantees against loss (see CEMA, *Arts in War Time*, p. 14). Even if CEMA did not pay any subsidies, however, it frequently offered 'moral sponsorship' to companies who agreed that any profits they made were at the disposal of CEMA; in return, since CEMA encouraged only work of a 'cultural' kind, these companies usually benefited by gaining exemption from Entertainments Tax (see Nicoll, Allardyce. '"In Association with CEMA".' *Theatre Arts* 28 (1944): p. 420).

107 See Marshall, *Other Theatre*, pp. 133–6. Regarding Thorndike's celebrated war work and especially her Welsh tours see Morley, Sheridan. *Sybil Thorndike. A Life in the Theatre*. London: Weidenfeld and Nicolson, 1977. pp. 111–20. On the occasion of her 1940 tour of *Macbeth* Thorndike wrote a 'plain clothes prologue' in which she tried to make the wartime relevance of the play clear to the miners: 'You needn't always think of dictators in terms of concentration camps and tanks and aeroplanes. Men don't change in a thousand years. What Macbeth wanted, what all such people want, is power. This is a play about a tyrant, a dictator' (ibid., pp. 111–12).

108 For a detailed contemporary account see Haskell, Arnold L. 'Ballet Since 1939'. Haskell, Arnold L., Dilys Powell, Rollo Myers and Robin Ironside. *Since 1939. Ballet – Films – Music – Painting*. London: Readers Union, 1948. pp. 9–56.

109 Jooss had headed one of the most influential dance companies in Europe when forced to leave Nazi Germany. After having worked in Münster during the mid-1920s he formed his first company in Essen and widely toured his prophetic work *The Green Table*. In 1933 Jooss took his headquarters in Britain (see Haskell, *Ballet Since 1939*, pp. 43–4).

110 From the beginning, ballet in Britain was influenced by foreigners, especially by the Russian school of Serge Daghileff and Anna Pavlova. Even the re-emergence of ballet during the war was largely due to foreigners. Ninette de Valois, who founded the first successful professional ballet company in Britain with the Vic-Wells Ballet, was Irish, Marie Rambert, the founder of the famous Ballet Rambert, was French, and Kurt Jooss was a German émigré. The growth of these companies is hardly imaginable without the war. Sadler's Wells, for example, grew from a small company of eight dancers into a substantial organisation appearing all over Britain during forty-eight weeks out of the fifty-two (see Marshall, *Other Theatre*, p. 142). Together with the emergence of important new names such as Frederick Ashton, Robert Helpman, Mona Inglesby and Margot Fonteyn contemporary commentators claimed that 'the British are once more a dancing nation'. It was even suggested that male dancers should be exempt from conscription, 'as their absence would jeopardise the existence of something precious for national artistic prestige in the future and useful for public morale in the present' (see Haskell, *Ballet Since 1939*, pp. 23 and 45. See also Williamson, Audrey. 'English Ballet, 1944.' *Theatre Arts* 28 (1944): pp. 733–6).

111 It has to be stressed, however, that Sadler's Wells presented scaled-down versions of the great opera classics on tour with an 'orchestra' of four and the décor for *Marriage of Figaro*, for example, only consisting of two chairs and a sofa (see Myers, Rollo. 'Music Since 1939'. *Since 1939*, p. 118). Tours of factory workers' hostels were high up on CEMA's list of priorities. Between July 1942 and December 1943 alone seven companies were sent on tour, and by 1945 sixty-nine hostels were regularly visited by parties associated with CEMA. Most of the hostels had well-equipped theatres with seating

capacities of up to 400 (see Marshall, *Other Theatre*, p. 229; CEMA, *Arts in War Time*, pp. 16–17; Landstone, *Off-Stage*, pp. 50–1).

112 In 1942–3 CEMA provided over 4,500 factory concerts, sometimes to audiences as large as 7,000 (see Minihan, *Nationalization of Culture*, p. 220). The number of concerts given under CEMA auspices rose to over 6,000 in 1944. It is interesting to note that an increasing level of support was offered by local councils to concert series of all kinds (see CEMA, *Fifth Year*, p. 8).

113 For Casals and Hess see Calder, *People's War*, p. 373; for Menuhin see CEMA, *Fifth Year*, p. 7. Commentators were quick to stress the importance for the war effort of the work carried out by musicians, and the significance of this work for post-war Britain, as 'musically, Britain has won her spurs and can now face the future with confidence. Gone are the days when it was possible for foreign nations to refer to her as the land without music' (Myers, *Music Since 1939*, p. 139).

114 Among the biggest theatrical successes in the hostels for factory workers, for example, were *Twelfth Night* and *Hedda Gabler*. Regarding the new audiences found, commentators noted after the war that 'some hundred centres are now enjoying regular concerts where, only ten years ago, nothing of the kind had ever been heard' (Russell, Thomas. *Philharmonic*. London: Penguin, 1953. p. 123). In fact the public demand for 'high' culture far exceeded any pre-war expectations (see Minihan, *Nationalization of Culture*, pp. 218–20 and 225).

115 CEMA saved the Bristol Theatre Royal from demolition, restored it, placed it in working order and ran the playhouse on a lease under its direct management (see CEMA, *Arts in War Time*, p. 10). It is interesting to note that all this happened in September 1942, a particularly difficult month for the Allies with the fall of Tobruk, the German advance towards Stalingrad, and Japanese supremacy in the Far East.

The inauguration in August 1944 of the Old Vic as a permanent repertory company in the heart of London's West End devoted entirely to the production of classics was not only a bold idea but also another indication of the theatre's wartime role. CEMA was aware that it 'would need bold and generous expenditure' to reach this goal. Lord Keynes 'spoke of good round sums, well into five figures', and agreed to pay 'an advance cheque of £5,000' immediately (see Landstone, *Off-Stage*, pp. 148 and 151). Perhaps the boldest part of the scheme was to secure the services of a star-studded company headed by two of theatre's most celebrated actors, Laurence Olivier and Ralph Richardson – although they were both on active service. So Lord Lytton, the chairman of the governors of the Old Vic, wrote to the First Lord of the Admiralty asking for their release. In doing so he used a dual strategy. First, he stressed the close links between the Old Vic and CEMA, which, 'I need hardly add, expresses the cultural policy of the Board of Education, and is financed by the Treasury.' Second, Lytton put forward artistic reasons as 'the importance need hardly be stressed of having such a company in existence while the war is in progress', adding that 'the many thousands of

Overseas visitors in London make it highly desirable that British drama, and particularly the Classics, should be presented in the best possible manner.' (letter dated 15 March 1944. Theatre Museum. Charles Landstone Archive THM/201. Box 4). The fact that these two actors were duly released from active service to become joint directors of the Old Vic indicates how much the political landscape had changed within a few years.

116 For a detailed overview of the developments in the run-up of the foundation of the National Theatre see the study by one of its most ardent supporters, Geoffrey Whitworth (*National Theatre*).

117 See Whitworth, *National Theatre*, p. 15. In a typical pre-war statement David Fairweather made his rejection of the National Theatre idea clear. He argued that if the nation really wanted a National Theatre it would have subscribed the needed £1 million already. The fact that only half of that sum had been found was an indicator that the people did not want such a theatre. It is interesting to note that the idea of a state subsidy as a possible solution to the funding problem does not seem to occur to him (see *Theatre World* January 1936: p. 3).

118 See Dean, *Theatre at War*, pp. 212–13. Dent even claims that 'if ever a body of men and women helped to revive and sustain the morale of the English people, during a time when this was most needed, those CEMA artists did' (see Dent, *Education in Transition*, p. 149).

119 In August 1940 the League mounted a conference to discuss the 'uses, opportunities, and responsibilities' of drama in wartime (see *Theatre World* August 1940: p. 46). The new demands were illustrated by the list of organisations in attendance: CEMA, ENSA, the Army Welfare Committees, the National Council of Social Service, the Federation of Women's Institutes, etc. More importantly, the conference took place at the Shakespeare Memorial Theatre at Stratford. Quite obviously, the League wanted to stress the link between Elizabethan England and the current conflict.

120 At first most of the concerts featured the established classical repertoire. Soon, however, the fact that most of these works were by German-speaking composers to some critics seemed inappropriate and contemporary British composers received commissions. Arnold Bax (*Work in Progress*), E. J. Moeran (*Overture to a Masque*) and Alan Rawsthorne (*Street Corner*), among others, wrote overtures especially for these occasions (see Dean, *Theatre at War*, p. 221).

121 Shellard, *British Theatre Since the War*, p. 4. See also Hobson, Harold. *Theatre in Britain. A Personal View*. Oxford: Phaidon, 1984. pp. 134–9; Landstone, *Off-Stage*, p. 151; Stephens, Frances. 'Over the Footlights.' *Theatre World* October 1944: p. 5.

122 See Rowell, George. *The Old Vic Theatre. A History*. Cambridge: Cambridge University Press, 1993. p. 138.

123 *The Observer*, 30 September 1945, and ibid., 7 October 1945. Similarly Dukes, Ashley. 'The Gielgud Macbeth.' *Theatre Arts* 26 (1942): p. 617 and 'Repertory at Last! The Scene in Europe.' *Theatre Arts* 29 (1945): pp. 22–31.

124 See Calder, *People's War*, p. 510.

125 After having been rather unsuccessfully posted in Paris and the US, Coward returned to Britain in 1941. He produced nationalistic songs, the successful play *Blithe Spirit* and the patriotic film *In Which We Serve*, which was one of the most successful films of the war (see Lesley, Cole. *The Life of Noel Coward*. London: Cape, 1976. Photos between pp. 172 and 173). In 1942 Coward's play *This Happy Breed* toured Britain for 26 weeks, and after that he went on concert-tours to Australia, New Zealand and South Africa (see Shellard, *Harold Hobson*, p. 50). For Dane and Priestley see Lesley, *Noel Coward*, p. 226 and Shellard, *Harold Hobson*, p. 50.

126 'Donald Wolfit's Great Achievement for the Theatre in War-time.' *Theatre World* January 1941: pp. 10–11). Wolfit and his company played extracts from different Shakespearean plays (see 'Lunch Time Shakespeare.' *Theatre World* December 1940: p. 128, January 1941: p. 8). Wolfit enjoyed the backing of CEMA for his enterprise (see CEMA meeting on 15 October 1940. AAD, EL 1/6).

127 See *Theatre Arts* 24 (1940): p. 225; Morley, Sheridan. *John G. The Authorised Biography of John Gielgud*. London: Hodder and Stoughton, 2001. p. 167. See also Noble, Peter. *British Theatre*. London: Knapp & Drewett, p. 23.

128 Among other journals the *Theatre Arts* used the photos. They showed the company travelling in an ordinary coach and being cramped into their dressing rooms, they depicted the scenery van and the basic halls they performed in. The intended honest down-to-earth image was further underlined by the captions: 'After the show, the members of the company will sleep in the cottages of their new-made audience friends, working men and women and their children, who have paid not more to see fine theatre than they would at their local cinema' (*Theatre Arts* 26 (1942): pp. 241–4).

129 The *Bulletin* was an information service for British officials serving throughout the world, which they were asked to disseminate. It was intended to inform them about the activities of the British forces as well as the impact of the war upon the home front. It was published by the British Library of Information in New York and obviously directed at the American market as the spelling was American throughout. The *Bulletin* reads like a propagandistic newspaper, it is desperately reassuring, features a simple typescript and no pictures.

130 See, for example, Brown, Ivor. 'In War, British Drama Finds a New Public.' *Bulletin from Britain*. no. 97. 8 July 1942. pp. 15–16.

131 At a conference at the Ministry of Labour with ENSA and the entertainments industry in March 1942, Bevin assured the delegates that the maintenance of civil entertainment was an important part of government policy. Bevin decided 'that artistes who offer to give six weeks' work each year to national-service entertainment shall have that taken into consideration when their applications for deferment are considered' (Dean, *Theatre at War*, p. 238).

132 The Committee was established in early 1940 and around a hundred artists

were asked to do specific works, some of which the Committee bought. Thirty artists were employed full-time on a salary, twenty-one of those became officers and were attached to the services (see Calder, *People's War*, p. 510).

133 Olivier was particularly praised for his morale-boosting portrait of *Henry V* in the 1944 film.

134 In York, for example, Manchester-based company Hills produced aircraft at Terry's, the chocolate manufacturer (as Ms Motherdale recalled in Wilson, Van, comp. *York Voices*. Stroud: Tempus, 1999. p. 94).

135 Programme notes had to be radically reduced in size. York's lavish twelve-page booklet was cut down – a fact which people recollect until today. Marjorie Leng was a regular theatregoer in the 1930s and 1940s and recalls 'the wartime programmes, some of them were single sheets, because of the paper drive' (see Wilson, *York Voices*, p. 117).

136 The press regularly featured articles about actors being called up, and also about the first casualties (see *YEP*, 10 April 1940, 16 April 1940, 17 April 1940, 8 May 1940, etc.). One example is York actor Michael Rennie. When he joined the RAF in November 1940 the press devoted long articles to his departure (see *YG*, 15 November 1940; *YEP*, 6 November 1940).

137 In a monthly bulletin CEMA published a list of all the events it supported. The May 1944 bulletin, for example, lists 30 different events in Yorkshire alone including the London Symphony Orchestra's visit to Hull's Queen's Hall, a YMCA concert tour in the East Riding, chamber music in different Leeds factories, a production of *The Shoemaker's Holiday* by Walter Hudd's company in Huddersfield, a five-week tour of northern towns by Ballets Jooss, and art exhibitions all over Yorkshire (see *CEMA Bulletin* May 1944: pp. 4–5, 10–11, 14 and 17). See also the Regional Directors' Reports (AAD, EL 3).

138 Commentators claimed that CEMA was 'the harbinger of a new form of adult education' (see Dent, *Education in Transition*, p. 58). CEMA also became engaged in organising exhibitions all over Britain. Here, too, the educational mission was obvious. Although the majority of exhibitions were concerned with visual art, interesting other examples included shows like 'Living in Cities', 'Rebuilding Britain' and 'War Artists' (see CEMA, *Fifth Year*, pp. 38–9). For an account regarding its educational concept see CEMA's own Lord Keynes in a talk given at the reopening of Bristol's Theatre Royal ('The Arts in War-Time. Widening Scope of CEMA. Re-opening of Bristol Theatre To-night.' 11 May 1943. Theatre Museum. Charles Landstone Archive THM/201. Box 4). Other institutions, too, embarked on their educational agendas. Perhaps most important of all – because of its ability to reach millions of people simultaneously – the BBC offered programmes intended to educate its listeners without being too patronising (a common point of criticism during the 1930s). The Corporation's wartime successes included the highly popular Promenade Concerts and the provision of

entertainment for factory workers with 'Music While You Work' (see Minihan, *Nationalization of Culture*, p. 227).

139 In its report on the work during 1944 CEMA puts special emphasis on 'new and unusual works' performed by its associated orchestras (see CEMA, *Fifth Year*, pp. 29–30).

140 For a typically glowing article on CEMA's work see Nicoll, *Association with CEMA*, pp. 417–21. An indication of the popularity of classical music is the sheer number of concerts and listeners. In 1944 alone the Hallé Orchestra, the Liverpool and London Philharmonics 'provided between them no less than 722 concerts to audiences totalling over a million' (Myers, *Music Since 1939*, p. 107).

141 Many commentators complained about poor standards at provincial repertory theatres. To improve this situation Landstone presented a scheme by which CEMA offered grants to repertory companies who decided to present a special play for a fortnight instead of only one week as usual. As this meant that the previous play would have to run for two weeks, too, and the takings in the second week were bound to be lower, CEMA paid the deficiency up to the average takings of the previous thirteen weeks. This 'Landstone Plan' ran successfully for four years. The scheme was part of an overall effort to make two- or three-weekly repertory attractive to regional theatres. The envisaged effect was not only to raise standards but also to provide an incentive to produce the classics. Especially after the war these plans bore fruit with the establishment of regional touring circuits and subsidiary playhouses. York's Theatre Royal, for example, took a lease at Scarborough and Northampton played the Savoy Theatre in Kettering.

142 CEMA supported the Old Vic's move to the North financially (see Landstone's detailed accounts in Landstone, *Off-Stage*, pp. 21–4, 28).

143 There were numerous provincial theatres which now became associated with CEMA, including Dundee Repertory Company, Glasgow Citizens' Theatre and, perhaps most important, the Theatre Royal in Bristol. It is interesting to see that CEMA did not support these theatres and companies unconditionally. To be eligible for association with CEMA they had to become non-profit organisations and had to agree to certain obligations as the Council reserved the right to review their finances, plans and policies annually. In return they received support that ranged from full financial responsibility to limited guarantees against loss (see Minihan, *Nationalization of Culture*, pp. 221–3). Apart from the gain in financial security, the theatres and companies were also assured that the support they received was a recognition of their work done in the interests of national service (see CEMA, *Fifth Year*, pp. 32–3).

144 CEMA, *Fifth Year*, p. 32.

145 See CEMA, *Arts in War Time*, pp. 15–16. Speaight claims that this possible exemption from a great burden in fact 'conferred a much larger financial benefit than anything CEMA could afford to give' (Speaight, *Drama Since*

1939, p. 22). As CEMA could not itself grant the tax exemption but had to apply at the Board of Customs, there were ongoing and increasing attempts to acquire control over this question especially during the later stages of the war. Ultimately, CEMA wanted to be in the position to cast the crucial verdict itself whether or not a play was educational, instead of leaving it to the Board of Customs. Although this change in legislation never materialised, it shows how self-confident CEMA had become by this point (see AAD, EL 1/7 Minutes Meetings 21–37).

146 The first conference of the Council was held in Birmingham in autumn 1944, the second meeting took place in York at the end of 1944. By then the membership had already risen from the initial seven to ten theatres (see Landstone, *Off-Stage*, pp. 104–5).

147 The inclusion of the York and Sheffield repertory companies in the 1948 'Festival of English Repertory' at the Shakespeare Memorial Theatre in Stratford indicates the success they enjoyed – also thanks to government funding.

148 CEMA, *Fifth Year*, p. 32. In an interesting 'Memorandum on Old Vic Policy', written by Tyrone Guthrie on 23 September 1943 and sent to CEMA's Lewis Casson, Guthrie states under the heading *Education v. Entertainment* that it 'will be seen the whole trend of this document is to advocate a policy related as closely as possible to the educational life of the country, and distinguishing as much as possible from other theatrical enterprise; i.e. a declared policy of *Education* as opposed to *Entertainment*. … By and large the audiences for whom we cater will be intelligent enough not to be frightened by the label *Education*; and the audience in search of a *spree* will not go to Shakespeare etc. anyway. BUT we must be on our guard against the attitude that a classic is only uplifting if it is dowdy; and the devotees who always cluster round a movement of uplift. In other words, our social service must be oblique – it must not reek of social service, but show itself in artistic vitality' (Theatre Museum. Charles Landstone Archive THM/201. Box 4).

149 See *The Civic Theatre Scheme* (Theatre Museum. British Drama League). Although the scheme was not adopted there and then it clearly influenced the 1948 Local Government Act.

150 At the annual meeting of the British Drama League Lord Esher vigorously made the case for municipal theatres after the war (see *Theatre World* January 1943: pp. 31–2).

151 Quoted in Marshall, *Other Theatre*, p. 206.

152 See Whitworth, *National Theatre*, p. 234. It is interesting to note that a similar act in support of municipal museums had already been passed in 1845 enabling Town Councils to found and maintain museums from the rates.

153 The *Theatre World* substituted its series 'New Plays in Town' with 'Plays on Tour' in October 1940 when only one London theatre remained open.

154 W.A. Darlington even claimed that the provinces turned into what London had been before the war with the capital becoming a mere 'touring date' (see

Darlington, W. A. *The Actor and his Audience*. London: Phoenix House, 1949. p. 170.

155 See Foulkes, Richard. *Repertory at the Royal. Sixty-Five Years of Theatre in Northampton 1927–92*. Northampton: Northampton Repertory Players Ltd., 1992. pp. 74, 78 and 82.

156 Although performances were also brought forward one hour this did not affect attendances which showed 'little deterioration' (see 'The Repertory Theatres.' *Theatre World* December 1939: p. 213). See also PRO. Home Office. HO 186 Air Raid Precautions. HO 186/742 Entertainment (1942). p. 3.

To counter the negative effect once-nightly performances had on box office receipts many theatres introduced higher ticket prices. York's Theatre Royal from August 1943 charged the following: Dress Circle 3/6, Circle 2/6, Orchestra Stalls 2/6, Pit 1/3, Upper Circle 1s and Gallery 6d.

157 See, for example, York's programme notes on 18 September 1939. At the beginning of the war the greatest and most immediate danger was thought to be a gas attack. The A.R.P. notice, therefore, warned patrons that admission might be refused for 'those not having one [a gas mask – A.H.] in their possession. These masks must be taken to the seats, and not left in the cloakrooms'.

158 Similar announcements appeared in theatres all over the country – and seemed to reflect the public mood. The following account of an incident at a theatre not further specified seems quite typical: 'A few days ago, an air-raid warning sounded. The performance was stopped and the spectators were informed they might leave for a shelter. Only two persons rose – two old ladies in a box, who asked if they could get seats in the "pit" … since they thought they would be safer there' (see *Bulletins from Britain*. no. 1. 3 September 1940. p. 1).

159 Contemporary witnesses such as Ms Mothersdale remembered that 'York was full of air force of every nationality'. The city was 'choc-a-bloc with forces' (Wilson, *York Voices*, pp. 94–5).

160 Hull suffered badly from various bombing raids (see Geraghty, T. *A North-East Coast Town. Ordeal and Triumph. The Story of Kingston upon Hull in the 1939–1945 Great War*. Hull: Hull Academic Press, 2002); Sheffield and York both experienced one heavy raid each. In December 1940 much of Sheffield's city centre was affected, and in April 1942 York was attacked in one of the so-called 'Baedecker raids' (see the confidential 'Report on the air raid on the city during the early hours of Wednesday, 29th April, 1942', *York City Council, Council Minutes 1941–1942*. See also 'York's Darkest Hour', Special Edition *Evening Press*, 29 April 2002. For a detailed Home Office report see PRO. Home Office/Ministry of Home Security. HO 199 Intelligence Branch. HO 199/40 Air Raids on York (1940/41); PRO. Home Office/Ministry of Home Security. HO 199 Intelligence Branch. HO 199/46 Air Raid on York (April 1942) and PRO. Home Office. HO 192 Air Raids. HO 192/1676 Air Raid

Assessment Report. Public Utilities York (1941/42). Similarly PRO. Home Office. HO 192 Air Raids. HO 192/1656 Air Raid Assessment Reports York – General (1942/43)).

161 See Hull City Archives. DFBN 79–99 Sundry Financial Papers, Miscellaneous. DFBN 81.

162 Interestingly the problems faced by repertory theatres were quickly acknowledged and appreciated by commentators ('Round the Repertory Theatres.' *Theatre World* January 1940: pp. 20–1).

163 York's company went on its first ENSA tour in January 1945 and did another six months later 'for troops and war-workers in Scotland' (*YEP*, 22 June 1945). Northampton's repertory company conducted an ENSA tour in October 1943 (see Foulkes, *Repertory at the Royal*, p. 82).

164 In York the popular comedian Hal Osmond became something of a regular feature, in Northampton Godfrey Kenton and Vivienne Bennett returned to their old theatre (see ibid., p. 74).

165 York's theatre patrons donated £85 13s 10d in September 1940 alone to the 'Lord Mayor's Spitfire Fund' (see programme notes, 9 September 1940).

166 York's event held in early 1942 featured a special show in the Theatre Royal including sketches, music and talks by members of the armed forces (see programme notes, 17 February 1942). Selby's 'Warship Week' in the same year supported the 'Tanks for Attack' campaign and the 'Submarine Sturgeon Comforts Fund' (*YP*, 29 July 1942).

167 See Calder, *People's War*, p. 347. See also Nicholson, Steve. 'Theatrical Pageants in the Second World War.' *Theatre Research International* 18 (1993): pp. 186–96. For a sketch of the proposed stage design and decorations see PRO. Ministry of Information. INF 3/316.

168 The organisers of the meeting screened Soviet films and collected money for the 'Help Russia Fund'. Admission was free on giving money to the fund (see *YEP*, 6 March 1942).

169 York's Council, for example, took a keen interest in planning and organising the event. Matters concerning the 'Holidays-at-Home' programme were extensively discussed in the Entertainment Committee (see York City Archives. BC 81. Corporation of York. Entertainments Committee-Minutes. 1944–1946). See also York City Archives. Acc 278. York 'Holidays at Home' Scheme (with accounts, press cuttings, photos, programmes and leaflets from 1942 and 1944).

170 See *The Observer*, 21 June 1942.

171 See PRO. LAB 26/47. *Making the Best of Holidays in 1942.*

172 CEMA provided support especially in connection with the open-air theatres, which, as the Council hoped, 'may well become permanent and indeed suggest a promising future for civic enterprise' (see CEMA, *Arts in War Time*, p. 9). Regarding CEMA's support for Birmingham's open-air theatre see Kemp, Thomas C. *Birmingham Repertory Theatre. The Playhouse and the Man.* 2nd rev. ed. Birmingham: Cornish, 1948. pp. 108–10. Substantial support,

too, came from the British Drama League (see Noble, *British Theatre*, pp. 168–9).

173 *YP*, 3 July 1942.

174 *YP*, 10 August 1942.

175 It included a fanfare of trumpets to 'herald a month of austerity holidaymaking' (*YEP*, 17 July 1942), open-air services, donkey rides, Punch and Judy shows, ventriloquists, children's sports, football and cricket games including an 'Aquatic Gala', variety entertainments, a model railway, and choir concerts, military dance bands, display of flags and bunting, military parades and a drumhead service with 1,500 personnel and several thousand visitors.

176 The actors gave the performance in their free time and were 'enthusiastically hailed by an audience of nearly 600' (see *YEP* as quoted in *Collection Nellie Woodhouse*, vol. VI 1941–2).

177 Mrs Crichton, then Lord Mayor, on the occasion of the civic send-off of the programme on 18 July 1942 (*YEP*, 18 July 1942).

178 *YEP*, 20 July 1942. Commentators hoped that 'as a result of the Holidays at Home Month the citizens would be recreated in mind and body and that they would return to their work refreshed and with renewed confidence in the future, so that they might feel that all would end well in the world conflict between the forces of good and evil' (article 'Holidays At Home Are Part of our War Effort' in *YG*, 24 July 1942).

179 See *YP*, 25 July 1942.

180 Harrogate's motto for the holiday season was 'relax without relaxing the war effort', with the programme arranged around that slogan (see *YP*, 31 July 1942). For further details regarding the 1942 programmes in Leeds, Huddersfield, Skipton, Halifax, Harrogate, Thirsk, Sutton, Bradford, Horsforth, Shipley, Wakefield, Keighley, Blackpool, Bingley, Norton, Malton, Castleford, Batley, Dewsbury, Mirfield, Otley, Luton, Blackburn, etc. see York City Archives, file York 'Holidays at Home' Scheme. Accounts and Press Cuttings 1942 and 1944. Photos, Programmes, Leaflets. Acc 278.

181 See *YEP*, 14 August 1944. The BBC, too, stressed that even a little leisure after a twelve-hour shift was part of the war effort as 'rest from work has become a precious thing – and, because the quality of work depends so largely upon it, one of great value' (see Gardner, Juliet. *The People's War. Pictures from the Past*. Devizes: Select Editions, 1995. p. 88). It is interesting to note that the scheme aroused the interest of the Nazis, too. One of the regular internal propaganda reports on the situation in England from summer 1943 claims its failure and refers to an article in *The Times*. The report claims that appeals to the people's reason regarding the attempted reduction of private rail use, as in the Holiday-at-Home scheme, did not have the expected success (see BArch [Bundesarchiv Berlin-Lichterfelde], R55/607, p. 70).

182 See Sladen, Chris. 'Holidays at Home in the Second World War.' *Journal of Contemporary History* 37 (2002): pp. 87–9.

183 See PRO. INF 1/292 (Part 2). Home Intelligence Reports. August 1941–July 1942. pp. 3–7, 342–5. Similarly PRO. INF 1/292 (Part 3). Home Intelligence Reports. July 1942–August 1943. pp. 1–5, 7–18, 27–32, 41–52, 430–6, 443–8 and 460–471; PRO. INF 1/292 (Part 4). Home Intelligence Reports. From September 1943. pp. 159–62 and 299–303.

184 See Minihan, *Nationalization of Culture*, p. 241.

185 In 1942 York's City Council started to plan in earnest for post-war cultural development in a way not too different from a German *Kulturamt*. The newly found enthusiasm is illustrated in the fact that the new committee met as often as ten times in the first year of its existence between July 1942 and July 1943 (see York City Archives. BC 71/1. Corporation of York. Civic (Cultural Development) Sub-Committee. Minutes 1942–1944). As an example of post-war planning regarding municipal theatre provision see Hayes, Nick. 'Municipal Subsidy and Tory Minimalism: Building the Nottingham Playhouse, 1942–1963.' *Midland History* 19 (1994): pp. 128–46. Hayes points out that the general atmosphere after the war was favourable to publicly funded local theatres.

186 See Rowntree, Seebohm. 'The Municipal Theatre Can Be a Success.' *Local Government Service* October 1943: p. 452. Some even dreamt of an open-air theatre on the Ouse (see Morrell, John B. *The City of Our Dreams*. London: Fountain Press, 1940. pp. 54 and 56).

CHAPTER TWO

History of Theatre in Westphalia

The history of German regional theatres roughly divides into three different periods. The first period starts with the foundation of the first purpose-built playhouses in the eighteenth century due to aristocratic patronage and against the backdrop of the Enlightenment. It ends at the turn of the twentieth century with changes in administration (especially regarding funding) and function in society. At many places this period was on the one hand characterised by financial difficulties, aristocratic control and censorship, on the other marked by the steady development of playhouses into municipal theatres against the background of social change and rising bourgeois influence. The second period is marked by the growing importance of theatres within independent civic communities and coincides with a time of economic growth and national hubris after 1871, which marked the foundation of the second German Empire. With regard to theatre provision, it is in this period that the majority of Germany's regional playhouses were opened, most of them either by municipal authorities eager to display their interest in the arts or by bourgeois pressure groups – or a mixture of both. The final period begins with the changes brought about by the revolution of 1918/19 and ends with the closure of all theatres by Nazi propaganda minister Joseph Goebbels in 1944. Although this periodisation may seem to level out the differences between the Weimar democracy and the Nazi dictatorship, it will be seen that, with respect to the theatre, the Nazi seizure of power in 1933 did not result in radical changes. After some short-term experiments with alternative forms and spaces the Nazis returned to the established formats. As a result, the development of regional theatres as municipal institutions was not affected by the 'National

Revolution' as much as one might expect – and as the Nazis had hoped.[1]

The Prussian province of Westphalia was home to five municipal theatres: Bochum, Bielefeld, Dortmund, Hagen and Münster.[2] Münster as the old Westphalian capital claimed a similar role for itself as York. Bielefeld in eastern Westphalia has always been a city of commerce, whereas Dortmund and Bochum (and to a lesser degree Hagen) have been important centres of heavy industry in the *Ruhrgebiet*, Germany's industrial heartland. The theatre in Münster is the oldest and was built at the end of the eighteenth century, whereas the playhouses in Dortmund, Bielefeld, Bochum and Hagen all opened around or after 1900. Both groups exemplify some fundamental issues in German theatre history.

EARLY HISTORY

Regional theatres in the eighteenth century: Münster's *Comödienhaus*

During the peace conference in the course of the Thirty Years War in the 1640s, in which Münster played a significant role as one of the venues of the talks, touring companies visited the town on such a regular basis that commentators claimed they represented its first standing theatre.[3] Later touring productions were transferred to the home of the merchants' guild, which housed performances for the next 130 years.[4] A substantial change took place at the end of the eighteenth century under prince-bishop Maximilian Friedrich, at a time when many 'enlightened' German princes increasingly became patrons of the arts and entered into competition with one another. Münster's first purpose-built theatre, the *Comödien- und Redoutenhauß*, was a result of such patronage. Its early foundation in 1775, at a time when interest in a German national theatre was growing,[5] is remarkable for such a small town. The *Comödienhaus*' architecture, too, is noteworthy because it reflected Lessing's idea of a *Volkstheater*, a theatre for the people. It was not only placed in the heart of town – and far away from the prince-bishop's residence, and thereby avoiding his immediate influence – but the architect Lipper also testified to the rising influence of the bourgeoisie by joining the pit with the dress circle and the boxes.

The *Comödienhaus*' fortunes, however, quickly changed. As

financial pressures grew, the standing company had to be disbanded. In a relatively small town like Münster with some 15,000 inhabitants, in 1815 the number of potential patrons was limited and the repertoire had to change quickly. Apart from this, commentators criticised the lack of concentration and discipline of both audiences and actors, and, generally, the rowdy performances.[6] Even impresario August Pichler, celebrated for his ambitious productions of the classics, had difficulty in maintaining his audiences when a company featuring dogs and monkeys came to Münster in 1851.[7] On the other hand audience expectations had risen so much that a provincial stage like Münster could not satisfy them any more and Pichler complained about bad business and empty seats in the dress circle.[8] The public support, which the theatre had enjoyed around 1800, had faded away half a century later. The bourgeois theatre did not draw the backing of the bourgeoisie any longer. Lessing's *Volkstheater*, which emancipated itself from the influence of the ruler to become a *Bildungsanstalt* – an institution with an educational mission – did not seem to be able to maintain its appeal. On the contrary, bourgeois patrons despised the mixed character of late nineteenth-century audiences and joined charity clubs or academic circles rather than sharing the theatre with the increasing number of working-class visitors.[9] It comes as little surprise, therefore, that on the demolition of the *Comödienhaus* in 1894 hardly anyone protested.

At the same time, however, there is proof of a growing popularity of performances elsewhere. From the mid-1850s onwards, a summer playhouse entertained audiences during the 'theatre holidays' of the *Comödienhaus*, dialect plays were staged by the 'evening society' and other more makeshift venues included restaurants, inns and halls.[10] The fact that the interest in matters theatrical found new outlets outside the established formats is interesting in terms of current research into alternative theatre spaces. The managers of the *Comödienhaus* had to react to meet the demands of the new audiences. Although they continued to complain about the upper classes failing to patronise the theatre, they also supported the opening up of the playhouse by a wide range of ticket prices, and thus gradually changed its character from an elitist institution to a place for (nearly) everyone.[11] Münster's theatre was thereby also taking account of the rising 'People's Theatre' movement with its intention to enable the working classes to visit the theatre.[12]

Comparative perspectives

The first period in the history of Münster's standing theatre shows many similarities with Yorkshire, but also points at some fundamental differences. Like York's Theatre Royal, for example, Münster's first theatre was owned by the city. It was leased to impresarios who took over full responsibility and were bound to make a financial profit. This often proved difficult as the overall costs were immense and even box office successes could not guarantee the theatre would break even.[13] Like Tate Wilkinson, Münster's impresarios resembled business managers rather than the artistic directors they would later become. Another parallel development accounts for one of the reasons for the survival of the theatre in its early stages. The resistance against the *Comödienhaus* as a playhouse forced upon them by the prince-bishop had been substantial, but the rising bourgeois population quickly acquired a taste for the new theatre. In a remarkable move, they formed the *Theaterkommission*, the theatre committee. To secure the theatre's financial position, all committee members bought season tickets and agreed to guarantee a certain income from the subscriptions. They deliberately constituted themselves as representatives of the general public who wanted to have a say in the theatre's development. Although the committee was soon dissolved, this act of showing responsibility for 'their' theatre proved that the population was not entirely prepared to accept the suspicious control of the civic authorities (e.g. regarding censorship) and the financial pressures exerted on the impresarios. They also declined to accept the influence of the prince-bishop, as, in contrast to York, German regional theatres were likely to be controlled by their local or regional princes who tended to regard them as their personal places of entertainment. This fact also hints at a major difference between the two countries, as, in contrast to York, it was the large sums Maximilian paid which largely accounted for the theatre's survival during the crucial years around 1800. Relating to these early years, the biggest difference between Yorkshire and Westphalia, however, is the immediate founding period of the respective theatres. Whereas the erecting of Yorkshire's early theatres was an enterprise undertaken by businessmen, the *Comödienhaus* was built by the prince-bishop against the will of both the city authorities and a large section of the population. They did not want to see 'voluptuous, vain plays and comedies which corrupt our youth' being performed in Münster.[14] Despite the resistance, the prince-bishop went ahead with his plan – a move hardly imaginable in Yorkshire.

Perhaps surprisingly, however, the decades from 1870 show many parallels between Westphalia and Yorkshire again. German cities were still far away from subsidising the performing arts. To commit themselves to municipal playhouses was out of the question. Although many became increasingly prepared to offer limited financial help if yet another season had ended in financial loss, this change of attitude does not mean that cities came to pursue an active cultural policy; it rather meant agreeing to waive the cost of the lease in one-off decisions. That Münster, for example, was not interested in any long-term commitments is illustrated by the neglect of the theatre building and its subsequent demolition.

THE BEGINNING OF MUNICIPAL THEATRE PROVISION

Münster's *Romberger Hof* and *Lortzing-Theater*

A new era for Münster's theatre began in 1895, when the new bigger theatre, the so-called *Lortzing-Theater*, opened in a former aristocratic

Figure 2.1 Lortzing-Theater, Münster, c.1900

residence.[15] The new playhouse's name indicated that it had become a theatre of the city – although not a municipal theatre as yet and still privately owned. The city council, however, changed the way the theatre was funded shortly after the re-opening and accepted a longer-term commitment for the first time. From 1899 the city paid an annual subsidy of RM (*Reichsmark*) 12,000 as a contribution to the running costs, and over the following years this subsidy rose substantially to more than RM 88,000 in 1911.[16] More importantly, the city bought the building in 1906 for RM 580,000 and renamed it *Städtisches* (civic) *Lortzing-Theater*. The city took over the basic equipment, which was put at the lessee's disposal, and paid for heating and lighting. The change of name indicated the city's obvious desire to demonstrate that the playhouse was no longer a private enterprise but had become a public undertaking, that it was transferred from the world of commerce into the sphere of education and social welfare. This claim, however, did not entirely correspond with reality as the business of running the theatre and the way it was organised did not change fundamentally. The theatre directors still had to take out a lease and could not afford to run their own company. After the ensemble of Essen's municipal theatre had performed in Münster until 1900, the theatre established a cooperation with Bremen and later with Osnabrück.[17] Although the new name was, therefore, misleading, it is nevertheless interesting that the council publicly expressed the desire to establish a connection between theatre and city. This desire does not only contrast with the councillors of a hundred years earlier but also with the situation in Yorkshire around the turn of the century. Although in Yorkshire some city councils became increasingly prepared to meet some of their theatres' needs, they hardly desired to take them over in order to run them as municipal theatres.

Until the outbreak of the First World War the *Lortzing-Theater* experienced successful times with rising attendances, sound management and artistic achievements.[18] The theatre undertook successful tours to the Netherlands, incorporated opera in the repertoire and received its own professional orchestra. The city council even considered erecting a new theatre building on Servatii Square, for which it had already acquired the land.[19] Although the outbreak of the First World War put these plans on hold, the city's involvement in theatrical matters had reached a remarkable degree within only a few years.

Figure 2.2 Dortmund municipal theatre, 1908

The other Westphalian theatres

After Dortmund had played host to visiting companies at different venues, a group of influential *Bürger* decided to campaign for a municipal theatre during the late nineteenth century. This issue became pressing after the *Kühn'scher Saal*, which had been extended for performances, had burnt down in 1903. The bourgeois group exerted pressure on the civic authorities to rebuild the playhouse as a municipal theatre and raised money to contribute to the building costs, which eventually funded half of the overall expenditure. The *Stadttheater* was opened in 1904 with all the pomp and circumstance Wilhelmine Germany could muster.[20] It was first leased to *Privattheaterdirektor* Hans Gelling before being taken over by the city administration three years later. This remarkably early step indicates that working-class Dortmund was ahead of other cities in the region in realising the potential of theatre. This impression is supported by the fact that the theatre was not closed during the First World War (unlike most other German theatres) but presented special programmes for workers in munitions factories – following a 'suggestion' by the war office.[21]

In contrast to Dortmund with its large manufacturing base,

Figure 2.3 Bielefeld municipal theatre, 1939

especially its coal and steel industry, Bielefeld has always been a city of commerce and a proud centre of eastern Westphalia. Perhaps not entirely unrelated to this observation, Bielefeld's city council more than other councils in the region kept a close eye on costs. Not surprisingly, the theatre owes its foundation to a bourgeois pressure group who – similar to Dortmund's – raised money and lobbied politicians. The council decided that they would not be prepared to build a theatre unless RM 200,000 (40 per cent of the overall building costs) had been provided by donations.[22] After these funds had been secured the *Stadttheater* opened in 1904 and was then leased to directors with the city paying a subsidy and waiving some of the costs including heating, lighting, water and the services of a fireman. Until the First World War the lease system reaped financial rewards for the directors and annual profits reached RM 60,000 in 1910.[23]

Hagen, an industrial city south of Dortmund, had its own theatre since 1911. In a similar scenario to other places, it owed its foundation to a bourgeois theatre society, who had established a limited company in 1909 and had successfully canvassed for donations. Franz Ludwig became the manager of this first commercial playhouse. The

Figure 2.4 Postcard of Hagen's municipal theatre, c.1910

municipal interest in the theatrical endeavours of the limited company became obvious, however, in the fact that a member of the city administration sat on its board.

THEATRE IN THE WEIMAR REPUBLIC

With the military defeat of Imperial Germany in sight, a socialist revolution broke out in 1918, and after the victory of the allied forces Germany became a republic. Although the revolution was not successful, it had lasting effects in some areas – one of which was the theatre. The former court theatres were transformed into municipal or state theatres, and most of the private theatres were taken over by towns and cities, too. To most of them, being run as a municipal institution promised increased financial security. At the same time, however, theatres were now linked to municipal budgets, which experienced various pressures during the 1920s, and their position proved to be far from safe. Public debates about subsidies as well as managers struggling to keep afloat became regular features.

Münster's *Städtische Bühnen*

Although conservative Münster was only marginally affected by the revolution, the city followed the national trend and, in 1922, took over full responsibility of the *Lortzing-Theater*. The city paid an annual subsidy, which entirely funded the playhouse, appointed an *Intendant* as manager and gave the theatre a new name: *Städtische Bühnen*.[24] The playhouse became a full *Drei-Sparten-Theater* with its own theatre, opera and dance companies in 1924, and annual subsidies reached RM 699,000 in 1926.[25] Under Hanns Niedecken-Gebhardt's management Münster became an acclaimed centre for the production of Händel operas, and was nationally acknowledged for the avant-garde dance performances of Kurt Jooss and the modernist set designs of Heinrich Heckroth.[26] Financial constraints continued, however, as rising subsidies were quickly eaten up by rising costs and demands. To save money the city council decided not to appoint another *Intendant* after Niedecken-Gebhardt had left.[27] As savings failed to materialise, the city even returned to the pre-war lease system.[28] Alfred Bernau, who joined the theatre in 1929, received reduced subsidies amounting to RM 560,000,[29] and his successor Fritz Berend even entered into another co-operation with the Osnabrück theatre to save money.[30] In view of these pressures and the difficult general economic climate it is remarkable that Bernau managed to open the Studio in 1930.[31] Bernau, too, however, had to quit eventually because of financial problems in 1932. To many residents it seemed as if chaos reigned in Münster's cultural life.[32] The Westphalian Theatre Company declared that the province was in a 'state of cultural emergency'.[33] Although Münster was affected by economic problems to a lesser degree than Bochum or Dortmund, unemployment and political radicalisation soon became problems here, too. A decisive move to the right became apparent, although the Centre party, which had been one of the pillars of the Weimar Republic, remained the strongest party until 1933.[34]

Münster's theatre was directly affected by economic pressures and political radicalisation. The *Städtische Bühnen* had to cope with declining attendance figures and cuts in the budget. As a result seasons were shortened to six months and staff were forced to look for alternative employment for the rest of the year.[35] Many of them became easy targets for Nazi propaganda, which promised new labour politics, social reforms and chances for everyone.[36] Meanwhile the move to the right was reflected in the repertoire as nationalist and *völkisch* drama was first produced during the 1931–32 season. The local group of Alfred Rosenberg's radical 'Militant League for German Culture' founded its own patrons' organisation in 1932 and tried to influence the theatre's repertoire through block bookings of specific performances once or twice a month.[37] They did not solely support *völkisch* drama, however, but also farces like *Lily-Liver Can't Help It*. In the same year the 'Touring Company of the Militant League' was founded, offering jobs to unemployed actors and touring with Hans Kyser's anti-Polish drama *Fire on the Border*.[38] The cultural atmosphere had noticeably changed.

The other Westphalian theatres

The theatres in Bielefeld, Dortmund, Hagen and Bochum more or less mirrored this development especially with regard to rising demands for subsidies in the late 1920s. Under the management of Johannes Maurach, Dortmund's *Stadttheater* experienced a successful, creative and for the most part financially stable period.[39] He realised the importance for a theatre to plan ahead and introduced closed performances for trade unions and big companies. In terms of public

Figure 2.5 Dortmund's municipal theatre by night, 1929

relations he was equally forward thinking with the publication of elaborate monthly programme notes.[40] When Maurach left in 1922 Karl Schäffer took over and established a second venue for the more entertaining fare at the *Burgwalltheater* – a courageous step in a city to which the love of the theatre did not come naturally.[41] When five years later Richard Gsell became manager, the playhouse undoubtedly experienced its most successful times in artistic terms with an avant-garde repertoire and clear aesthetic concepts.[42] At the same time Gsell's conflicts with the city council about funding, especially during the economic crisis in the early 1930s, grew increasingly fierce. As a city dominated by its heavy industry, Dortmund suffered particularly hard. It was no longer prepared to treat itself to the 'luxury' of a second theatre venue and the *Burgwalltheater* was closed.[43] Although Gsell fully realised the new financial constraints and admitted that 'the focus of the theatre manager has to be on the balancing of the budget' rather than on aesthetic considerations to ensure the required revenue,[44] he was soon the object of public criticism because of his alleged 'lack of principles in artistic questions'.[45] As in many other cities, Dortmund's theatre suddenly seemed to be in utter disarray.

Bielefeld's *Stadttheater* was taken into municipal control in 1918 and under the joint directorship of Max Cahnbley and Richard Starnberg developed into a bold statement of civic pride in artistic excellence.[46] Despite financial crises the theatre aimed at producing drama and opera of the highest possible quality. This came at a price: although still moderate in comparison to other cities, the municipal subsidy rose quickly, from RM 91,000 in 1924–5 to RM 155,000 in 1925–6.[47] As an average of 40 per cent of the seats remained empty, however, the much-needed revenue did not materialise. Public discussions ensued all through the Weimar years, a limited company was founded but only proved viable for a few years, the city imposed wage cuts, shorter seasons and redundancies, and to many the theatre appeared in constant crisis. The city administration, it has to be noted, failed to counter these criticisms, appeared to be in permanent arguments about the theatre's finances and indeed its future and proved an easy target for Nazi propaganda.[48]

Bochum's *Stadttheater* was opened as a municipal theatre in 1919.[49] From the beginning financial pressures in a large industrial city with high unemployment were substantial and the theatre was required to keep costs to a minimum.[50] The playhouse entered into a partnership

Figure 2.6 Bochum municipal theatre, c.1925

with Duisburg in 1921 (which remained in place for thirteen years) and visited other cities in the Ruhr area for additional revenue. At the same time, manager Saladin Schmitt from the beginning tried to establish Bochum as a leading regional stage with an ambitious repertoire. He combined this approach with a strong educational, quasi-religious, mission and put high demands on his patrons in a drive to create new audiences.[51] Schmitt laid particular emphasis on the classics and honoured Shakespeare in the first of a series of festivals in 1927.[52] He quickly made a name for himself although audience figures were lower in comparison to the other theatres in the region.[53] The municipal subsidies, however, rose exponentially from RM 150,000 in 1919 to RM 949,000 in 1928.[54] Interestingly though, and in contrast to other cities, Bochum's councillors did not seem to be too much alarmed by these extraordinary sums. To reduce costs they merely suggested increased advertisement.[55]

Of all the Westphalian theatres Hagen seemed to have encountered the most serious troubles during the Weimar Republic and epitomised many of the problems the Nazis later used in their propaganda. Although still a limited company, the links between Hagen's theatre and the city administration became closer in the early 1920s, when the city obtained the right to appoint theatre managers and agreed a guarantee against loss to safeguard staff salaries.[56] However, this security did not prevent the 'theatre crisis' of 1922–3 when the playhouse was turned into a receiving theatre, after the city council had refused to pay the annual subsidy, and *Intendant* Ludwig was forced to go – although the authorities claimed the termination of his contract had happened 'by mutual agreement'.[57] Shortly after that however, the situation calmed down, the playhouse became a fully municipal theatre in all but name in 1924 and experienced more steady times under the popular management of Hanns Hartmann (1927–30).[58] Financially, the theatre's position was not bright though and annual subsidies amounted to over RM 350,000 at the end of the 1920s.[59] To save money, therefore, the new *Intendant* Smolny entered into a co-operation with Dortmund's theatre, which took effect in September 1931, and subsequently subsidies did indeed decrease. The next crisis, however, loomed as soon as summer 1932 when the city declared it was unable to continue paying 'subsidies at the current level' any more. The solution was a different form of organisation as a co-operative with all employees as members. Willie Schmitt and W.G. von Keller took over the directorship.[60] Eventually Hagen seemed to have found a workable model which produced the desired results as municipal subsidies declined to around RM 130,000 during 1932–3. Not surprisingly, the municipal theatre council suggested a continuation of the arrangements as late as January 1933.[61]

THE NAZI TAKE-OVER

On 30 January 1933, President Hindenburg appointed a cabinet under Adolf Hitler as chancellor – the so-called *Machtergreifung* (seizure of power). Many theatre staff welcomed Hitler in the hope of a change. Those, however, who expected clear policies and immediate decisions were soon disappointed. Not only were these policies missing, but also the situation in the new cultural administration was chaotic and inconsistent. Until the end of 1933 matters concerning the theatre were handled by at least four different authorities: Alfred Rosenberg, Joseph Goebbels, Robert Ley and Hermann Göring. Rosenberg was the party hardliner fighting for 'pure' German art and ideologically 'sound' repertoires, Goebbels appeared less radical at first but eager to increase his power and remain close to Hitler, Ley headed the mass organisation 'Strength Through Joy' (*Kraft durch Freude*) and wanted to exert his influence on the leisure sector, and Göring played an important role as Prussian Home Secretary.[62] In September 1933 Goebbels founded the 'Reich Culture Chamber' in an attempt to gain complete control over Germany's cultural life. This organisation comprised seven different chambers, including one for the theatre. Part of the Propaganda Ministry and, therefore, under Goebbels' direct control was the *Reichsdramaturgie*.[63] Officially, the National Dramaturg's office had to oversee the programmes of all the German theatres and ensure the 'right' plays were chosen. Although total control of repertoires proved impossible and the office was poorly equipped, the system proved efficient as many managers were anxious to avoid problems with the authorities and presented a programme they considered safe.[64] The last step on Goebbels' way to complete control was the 'National Theatre Law' of May 1934, which, in theory, put every theatre under the influence of the Propaganda Ministry. This does not mean, however, that diversification in cultural administration came to an end.[65] One reason for this was that, traditionally, only a few state theatres were under direct supervision of the national authorities. The vast majority of playhouses were municipal theatres where state intervention could rarely be exerted. The only possible means of direct intervention was via the police when performances were 'disrupting public order'. With the take-over, the police came under Nazi control, and Westphalia's forces were now under Göring's direct rule as Prussian Home Secretary. Additionally, the boundaries between SA (the Nazi 'Storm Troopers') and police became blurred, which opened up another possibility for interference. Outright control, however, would have resembled measures in a dictatorial police state – an image the Nazis tried to avoid at all cost. This neither means that the local level was free of Nazi influence nor that it was free of disruptions and irritations. Regional theatres were not only supervised by the city authorities and the *Intendant* alone,[66] but also the *Gauleiter* (district party head) was keen to play his part, party organisations like 'German Stage' or 'Strength Through Joy' were eager to affect the repertoire and even minor local party officials wanted to have their say.[67] Münster's Willi Hanke, for example, was not formally announced *Intendant* until the mayor, the *Gauleiter* of

Northern Westphalia (of which Münster was the capital), the president of the province Westphalia and the *Gau* head of cultural affairs had given their consent.[68]

Although positive theatre policies seemed non-existent, the Nazis' negative policies had direct and manifold consequences. The Jewish participation in German cultural life was brought to an abrupt end. According to the euphemistically entitled 'Law for the Restoration of the Career Civil Service' from April 1933 all 'non-Aryan' theatre staff were made redundant – like Münster's manager Fritz Berend, who was Jewish and who had been in office for only one year. Although not within the law, eager Nazi councils interpreted the legislation rather loosely and also fired *Intendanten* who were not Jewish but regarded as 'unfit' – such as Bielefeld's Max Cahnbley and Dortmund's Richard Gsell. Berend was replaced by an 'Aryan' theatre manager who followed the party line: Otto Liebscher. Berend was allowed, however, to stay on for another three years as director of music before he was forced to leave. This event shows that exceptions from the rule were possible during the first years under the Nazis if they suited the regime; in this case the theatre was dependant on Berend's musical competence.[69] For the repertoire the radical turn against anything Jewish meant that works by Jewish dramatists and composers were banned from the stage. This move affected a substantial number of comedies and operettas especially.[70] Left-wing drama, too, was immediately forbidden, and works by avant-garde dramatists were burnt at the *Bücherverbrennung* on 10 May 1933.[71] In this respect, the take-over was indeed a clear break.

Danger of closure, renovation and propaganda in Münster

The Nazi take-over had an immediate effect on all German theatres and seemed to have lasting consequences. For Münster's patrons, however, these considerations seemed secondary in 1933. They feared for the bare existence of their theatre. Until July the continuation of the Berend era seemed certain, but when his dismissal became public and no other information concerning future plans for the theatre had been heard of, Münster's citizens feared for the worst – especially as the new Nazi magistrate made it clear that they were not prepared to offer substantial funds.[72] After a public appeal to save the theatre had proved successful, however, the Nazis quickly seized this opportunity to take over the campaign and presented themselves as the saviours of Münster's theatre. The union with Osnabrück was cancelled and the *Städtische Bühnen* came under Münster's sole municipal control again. Although this decision resulted in rising costs, it proved popular and was, therefore, a clever tactical move by the new authorities. As mentioned before, the chief purpose of the union had been to save money by suspending Münster's opera ensemble and letting Osnabrück's company play both theatres. However, opposition in Münster, where opera had traditionally been highly popular, was considerable.[73] The return of a standing opera company was, therefore, not only welcomed by patrons but also attributed to the new administration. The new Nazi mayor Hillebrand together with the city's executive for cultural matters Aschhoff and *Gauleiter* Meyer, however, did not stop there. Over the summer the theatre was expensively refurbished and redecorated,[74] for which the administration received national press coverage and recognition.[75] In line with Nazi ideology they stressed that the building programme was made possible by the wave of public support it received – the *Volksgemeinschaft* working together for their *Volkstheater*.[76] Additionally, the weeks before the beginning of the 1933–4 season were accompanied by massive propaganda such as rallies of 'Hitler Youth' (HJ) and SA storm troopers, a special issue of the local arts magazine *Beautiful Münster*, the establishment of a local branch of the 'German Stage', publicity and fund-raising campaigns, and even home visits to prospective season ticket holders. The campaign was immensely successful and the number of season tickets reached 5,377, which meant a rise of 407 per cent in comparison to the previous year.[77] At the end of the campaign a 'victory party' was organised, which included a pageant through the city with actors in historical costumes and a sold-out concert in the city hall for 8,000 people.[78] In view of these impressive figures the new *Intendant*, Otto Liebscher, opened the season as the beginning of a 'new era'.[79]

The apparent successes with the renovation programme and the public support expressed in donations and soaring ticket sales also made it easy to condemn the theatre politics of the Weimar years. The new civic leaders and the new theatre management were anxious to stress the break with this 'decadent' past. The head of the municipal theatre department, for example, claimed that up until 1933 the theatre had suffered from a catastrophic financial administration, had regularly received additional payments on top of the 'fabulous sums', which had been reserved for it in the budget anyway, and had presented a repertoire characterised by 'cheap sensational hits' which were continually moving away from audience demands. As a result, attendances had 'consistently declined'.[80] Although these claims could easily be proved wrong, countless similar statements appeared at the beginning of the 1933–4 season and they almost certainly left their mark.[81]

The take-over at Bielefeld

Bielefeld's long-standing manager Max Cahnbley was made redundant in 1933 despite the fact that he was not Jewish; the mere 'accusation' of some local Nazis of having employed too many 'non-Aryans' was sufficient to get rid of him. Interestingly, however, Cahnbley did not go without a fight. On production of his 'proof of Aryan descent' it became clear that he could not be fired with immediate effect and that he was entitled to a pension.[82] Cahnbley was succeeded by Leon Geer, a Nazi party member and cultural functionary since 1931, who immediately tried to turn the playhouse into a political tool.[83] After it had been run as a limited company since 1926 he took the theatre back into municipal ownership and, through this, hoped to provide sufficient proof of the new administration's commitment towards the arts.[84] In a preview for the 1934–5 season Geer stated that the high aims set for the theatre by the *Führer* gave his work 'meaning and purpose'.[85]

The take-over at Dortmund

Richard Gsell in 1932–3 not only had to fight criticism of his personnel policy and alleged lack of principles in artistic questions, he also had to face additional problems caused by the rising influence of the Nazis. Their claim of Gsell being a typical exponent of Weimar decadence was difficult to counter. Despite this atmosphere Dortmund's repertoire remained remarkably free of Nazi influence – on the contrary. In January 1933 Gerhart Hauptmann on the occasion of his seventieth birthday was publicly celebrated as a Naturalist dramatist, and in March the theatre still performed Lessing's *Nathan the Wise*, a play frowned upon by the Nazis for its 'Semitic' theme.[86]

Shortly after that, however, the atmosphere changed markedly as the *Stadttheater* produced Hanns Johst's nationalistic showcase drama *Schlageter* on the occasion of Hitler's birthday and celebrated the 'National Socialist Day of the Arts' with a matinee.[87] At this point Gsell had already been forced out of his job.[88] As in Münster, however, the Nazis did not seem to know what to do with the theatre and consequently decided to close it down altogether following a decision by the city council on 23 May 1933.[89] The cultural façade, which the Nazis wanted to portray, began to show cracks. In line with a general development, however, official policy soon changed as Dortmund's magistrate made Bruno Bergmann the new *Intendant* and planned to renovate the theatre.[90] With Bergmann the Nazis had obviously found the ideal candidate for a new start. Commentators praised his artistic expertise, his communicative character and – as a party member since 1932 – his political reliability: the ideal candidate to start a new era of 'truly' national theatre.

The take-over at Bochum

Saladin Schmitt, who had successfully withstood attempts to modernise his repertoire and who had made a name for himself for monumental productions of 'timeless' classics, seemed the perfect choice for some to stay on as manager. For Nazi hardliners, however, who would have preferred a young manager ready to put on *völkisch* plays, it was exactly this conservative repertoire policy, together with Schmitt's nationwide recognition, which made it difficult to get rid of him. In terms of financial management the theatre sent out a mixed message, too. Although the municipal subsidies had been reduced from over RM 900,000 in 1931 to just under RM 700,000 in 1933, the revenue had declined just as well, from RM 345,000 in 1931 to RM 267,000 in 1933.[91]

The take-over at Hagen

Less than six months after Schmitt and Keller had taken over the directorship, they were made redundant in spring 1933 amidst official claims that they had fallen out with their staff in spite of earlier praise.[92] They were replaced – on short-term contracts until the end of the season – by the singer Hermann Bender and the actor Albrecht

Bethge. After their contracts had expired, however, the new administration did not have any clues concerning the theatre's future – despite later claims to the contrary. In April and May 1933 several possible candidates for the manager position enquired at Hagen's city council whether the post would be advertised soon. The staple reply by councillor Dönneweg was that the current situation was unclear and that decisions had not been taken so far.[93] Then, suddenly, the politically 'reliable' Bender was announced *Intendant* – despite the fact that Hagen's municipal theatre council had reservations about his appointment.[94] Keen to mark this 'new' beginning Bender wrote a glowing retrospective report about his start, stressing the 'disarray' he had found the theatre in and his successful groundwork. A staunch Nazi, Bender claimed Hagen's theatre had 'collapsed' at the end of the Weimar years and had to be 'rebuilt' by the new Nazi administration.[95] Hagen seemed to have found the perfect candidate for the job.

COMPARATIVE PERSPECTIVES II

If we take the claim of the beginning of a 'new era' and apply it to the situation in Yorkshire at the beginning of the 1930s interesting parallels appear, despite the increasingly incompatible political circumstances. The pressure on theatres in both regions mounted with the beginning of the new decade. The common problem was the economic crisis, which resulted not only in declining audiences (more of a problem to British theatres) but also in lower subsidies (which were only a problem in Germany). As a result, the closure of playhouses was a real danger in both regions. Another interesting parallel is the solution found: rescue programmes initiated and paid for by the citizens. In Münster – putting the propaganda purpose of the allegation aside for a moment – the new authorities' claim that without the huge public support the whole building programme would not have been possible was a correct statement, which corresponded to the increasingly desolate financial situation of the city. It was a group of actors who took the initiative in autumn 1932 and who appealed for public donations.[96] And, as in York, the public followed the appeal. Citizens donated money, bought shares and imaginary 'building blocks', companies printed flyers for free, provided money, building materials, fabrics, tools and even a grand piano.[97] Although the main difference is that the Münster initiative was soon taken over by the municipal authorities whereas in York local businessmen ran it, the fact that in both cities similar schemes were inaugurated is quite remarkable.

THE FIRST 'NATIONAL SEASON'

Liebscher in Münster

The start into the 1933–4 season could not have been better for the Nazis and for Otto Liebscher in particular.[98] To make the alliance between Nazi administration and theatre clear the inauguration of the renovated theatre included the 'consecration' of a flag and a performance of *Patriotic Music for Orchestra* 'dedicated to the Third Reich'.[99] It also became evident that the promises of this remarkable beginning had to be fulfilled during the course of the season. Liebscher himself made it known that attention now had to turn to finding ways of expressing the 'National Revolution' on stage.[100] In accordance with this claim he presented a repertoire clearly characterised by Nazi ideology. To be successful as a manager, however, Liebscher needed the support of his patrons. Without it the claim of a new *Volkstheater* would seem ridiculous – as it indeed did.

Attendance at the ideological plays especially was poor, and the 20 per cent they made up in the production figures did not contrast favourably with the 11 per cent they reached in the ticket sales.[101] This striking discrepancy illustrates that the audience did not want to follow Liebscher's course. They stayed away or went to see other plays instead.[102] The two most successful plays of the season were light comedies. It is not only this discrepancy, however, which is striking: the overall attendance figures only reached 134,000, which was 20 per cent more than during the last season, but still well below the figures of the years before when 170,000 or more patrons visited the theatre. Taking the high number of season tickets into account, the enormous propaganda effort, and the appeal of a newly renovated theatre, which was supposed to attract packed houses, these results were disappointing. It was obvious that Liebscher had failed, and in a bitter review of the season he admitted that he had not met the high expectations.[103] At this point, however, the Nazi magistrate had already decided that Liebscher had to be sacrificed. The reasons for his dismissal were not made public and the official statement remained as vague as possible[104] in an obvious attempt to play down an incident which was a blow to the Nazis' cultural ambitions.[105] Behind the nonchalant façade, however, the administration was furious. Despite their excellent starting position they were unable to capitalise on it. Even worse, the theatrical venture, which should have been a showcase of successful National Socialist cultural politics, was in danger of developing into a propaganda nightmare. Against this background it not only becomes clear that Liebscher's dismissal was a political decision, it is also obvious that he was dismissed for one chief reason: he had failed to present a programme which was both *völkisch* and popular. The Liebscher case clearly shows that the 'right' choice of programme was not enough – the statistics were crucial.[106]

It is interesting to note in this respect that the chaos the Nazis constantly attributed to the Weimar years really only started after the take-over. At first nothing seemed to have changed in Münster apart from an early end to the 1932–3 season. Then, suddenly, news broke that Berend was dismissed as theatre manager in Osnabrück and Münster. A few days later the information proved to be a false alarm and Berend's position in Münster seemed secure – for the time being. The building and renovation work at the theatre started and the advertising campaign for season ticket holders took off. Then, once again unexpected, Berlin asked Münster to dismiss Berend on racial grounds at the end of July and with the start of the new season only a few weeks away. The nervous magistrate quickly appointed Liebscher – probably the only person they could get at this stage with preparations for the following season well advanced.[107] The chaos, however, did not end with the appointment of Liebscher, who was presented to the public only three weeks before the season's start.[108] As early as September 1933 criticism regarding the poor quality of both productions and ensemble emerged in the press, Liebscher's casting policy and choice of programme was questioned, and commentators insinuated a renewed crisis.[109] Above all the young chief musical director Eugen Jochum, who enjoyed the support of the Nazi magistrate, proved to be a failure.[110] Regarding a production of Wagner's opera *Tristan and Isolde*, the press asserted that the decision to produce this work was courageous in view of the poor quality of the present company.[111] Liebscher's position, however, did not seem in danger at this point and in January 1934 the city even agreed to renew his contract for another three years.[112] Then, suddenly, they changed their minds and dismissed him in March. The city's embarrassment was complete when the Prussian Theatre Council reminded Münster's authorities of a clause in their contract with Liebscher, which stated that for a dismissal to take effect with the start of the following season it had to be expressed by 1 February. The Prussian Theatre Council, therefore, made it clear that they expected Liebscher to stay for at least another year.[113] The city authorities, however, did not take any notice and a few weeks later – long before the season had ended – Münster's astonished press were introduced to Willi Hanke.[114] This was to be the start of a 'new era' – for the second time within only one year. In the course of a few months the Nazi authorities had produced more confusion and disorder than all the previous administrations together since the theatre had come under municipal management in 1922.

But it was not only within the theatre itself that things did not develop according to plan. In a situation mirrored all over Germany, the activities of the 'German Stage' proved ineffective, despite promises that they would offer reduced tickets to low income residents.[115] In January 1934 the Prussian Theatre Council noted that the Münster branch of the 'German Stage' only had a disappointing 160 members.[116] The situation in other cities was not much better. Although the Nazis had declared in summer 1933 that the responsibility for the organised theatre visit from now on rested entirely with the 'German Stage', the organisation in most cities not only failed to recruit sufficient patrons, but also made demands on theatre managements.[117] The Prussian Theatre Council, aware of the competition and in fear of losing its grip on theatres, sent a questionnaire to all Prussian playhouses in early 1934 to learn more about the activities of the 'German Stage'. Numerous theatre managers were only too happy to list the problems they faced.[118]

Bergmann in Dortmund

The chaos in Münster was no exceptional case; the situation regarding both the new personnel and the new repertoire was mirrored at other Westphalian theatres. In Dortmund theatre manager Bergmann turned out to be a complete failure. He had been a typical case of a career Nazi promoted to a leading position without any previous managerial experience (he had been a singer at Essen's theatre until 1931, before becoming unemployed) and the Prussian Theatre

Council soon became aware of his lack of ability. In a report for the council Herr Leutheiser stated that although Bergmann was a 'splendid character' it was no longer acceptable that he rarely called meetings and failed to check the quality of plays.[119] Even worse, it transpired that Bergmann, according to the Theatre Council's own regulations, should never have been appointed in the first place. The council had made it clear that only experienced *Intendanten* could be considered for theatre managements, even if leading regional party officials intervened on behalf of certain people.[120] The only reason why things did not get out of hand entirely was the fact that with Willi Hanke (drama) and Georg Hartmann (opera) Bergmann had two experienced directors at his side.[121]

Geer in Bielefeld

In the same way as Dortmund Bielefeld's *Stadttheater* relied on the services of a singer to get it off to a good start into the 'Thousand Year Reich', Leon Geer failed in similar fashion. Even commentators not as critical of the Nazi era showed unease regarding Geer's egotistic and choleric manner and concluded that he was simply not suited for the position.[122] Although he hung on to his job until 1936 and produced popular romantic operas, his concentration on *völkisch* drama proved disastrous. There was no beating about the bush either. The press made it clear that during the first months of the 1933–4 season 'audiences had been catastrophic' and criticism of the theatre's economic position was substantial.[123] Even with massive propaganda campaigns ticket sales remained dire – and so did the theatre's financial situation, despite rising subsidies.[124] An exodus of leading actors and singers in late 1934 was attributed to the failures of the management and prompted a public explanation by Geer in an act of obvious damage limitation.[125] To improve the theatre's finances the city even applied for extra funding at the Propaganda Ministry.[126] At first the municipal theatre council, to which Bielefeld's *Intendanten* were ultimately responsible, tried to attribute this malaise to the press and one newspaper in particular, whose criticism was 'in large parts responsible for the fact that audiences had turned away from the theatre', but it quickly became clear that Geer himself was to blame. It transpired that Geer needed another RM 89,000 on top of the current subsidy to break even.[127] Like Liebscher's dismissal Geer's failure was an embarrassment to the Nazi administration and it comes as little surprise, therefore, that he disappeared in a similar – quiet – fashion.[128] There were no official statements, no explanations, and this time not even the press reported anything in their reviews of the season.[129]

Bender in Hagen

In a now familiar scenario Hermann Bender was similarly hapless. In a national survey of theatre ticket sales Hagen came out at rock bottom. Of every hundred available tickets Hagen sold just thirty-two, which did not compare well with other cities in the region which sold well over 80 per cent.[130] Bender himself claimed the 'warm weather' had kept people away and lamented that a large part of Hagen's audiences were still ideologically unreliable and had, therefore, 'boycotted' the new *völkisch* drama which subsequently 'had to be replaced with lighter fare'.[131] In contrast to Geer, Liebscher and Bergmann, however, Bender somehow managed to stay on.

Schmitt in Bochum

Bochum remained the exception, as nothing much seemed to change. At the same time Schmitt was happy to pay tribute to the new regime. Contemporary commentators claimed that

> Bochum in 1933 was in no need of transformation and adjustment. When Otto Laubinger, the first president of the Reich Theatre Chamber, wanted to introduce the *Führer* to distinguished and future theatre managers Saladin Schmitt – who was honoured with the title of 'Professor' on 30 January 1938 – was among the first names.[132]

'NORMALISATION'

After Hindenburg died in August 1934 Hitler became officially head of state and established an absolute dictatorship. The socialist wing of the Nazi party was silenced, SA calls for a second revolution and a 'night of the long knives' were brutally suppressed. Hitler's aim was to present the NSDAP not as a radical party advocating revolutionary change any longer, but to recommend it to the bourgeois classes as an established people's movement. For the theatre this development had implications, too. After Goebbels had successfully concentrated the decisive powers in his ministry by the mid-1930s, all experiments with alternative forms of theatre ended, especially the *Thing* movement, which had aimed to develop a genuine Nazi form of cultic theatre.[133] It made way for a restoration of the bourgeois theatre and its established forms.[134] The new Nazi-dominated city councils were forced to realise that radical changes only alienated them from their target audiences as they increasingly tried to make use of existing structures. The dissolution of Rosenberg's 'National Socialist Culture Association' (NSKG) and its assimilation into the less ideological 'Strength Through Joy' in 1937 perfectly marked the new trend. In addition to rising municipal subsidies and increasing audiences, Goebbels introduced his own direct payments to theatres not only as a means to help those in need but also as a reward and control system.[135] All Westphalian playhouses at one point profited from sometimes quite generous gifts. Dortmund, for example, was in receipt of annual payments, which reached RM 80,000 in 1939, as its administration declared itself unable to pay the full subsidy alone.[136] Gelsenkirchen's city fathers, on the other hand, cleverly banked on claims that the municipal theatre brought high art to the working classes (the city was dominated by its coal and steel industry with 55 per cent of jobs in these areas) and subsequently received an annual RM 60,000 subsidy from the Propaganda Ministry.[137]

Willi Hanke in Münster

After the mess of the 1933–4 season the Nazi administration was in urgent need of theatrical success stories, and Hanke was prepared to deliver. He achieved the longed-for record attendances, which increased to 210,000 – although Nazi propaganda claimed they even reached 300,000[138] – and the city claimed to have the highest number of theatre visits per head in any western German city.[139] In January 1937 alone the theatre put on a record total of 74 performances with an overall attendance of 27,000.[140] Equally important in terms of propaganda was the fact that Hanke became president of the *Land* theatre chamber, offered new employment and introduced twelve-month contracts.[141] The 'German Stage', too, intended to improve on their performance and presented themselves as the only visitors' organisation – although this claim could hardly be sustained.[142] By 1936 there were again four different groups who canvassed prospective season ticket holders. Although their number declined, it remained at an average of 3,600 until 1939 – double the figure of the Weimar years.[143] It is interesting to note, however, that the Nazis prohibited all other advertisements for cultural events before the start of each season in order to secure the subscription campaigns the best possible success.[144]

Hanke remained in Münster for several years, was successful and popular and knew how to please the authorities.[145] The question remains, however, why Hanke was able to achieve something which Liebscher had failed to do.[146] The chief reason seems to lie in the choice of repertoire, which avoided too much open propaganda, but the programme notes, too, showed a changed outlook. Whereas Liebscher accompanied his 'national' choice of repertoire with corresponding articles, Hanke concentrated on information and entertainment instead. Liebscher regularly included quotes (and photos) of Hitler, Goebbels and *Gauleiter* Meyer, he sometimes reprinted whole speeches and gave many of the new *völkisch* playwrights a forum for their – mainly rather boring – programmatic articles. Furthermore, the notes' tedious layout with pages and pages full of text without any illustrations did not help to make them popular. Hanke for his part included press reviews, photos of actors and rehearsals, as well as theatrical anecdotes,[147] and in 1935–6 extended the volume of the notes considerably.[148] Interestingly, in their outward appearance they began to resemble the look of the 1920s' programme notes again. Although this was certainly not intended, the notes suggest a continuity with a past Liebscher wanted to leave behind at all cost. The revolutionary character of a radical break and new beginning had given way to an approach which avoided open propaganda, tried to stress continuing elements and aimed at entertainment. In summer 1938 Hanke left Münster and handed over to Erich Pabst. It is interesting to note that Münster had been an important step in Hanke's career. After a brief stay in Graz he headed for Nürnberg, which, as the 'Capital of the Movement', was a city of high prestige.[149] Pabst came from Berlin where he had managed a private theatre. He remains a somewhat obscure figure and his political allegiances are difficult to pin down. On the one hand he seems to have been a loyal democrat during the Weimar Republic, on the other he appeared almost a devoted admirer of Hitler in the latter half of the 1930s.[150] In any case, Pabst was prepared to manage the theatre according to the 'spirit of the time'.[151]

It was about this time that in several respects Münster's theatre reached its peak as a cultural institution. The municipal subsidies were as high as ever, Münster even received extra funding from Berlin,[152] and Hanke cleverly seized the theatre for propaganda purposes. One convenient opportunity was to claim that the popular dialect comedies, produced in the municipal theatre by the 'Low German Stage', could be incorporated into the 'Blood and Soil' ideology as they stressed the connection with the Westphalian *Heimat*.[153] Another opportunity was to offer productions as closed performances to the army, large companies or party organisations such as the 'German Work Front', 'Strength Through Joy' or the HJ.[154] In 1937, for example, Hermann Burte's nationalist play *Katte* only made it to a successful run of nine performances because it was booked by entire HJ units.[155] Last but not least, both Hanke and Pabst managed to place the *Städtische Bühnen* in a long theatrical tradition. They referred constantly to the past and, thereby not only glorified Münster's theatrical history, but also firmly established the present situation as part of this development.[156] Ultimately the function of this contextualisation was to present the current theatre as the fulfilment of the promises of the past. By contrast and against the background of this century-old success story the 'decadent' Weimar years seemed an anomaly.[157]

Georg Hartmann and Peter Hoenselaars in Dortmund

After having been Bruno Bergmann's deputy from early 1934, Georg Hartmann took over the theatre management in 1935. Although not a party member, Hartmann was willing to toe the line and placed his artistic expertise at the regime's disposal.[158] He left Dortmund in 1937 for Duisburg and Peter Hoenselaars took over. Even more than his predecessor, Hoenselaars combined artistic with political reliability.[159] A party member and SA officer, he opened his first season in a completely refurbished theatre and furnished with a new title: *Generalintendant*.[160] Hoenselaars tried to present 'his' theatre in perfect symbiosis with the regime and opened the 1937–8 season as the 'culmination of the cultural reconstruction process'.[161] Theatre and politics, art and state became synonymous. Although audiences did not rise significantly and remained at a respectable but not spectacular level of around 220,000,[162] Hoenselaars did not have to wait for the due rewards for long – until 1939 the theatre received large annual payments from the Propaganda Ministry. In a city whose working classes had largely supported the Social Democrats and the Communists before 1933, and which had always struggled to maintain its theatre, this engagement seemed particularly profitable for the regime.[163] At the same time the Ministry wanted to keep an eye on the repertoire and received lists of all the season's productions. Although this does not seem to have been a prerequisite, Hoenselaars wanted to illustrate that the money was well spent – and make sure that the subsidy was granted again the following year. This obvious compliance, however, does not mean that the city officials did not complain if they thought they were treated unfairly or did not get enough.[164] When told that they would not receive any more payments due to the annexation of Austria in 1938 (the Propaganda Ministry claimed the money was needed at Austrian theatres) officials did not take 'no' for an answer, they complained and received what they wanted.[165] The situation in Dortmund clearly illustrates that even at the outbreak of the war the image of the theatre characterised by blind obedience in a total dictatorship needs to be adjusted.

Alfred Kruchen in Bielefeld

In 1936 Alfred Kruchen, who like Hanke trod more carefully and appeared less dogmatic and political, succeeded Leon Geer.[166] He was also responsible for technical improvements to stage, auditorium and rehearsal spaces and was credited with a successful first season.[167] His concentration on a repertoire dominated largely by entertaining fare proved highly popular and the *Stadttheater* now regularly sold 90 per cent of its tickets. The great importance the city administration attributed to rising audience figures – and increased revenue – can be gathered from the fact that this was seen as a prerequisite for increased subsidies.[168] Therefore, even under the Nazis, financial profit was not entirely discarded. It was in fact vital and closely monitored. It was only due to Kruchen's successful policy that a rise in subsidy seemed possible again in 1938.[169] At the same time Kruchen managed to place the theatre firmly in the new political arena. Like Hanke in Münster,

Figure 2.7 Bielefeld municipal theatre covered in swastika flags on the occasion of a district meeting (*Kreistreffen*) of the Nazi party (NSDAP), December 1936

Kruchen realised the potential of high-profile engagements in national festivals and tried hard to make a good impression on the regime's representatives.[170] Bielefeld's theatre regularly took part in the annual Grabbe Festivals and Wagner Weeks at Detmold.[171]

Bochum

Saladin Schmitt was happy to continue with his *Festwochen*, which could be easily incorporated into Nazi propaganda and conveyed cultural laurels to working-class Bochum, which had become the capital of the *Gau* Southern Westphalia. The theatre hosted special events,[172] was invited to national and international festivals[173] and received wide recognition. Bochum attracted rising audiences, and after a drop in municipal subsidies, they quickly returned to the levels paid in the early 1930s.[174] In 1938 the theatre also underwent an extensive renovation programme. Although Schmitt did not object to his theatre and his person being used by the regime in this way, he never became a party member and, at least in his view, seemed to have kept out of politics. This in turn annoyed some party circles.[175]

Hagen

Hagen's Hermann Bender is a perfect example of a manager whose political credentials were enough to secure his survival as *Intendant* until the end of the Third Reich despite a horrendous track record. After subsidies had been successfully reduced in the early 1930s they were soon back at record levels despite disappointingly low audience figures – even by Hagen's standards. In fact attendance was even lower than during the 1920s.[176] At the same time, and despite constant financial struggles in a city under strict budgetary control by the regional authorities (who had a close eye on its spending on cultural matters in particular), Bender managed to squeeze growing subsidies out of the city.[177] Although they rose from RM 150,000 in 1933–4 to RM 380,000 in 1936–7, Bender constantly asked for additional payments. In May 1937, for example, he applied for (and received) another RM 42,000.[178] The city authorities were well aware of the discrepancy between sharply rising subsidies and static revenue,[179] and after subsidies had reached RM 569,000 in 1939–40 the city treasurer finally called a halt.[180] At about this time the administration countered credible rumours that Bender was to be replaced as soon as prospective candidates applied for his post.[181] Bender himself, however, was quite unfazed by the criticism, and instead praised his own successful work claiming a general 'upswing' in Hagen's theatre.[182]

COMPARATIVE PERSPECTIVES III

Although the differences between Britain and Germany are more than apparent at the end of the 1930s, especially regarding the influence of local government and party politics, there are still interesting similarities regarding the importance attached to the revenue generated through ticket sales and rising audience numbers. The Nazis regarded the theatre as a prestigious asset on which they were prepared to spend sums unheard of during the Weimar years, but they still monitored expenditure closely in order to make sure that they received value for money. In particular the rise in audiences, which was of such a high propaganda value, became crucial for theatres in order to argue for equally rising subsidies, as the case of Bielefeld clearly shows. Luckily for the Nazis, most theatres delivered and attendances at regional playhouses in general increased substantially during the second half of the 1930s. It is interesting to see that this trend is mirrored in Britain where theatre audiences, especially at repertory theatres, rose too from the mid-1930s. Seebohm Rowntree in his seminal study about social life in York, for example, stated that the Theatre Royal attracted up to 10,000 people to its shows in good weeks.[183] It seems that regional theatres in both countries on the eve of the Second World War had successfully developed distinct characteristics which distinguished them from the cinema.

THEATRE AT WAR

In contrast to Britain, German regional theatres seemed to continue as if nothing had happened at the outbreak of the war – on the contrary: many of them received even higher subsidies and seemed strangely remote from any conflicts.[184] Hitler was at pains not to let everyday life be affected by the war.[185] It was understood that morale could only be sustained if life continued to run smoothly.[186] Whereas in Britain all places of entertainment closed in September 1939, it was Goebbels' expressed wish that German theatres should carry on as usual.[187] Despite these claims Westphalian theatres *did* immediately become affected by the war and increasingly played a political role.[188] As part of their war effort they presented a growing number of special, mainly entertaining, shows for the armed forces and war workers and variety shows, dance performances and comedy events – often staged in factories and garrisons – were jointly organised with 'Strength Through Joy' and the 'German Work Front'.[189] Bochum's theatre ensemble even opened the season in the occupied French city of Lille in 1941, and performed in Holland during the following years. These performances grew into an important factor with respect to the function of the theatre as a cultural institution during the war.

As air raids hit more frequently, schools closed and pupils were sent away to areas less affected. Some Westphalian cities experienced almost daily raids from 1943.[190] Consequently, many theatres stopped their evening performances and turned to matinees instead.[191] Eventually, on 31 August 1944, the final curtain came down when, following Goebbels' declaration of 'total war', all places of entertainment were closed for good.[192] In an ironic twist of history, the Nazis finally had to tear down their cultural façade and close all theatres – a move that Britain had already dared to take in 1939.

Figure 2.8 Münster's theatre during the war,
possibly after the July 1941 raid

Münster

The first war season began with yet another sharp rise in municipal
subsidies, which were up RM 300,000 compared with two years earlier
and now reached RM 1 million.[193] Additionally, a lavish 'year book'
was published in 1940 – in praise not only of the successful work at
the theatre but also of the *Führer* who had just won the campaign in
the West.[194] In line with efforts to be seen to be doing its bit, the
theatre took part in the annual *Gaukulturwoche*, sent productions to the
Detmold Grabbe Festival and asked actors to raise money for the
Winterhilfswerk.[195]

In July 1941, however, Münster became drawn into the war to a
much greater extent. The devastating British air raid on the city not
only destroyed most of the theatre building, but also the equipment,
the workshop, stage properties and sets were lost, too. Although plans

were hastily drawn up, the city proved unable to rebuild the theatre during the war.[196] From then on, the city hall was used as a provisional venue, but its technical equipment was poor, stage lighting barely existed and the changing of sets was impossible. At times the hall could not be used at all due to a lack of coal to heat the building.[197] To make matters worse the theatre also increasingly suffered from a loss of staff. By summer 1942, fifty-seven men had been called up and five were already dead.[198] To find replacements proved increasingly difficult. At the same time, however, the theatre was able to secure the services of replacement musicians as late as summer 1944. It is also interesting to note that the municipal orchestra in the same year still had forty-nine members – only six fewer than 1939 – and that they had even been raised to a higher income group. The theatre struggled but did on the whole succeed in lending credibility to the claim of a culturally minded city, even during the later stages of the war.[199] And only weeks before the final closure, the company still went on a trip twenty miles south to Hamm to give a guest performance.[200]

The other Westphalian theatres

In general, and until they suffered from the growing number of air raids, theatres experienced increasing audiences, increasing subsidies and increased political demands – which most of them were happy to comply with – after 1939.[201] The regional propaganda offices proudly reported to their superiors that performances regularly sold out and that theatres readily agreed to play their part in the war effort.[202] At the same time theatres suffered from scarce resources and 'called-up' staff, which increasingly affected the quality of performances.[203]

During the first years of the war, Bielefeld appeared like a normal city with a thriving theatre. Subsidies and audiences reached record levels.[204] Salaries of theatre staff also rose substantially during the war between 1941 and 1944 by an average of 17 per cent.[205] Although the city increasingly suffered from air raids and the city centre lay in ruins after a particularly heavy raid on 30 September 1944, the theatre survived the war almost unscathed. Alfred Kruchen made the most of the fact that the *Stadttheater* remained unaffected by the bombings for so long. He led the theatre to record attendances (quickly seized upon by Nazi propaganda) as the number of tickets sold reached 296,356 in 1942–3 – double the figure of 1933–4. At the same time, staff worked

Figure 2.9 Dortmund municipal theatre,
destroyed after air raid, c.1944

night shifts as air raid wardens and performed for soldiers in hospitals, as the theatre played its part in the war effort.[206] Kruchen, however, also had bigger things in mind. In line with his efforts regarding the Grabbe and Wagner Festivals, he did his best to impress the regime and recommend himself for higher laurels.[207]

In Dortmund *Generalintendant* Hoenselaars was similarly successful during the first war years as the theatre remained unharmed until 1943. In May of that year, however, it burnt down completely after an air raid and a frenzied search for a suitable alternative venue ensued – even Luxembourg seemed a possible location.[208] From early 1944 theatrical performances took place in the foyer of the destroyed *Stadttheater*, and in June opera received a new home in the *Deutsches Haus*. Before this venue could be opened, however, it was destroyed in another raid.[209] Again plans were hastily drawn up to open the 'New Theatre' a few weeks later but by then Goebbels had already declared 'total war'.

Bochum, like Dortmund, was a prime target for Allied bombers because of its heavy industry. With the beginning of the 1942–3 season, air raids became increasingly frequent. There were heavy raids in May and September 1943 that damaged the playhouse and led to temporary closures, and in November 1944 the building was completely destroyed. These raids affected the day-to-day business with rehearsals taking place in the mornings and performances in the afternoon. Additionally, artistic personnel were reduced from forty-five in 1939–40 to twenty-six in 1943–4. Until then, however, the theatre had performed successfully in quantitative terms and had managed to raise attendances from 148,000 in 1932–3 to 212,000 in 1942–3.[210] Saladin Schmitt for his part relished the honours the regime bestowed upon him.[211] At the same time, Bochum's showpiece theatre came at a price. By 1940, the municipal subsidies had risen beyond the level paid during the 'decadent Weimar years' with an increasing reliance of the theatre on these payments (their share in the overall income increased from 56 per cent in 1925 to 78 per cent in 1940), and increasing salaries (as in Bielefeld) meant the share of personnel costs in the overall budget went up from 42 per cent in 1925 to 63 per cent in 1940.[212]

Following the city treasurer's advice from before the war, Hagen duly reduced its subsidies, although they were still well beyond anything paid before 1933. The war also influenced the theatre's attendance figures, which finally recovered. During 1941–2 the theatre generated RM 230,000 from tickets sold.[213] In other ways, too, Hagen remained a 'normal' playhouse even in the later stages of the war. In 1942–3 it still employed fourteen actors, eight opera and seven operetta singers, three conductors, a set designer, a prompter, a full ballet ensemble and a chorus plus other administrative and technical staff. Wages were average and ranged from a monthly wage of RM 150 for a female chorus member to RM 750 for a tenor soloist in the operetta.[214] The theatre was only destroyed in March 1945 after it had already been closed due to the 'total' war effort.

CONCLUDING REMARKS

In conclusion, we have seen that – possibly in contrast to expectation – German city councils took a long time to accept responsibility for the theatre. Until the first regular payments came into effect in the late nineteenth century, organisation, administration and financial problems in Westphalia's theatres were quite similar to their Yorkshire counterparts. Indeed, the similarities outweigh the differences by far, despite differences in patronage, social function and educational mission. Only after the turn of the century did theatres slowly begin to develop in another direction. Although they started to receive annual subsidies and were eventually taken over by the city authorities, however, financial problems still troubled Westphalian playhouses. The difficulties culminated in the early 1930s and resulted in radical proposals. Whereas many theatres in Yorkshire were on the brink of being turned into cinemas, Westphalian magistrates discussed possible mergers with other theatres in the region. Some politicians wanted the theatres of Bochum, Dortmund, Essen and Duisburg to join forces while others favoured a working together of Münster, Hagen, Dortmund and/or Bochum.[215] Other experiments included a return to the lease system or the total abandonment of a theatre manager. At the same time, these constant experiments and discussions conveyed the impression to many residents that money was the only matter councils cared about. Cultural politics, therefore, became an easy target for Nazi propaganda in the early 1930s. Promises to save theatres in connection with calls for a nationalistic, traditional and 'clean' programme went down well with many bourgeois residents not normally close to Hitler. In turn their support made the Nazis acceptable to many other critics. They applauded renovation programmes, supported the propaganda campaigns for a 'new' theatre and approved of increased subsidies, rising audiences, prolonged seasons and improved working conditions for actors. To most of them it seemed as if the Nazis had indeed delivered and kept their promises to lead theatres to 'golden times'. And the Nazi propaganda worked as, until well after the war, many residents failed to link 1933 to the destruction of their theatres in the 1940s.

During the war, it is remarkable that Westphalian theatres managed to continue their work despite the critical situation caused by the shortage of raw materials and disruption by air raids. Many theatres profited from special subsidies directly paid to them by the Propaganda Ministry in compensation for destruction caused by bomb damage.[216] In contrast to Yorkshire's theatres drastic measures, such as the cancellation of evening performances and, eventually, the closure of playhouses, were avoided as long as possible and only introduced when cities already lay in ruins. One could argue, therefore, that the theatres' dramatic zeal was not limited to their stages but that Westphalia's playhouses took part in a national performance of make-believe. This business-as-usual mentality corresponded to Hitler's demand not to let the home front be too much affected by the war. Even amid increasingly disastrous air raids, every effort was made to stage lavish opera productions and revive the great classics. Münster's Pabst, for example, was praised by the city authorities for his being prepared to keep going and was even nominated for a war medal.[217] This event also illustrates how much theatres had become part of the war effort by the early 1940s. They had developed into institutions deemed vital for propaganda, diversion and moral edification – until the 'final victory'.[218]

NOTES

1   This was a general development on German stages. The Nazis failed to transform the theatre into a specifically *völkisch* art form but made use of existing structures (see, for example, Dussel, Konrad. *Ein neues, ein heroisches Theater? Nationalsozialistische Theaterpolitik und ihre Auswirkungen in der Provinz.* Bonn: Bouvier, 1988; London, John, ed. *Theatre under the Nazis.* Manchester: Manchester University Press, 2000). Although research now largely agrees on the Nazis' failure to transform the theatre according to *völkisch* concepts, some scholars still claim that the take-over resulted in a complete shake-up. These issues have not so far been resolved as recent attacks by Henning Rischbieter and Thomas Eicher on Konrad Dussel's work show. Rischbieter claims that Dussel's categories were too 'simple', that his study lacked in depth and was playing down the Nazification of theatres after 1933 (see his foreword to Rischbieter, Henning, ed. *Theater im 'Dritten Reich'. Theaterpolitik, Spielplanstruktur, NS-Dramatik.* Seelze: Kallmeyer, 2000. p. 8). In the same book Eicher accuses Dussel of 'coarse generalisations' and outright mistakes regarding the claim not to see 1933 as a clear break (see Eicher, Thomas. 'Spielplanstrukturen 1929–1944'. Rischbieter, *Theater im Dritten Reich*, pp. 482–4).

2   As Gelsenkirchen received its own theatre as late as 1935 it will be largely left out of this study.

3   Prinz, Joseph. 'Die Geschichte des münsterschen Theaters bis 1945.' *Das neue Theater in Münster. Festschrift zur Eröffnung des Hauses.* Vernekohl, Wolfgang, ed. Münster: Werbe- und Verkehrsamt, 1956. p. 28.

4   See Müller, Eugen. 'Das Theater in Münster 1534–1927.' Intendanz des Theaters, ed. *Almanach 1927. Theater der Stadt Münster.* Münster: Städtische Bühnen, 1927. p. 28.

5   The end of the eighteenth century was a time of new departures. The idea of a unified German nation – and with it the idea of a national theatre – increasingly gained ground. Lessing wrote his *Hamburger Dramaturgie*, Goethe and Schiller had their first successes and National Theatres sprang up in Hamburg, Mannheim and Vienna.

6   The actors had to sign a contract, which laid down strict rules of conduct (see Brockpähler, Renate. 'Opernaufführungen im münsterischen Komödienhaus (1775–1890).' *Westfalen* 44 (1966): pp. 357–8).

7   See Jeismann, Michael. '"Bürgerliche Kultur" und Kultur des Bürgertums – Theater und Museen im 19. Jahrhundert.' *Geschichte der Stadt Münster*, vol. 2, p. 497.

8   See Müller, *Theater in Münster*, p. 38.

9   The distinction between bourgeois culture and the culture of the Bourgeoisie is the underlying idea of Jeismann's article. He points out that the bourgeois attitude towards the theatre changed notably over the course of time from enthusiastic support, to indifference, to general acknowledgement of its importance.

10   See Müller, *Theater in Münster*, pp. 45–9.

11   Further reductions were available for the *Volksaufführungen*, which presented a classical repertoire at reduced prices for people with a lower income.

12   The *Freie Volksbühne* society was founded in Berlin in 1890 with a social as well as an educational agenda. The 'People's Theatre' movement not only wanted to enable workers to see the German classics and Shakespeare, but also intended to expose middle-class audiences to the new Naturalistic plays by Hauptmann and confront them with the social issues of the working classes.

13   See Jeismann, *Bürgerliche Kultur*, p. 494.

14   Quoted in Sauer, Wilhelm. 'Das Theater zu Münster zur Zeit der letzten Fürstbischöfe.' *Zeitschrift für die Kulturgeschichte* NF (1873): 553–70.

15   A composer of romantic operas, Albert Lortzing had lived in Münster for a few years in the first half of the nineteenth century – a fact that the people of Münster are still proud of.

16   In 1911 the city paid RM 88,126 to the theatre. After that contributions fell to RM 67,700 in 1912 and RM 40,000 in 1913 (see Prahl, Anton. *Die eigenwirtschaftliche Tätigkeit der Stadt Münster in Westfalen*. Diss. U Münster 1936. p. 34).

17   See Prinz, *Geschichte des münsterschen Theaters*, p. 59. Other co-operations existed with Krefeld and Elberfeld.

18   During the 1913–14 season figures rose to 79,819, which was regarded as unusually high (see Prinz, *Geschichte des münsterschen Theaters*, p. 60).

19   Until 1929 plans regarding a new theatre building remained an object of public discussion (see, for example, 'Um den Theaterplatz!', *Münsterischer Anzeiger* [MA], 27 April 1929; 5 May 1929). After 1933 plans for a new building resurfaced and a planning committee was established (see

Stadtarchiv Münster [StdAMS]. *Verwaltungsbericht der Stadt Münster 1926–1945* (written by Verwaltungsrat a.D. Wangler, 1964). p. 223).

20 See Högl, Günther. 'Nimmer entbehre die strebende Stadt der veredelnden Künste. Opferfreudiger Sinn baute den Musen dies Heim.' *Heimat Dortmund* 2/2004. pp. 14–17, and Schwarz, Karin. 'Die Eröffnungsfeier des Dortmunder Stadttheaters.' Ibid., pp. 18–19.

21 These shows appeared for the first time in 1917 (see Dortmund's Theatre Archives [Theaterarchiv DO]. Box programme notes 1913–14 to 1918–19).

22 In the end the 240 people providing RM 170,000 was enough for the project to get the official go ahead (Schütze, Peter. 'Annalen des Stadttheaters.' Bühnen der Stadt Bielefeld, ed. *75 Jahre Stadttheater Bielefeld 1904–1979.* Bielefeld: Kramer, 1979. pp. 30–6).

23 The municipal subsidy amounted to RM 24,000 on average until 1914, the surplus reached RM 46,000 in 1906–7 and RM 60,000 in 1909–10 (see Schütze, *Annalen*, p. 40). These profits came at a price, however, as rehearsal times remained short and as a rule did not exceed four rehearsals for every production as Fritz Brinkmann recalls (quoted ibid., p. 38).

24 In German-speaking countries the *Intendant* is the manager of a publicly funded theatre. From the 1920s every theatre manager was called *Intendant*.

25 See StdAMS, *Verwaltungsbericht 1926–1945*, p. 133.

26 See, for example, *Blätter des Theaters der Stadt Münster 1925/26*: programme nos. 14 and 15. Both Heckroth and Jooss embarked on international careers and emigrated to Britain after 1933. Niedecken-Gebhardt continued his career in Nazi Germany and in 1939 came to the attention of Goebbels who made him director of a Dance Academy (see *Die Tagebücher von Joseph Goebbels. Sämtliche Fragmente. Teil 1. Aufzeichnungen 1924–1941.* Fröhlich, Elke, ed. München: Saur, 1987. vol. 3. Entries 14 and 19 December 1939, pp. 665 and 669). See also *WL*, August 1933 (series of articles).

27 Münster's subsidies, however, were not extraordinarily high. Some cities of similar size and importance (in 1933 Münster had 106,000 inhabitants) paid even more for their theatre. In 1930–1, Karlsruhe (156,000 inhabitants) paid RM 1.3 million, Aachen (155,000) RM 781,000 and Krefeld (152,000) RM 544,000 (see Dussel, *Heroisches Theater*, p. 160). Within Westphalia, however, Münster's expenses for *Kulturpflege* (cultural matters) in the mid-1920s scored top marks: with an expenditure of RM 7.56 per head Münster topped the 'league table'. The share of *Kulturpflege* in the general budget stood at 7.2 per cent (see Staatsarchiv Münster [StAMS], *Oberpräsidium no. 5501. Theaterplanwirtschaft.* p. 102) – a substantial figure even by today's standards. In 1990, the share of *Kulturpflege* in the budget was 6.1 per cent (see Teppe, *Politisches System*, p. 63).

28 The subsidies amounted to RM 639,000 in 1927 and to RM 706,000 in 1928 and, therefore, remained on similar levels as before (see StdAMS, *Verwaltungsbericht 1926–1945*, p. 133).

29 See StdAMS, *Verwaltungsbericht 1926–1945*, p. 133.

30 As a result, the subsidies could be reduced to RM 371,000 in 1932 (see StdAMS, *Verwaltungsbericht 1926–1945*, p. 133). Both theatres were under Berend's management but kept their independent ensembles. Osnabrück's opera company, however, played both theatres, and they also shared costumes and properties (see StAMS, *Oberpräsidium no. 5501. Theaterplanwirtschaft*, p. 326).

31 The Studio had a seating capacity of 200, it was not an integral part of the main theatre building, although still within walking distance. It soon became popular with patrons – as did Bernau who was praised as a gifted and successful manager and actor (see *MA*, 6 April 1930).

32 Because of lacking funds Bernau had to finish the season two weeks earlier than scheduled. This happened at such short notice that unsuspecting patrons, who had already turned up to see that evening's performance, were sent home again (see *MA*, 2 May 1932). Bernau had been unsuccessful in his negotiations with the city administration to renew his lease. On his abrupt leave he left the city to pay the overdue fees (see Grevelhörster, Ludger. 'Die Zeit der Weimarer Republik (1918–33).' *Geschichte original – am Beispiel der Stadt Münster*. vol. 19. Münster: n.p., 1995. Table 24. Chapter 'Städtische Theaterwirtschaft in der Zeit der großen Krise'). Bernau continued his career after 1933. In 1942 he was manager of the *Renaissance-Theater* in Berlin (see BArch, R 55/20434, p. 237).

33 The *Westfälische Landesbühne* was a subsidised travelling theatre company which performed all over Westphalia in towns without a standing theatre (see 'Tätigkeitsbericht für die Jahre 1930 und 1931.' StAMS, *Oberpräsidium no. 5501. Theaterplanwirtschaft*. pp. 264–5).

34 By May 1933, however, nine out of the nineteen Centre councillors had left the party, four of them joined the Nazis (see Kuropka, Joachim. 'Münster in der Nationalsozialistischen Zeit.' *Geschichte der Stadt Münster*, vol. 2, pp. 287–92).

35 Out of 17,000 theatre staff in Germany 7,000 were unemployed. Even those with a job, however, experienced difficulties as most of the theatres only offered short-term contracts – like Münster (see *Theater der Stadt Münster* 9 (1932/33): programme no. 20).

36 Unemployed actors were offered a small payment from the city's Social Services after the early end of the 1931–2 season (see *MA*, 2 May 1932). In these circumstances the offer to work for the Nazi 'Touring Company of the Militant League' was appealing for actors even if they did not support Hitler.

37 The fact that the 'Militant League' wanted to influence the repertoire was by no means hidden from the public but clearly spelled out in their programme (see *Aufruf zur Gründung der 'Kampfbund-Bühne', Ortsgruppe Münster i.W. im 'Kampfbund für deutsche Kultur e.V., München'*. StdAMS , Zentralbüro no. 135, Bd. IV. p. 157).

38 *Fire on the Border* was set on the German–Polish border, portrayed the alleged suppression of German peasants and endorsed the return of the former

German territory now belonging to Poland. The 'Touring Company of the Militant League' soon had 683 members (see *15 Jahre NSDAP Münster 1922–1937. Kreistreffen 15. –17. Oktober 1937*. Münster: n.p. pp. 37, 38; also Kuropka, Joachim. 'Auf dem Weg in die Diktatur. Zu Politik und Gesellschaft in der Provinzialhauptstadt Münster 1929–1934.' *Westfälische Zeitschrift* 134 (1984): p. 197). For press reviews and the company's tour plan see BArch, R56 I/46, p. 122.

39   See Häußner, Werner. 'Das Dortmunder Theater 1919 bis 1933. Personen und Entwicklungen.' *Heimat Dortmund* 2/2004.

40   See *Bühnenblatt des Stadttheaters Dortmund*, published in 1921–2 for the first time (see Theaterarchiv DO, box programme notes 1919–20 to 1926–7).

41   But also a step which did not come cheaply as subsidies increased more than fourfold from RM 200,000 in 1924–5 to RM 860,000 on 1925–6 (see Stadtarchiv Bochum [StdABO]. St 10/1 Theater-Haushaltspläne. p. 196).

42   See Theaterarchiv DO, box programme notes 1927–8 to 1932–3. For a contemporary largely positive assessment of Gsell's work see *Dortmunder Zeitung* [DZ], 17. February 1929.

43   In the summer of 1930 Dortmund's city council required the public to buy season tickets as the theatre's current utilisation of 55 per cent was not sufficient to justify the municipal subsidy any longer (see Stadttheater Dortmund, ed. *Einladung zur Zeichnung der Vormiete für die Spielzeit 1930/31*. Dortmund: Lensing, n.d. [1930]).

44   See Gsell, *Kassenreport*.

45   See Schneider, Ernst August. *Das Dortmunder Schauspiel*. p. 3 (unpublished manuscript, Stadtarchiv Dortmund [StdADO]. Mämpel bequest 481. no. 165).

46   The theatre's programme notes corresponded with this ideal (see *Blätter für Theater und Kunst* and *Bielefelder Blätter für Theater und Kunst* for the early 1920s and *Die Pause. Programmschrift des Stadttheater Bielefeld GmbH* thereafter).

47   See StdABO, D St 10/1 Theater-Haushaltspläne, p. 196.

48   In early 1926 the situation seemed in complete disarray. On 26 January the city's Council for Theatre and Music after a long discussion decided to keep the municipal theatre and two days later narrowly voted in favour of a RM 300,000 subsidy. Two weeks later, however, the council decided to get rid of the municipal theatre and instead advertised for the position of a theatre director to take out a lease (see Stadtarchiv Bielefeld [StdABI]. Stadt Bielefeld. Theater- und Musikausschuss. Prot 0067. Protokollbuch 1901–33. pp. 179–84).

49   There had only been two minor private theatres in Bochum before.

50   In the 1920s the theatre gave away tickets to those in need. The number of these free tickets grew from 200 to 1,000 (see StdABO, D St 13/1 Theaterangelegenheiten).

51   Schmitt was aware of his value for Bochum. Already in 1920 the city

administration increased his annual salary by 50 per cent (see StdABO, D St 10/1 Theater-Haushaltspläne, pp. 35–7).

52 See Schmidt, Bernd. *Die Entwicklung des Bochumer Theaters bis 1944. Unter besonderer Berücksichtigung der Festwochen in der Zeit von 1933 bis 1944.* Unpublished MA thesis FU Berlin (n.d.)

53 After a quick rise from 152,000 in 1922 to 186,000 in 1923 attendances declined again (see ibid., pp. 28–9). Between the mid-1920s and early 1930s they settled at an average of 150,000 per season (see StdABO, D St 10/1 Theater-Haushaltspläne, p. 191; StdABO, BO 20/234).

54 See StdABO, D St 10/1 Theater-Haushaltspläne, pp. 17–22, 34, 177 and 193–8.

55 See minutes of the municipal music and theatre commission, 8 December 1928 (StdABO, D St 13/1, p. 16).

56 See the official permit from the regional authorities 'allowing the running of a theatre enterprise' in Hagen from March 1921 (Stadtarchiv Hagen [StdAHA], Ha1/9230).

57 Letter of the *Regierungspräsident* to the German Stage Association who had filed charges against the city because, in their view, Hagen had violated the theatre's concession (StdAHA, Ha1/9230).

58 See *Westfälisches Tageblatt*, 28 June 1930.

59 See minutes from the board meeting of the *Stadttheater AG*, 26 June 1930 (StdAHA, Ha1/9297). For a full list of subsidies between 1924 and 1942 see StdAHA, Ha1/9272.

60 This did not mean, however, that the city authorities gave up their involvement in the theatre, which included supervision of the repertoire and even attending production meetings (see contract for the 1932–3 season signed in September 1932. StdAHA, Ha1/9230).

61 See StdAHA, Ha 1/9280.

62 Göring claimed control over all Prussian theatres. This made him a major player in the culture sector as Prussia comprised about two-thirds of the German territory. In a telegram to the heads of all Prussian districts in April 1933 Göring made it clear that 'all affairs of the municipal theatres are with immediate effect subject to my control entirely' (StAMS *Oberpräsidium no. 5501. Theaterplanwirtschaft*. p. 327). Göring repeatedly renewed this claim in official circulars. In May he publicly warned Rosenberg's organisations against exercising influence on municipal theatres and in July 1933 he stated that every senior official in a Prussian theatre was subject to his confirmation (see StdABO, D St 15, p. 28; Wulf, *Theater im Dritten Reich*, pp. 63 and 83). Göring's statements were widely publicised and reprinted, even in local programme notes. After Goebbels had successfully established his pre-eminence in the culture sector Göring continued to play an important role regarding the Prussian state theatres in Kassel and Berlin, where Gustav Gründgens was his famous protégé.

63 For contemporary statements regarding the duties of the National

Dramaturge see Laubinger, Otto. 'Die Aufgaben der Reichsdramaturgen.' *Der Autor* September 1933: pp. 4–6. Laubinger was the first president of the Reich Theatre Chamber. Rainer Schlösser was National Dramaturge between 1933 and 1945.

64 See Dussel, *Heroisches Theater*, pp. 89–100. The question of the actual powers of the National Dramaturge is still contested. Eicher, for example, claims that Schlösser's influence had been 'extraordinary' (see Eicher, *Spielplanstrukturen*, p. 484. Similarly, Rischbieter, Henning. '"Schlageter – der erste Soldat des Dritten Reiches." Theater in der Nazizeit.' Sarkowicz, Hans, ed. *Hitlers Künstler. Die Kultur im Dienst des Nationalsozialismus*. Frankfurt: Insel, 2004. p. 218).

65 See, for example, an internal report on the chaos within the Reich Theatre Chamber written by its deputy head Helmuth Steinhaus in 1936 (see BArch, R56 I/91, pp. 150–8). Another report less than six months later illustrates the continuous chaotic financial situation (see BArch, R56 I/128, pp. 46–50).

66 It is interesting to note that this 'supervision' by the city authorities could result in outright censorship during the Weimar years, too. When Münster's Alfred Bernau was appointed manager in 1929 his proposals for the repertoire were subject to approval of the municipal Theatre and Music Council (see *MA*, 28 April 1929). In that sense Nazi demands on the arts were not necessarily felt to be an anomaly but something theatres had been used to to a certain degree.

67 In spring 1933 the 'German Stage' came into being through the forced merger of the two most important visitors organisations, the 'Association of Free People's Theatres' and the conservative *Bühnenvolksbund* with the 'German Stage', which was part of Rosenberg's 'Militant League for German Culture'. This move suddenly created a mass organisation with some 800,000 members (figures as at 1932, quoted in Rischbieter, Henning. 'NS-Theaterpolitik. NS-Theaterpolitik als Prozeß, Theatermetropole Berlin, Die deutsche Theaterlandschaft 1933–44.' Rischbieter, *Theater im Dritten Reich*, p. 30).

68 See *Westfälischer Kurier* [*WK*], 10 April 1934.

69 The 'Berend case' is indeed interesting as it not only illustrates the devastating consequences of Nazi persecution but also shows the inconsistency of official policy. Berend, who jointly managed the theatres in Osnabrück and Münster, was made redundant by Osnabrück's city council – but only as manager of the theatre there. After the press had wrongly announced that he was to leave both posts (see *Dortmunder Generalanzeiger* [*DG*], 8 April 1933), the same newspaper hurried to correct its mistake a few days later and confirmed that Berend would remain manager at Münster. The paper even added that Berend now wanted to concentrate on 'great opera' (see *DG*, 18 April 1933). Berend himself tried to fight the dismissal by Osnabrück's city council and on 12 April 1933 wrote to mayor Gaertner. Berend claimed that as a highly decorated soldier of the First World War he

was exempt from the April law – and he was right. President Hindenburg made his consent to the law dependent on this exemption and signed it only after the Nazis had granted it. Gaertner, however, suggested not to pursue the matter any further as it would lead to nothing. We do not have Berend's reply to this letter, but on 26 April Gaertner asked Berend to request his own dismissal. The reason given was a typical example of Nazi perfidy. A Dortmund newspaper had announced which plays Berend wanted to produce for the celebrations on 1 May 1933 without him knowing about or agreeing to it. The accusation was that someone had given the press release to the paper without Berend's knowledge, which should not have happened because he was the manager. At this point Berend must have realised that the letter of the law no longer counted under the new regime. A few days later he asked for his resignation and was 'granted leave for the time being' (for the whole dossier see BArch, R56 I/54, pp. 89–91). In Münster, however, Berend continued as theatre manager. The city authorities believed they acted according to the law when continuing to employ the decorated World War One officer. They even wanted to renew Berend's contract for the 1933–4 season (see BArch, R56 I/54, pp. 86–8) when – suddenly – Berlin interfered. The Prussian Theatre Council made it clear that 'under no circumstances must a German theatre be led by an *Intendant* who is not of Aryan descent' even if he participated in the World War (BArch, R56 I/54, p. 82). This decision was clearly not expected in Münster and stands as another example of the unpredictability of the regime. The council had to act quickly in view of the start of the next season and the city's executive for cultural matters, Aschhoff, immediately headed for Berlin to look at the applications of possible candidates. Only a few days later, Otto Liebscher was announced as the new manager (see *MA*, 25 July 1933). Berend eventually left in 1936 and worked at the theatre of the Jewish cultural association in Berlin until 1937. He then emigrated to Britain where, after years of uncertainty, he eventually managed to secure a position as a musical director at the Welsh National Opera (see *Westfälische Nachrichten* [*WN*], 6 January 1956). It was not until 1953 though that Berend returned to Münster for a brief visit. Although announced at the time a return visit to conduct an opera at the theatre never materialised (see *Münsterische Zeitung* [*MZ*], 8 July 1953). Berend died in London in 1956.

70 At the same time, however, agreement on who was 'Jewish' was not always reached. The radical 'German Stage', for example, in December 1933 wrote a letter to the Prussian Theatre Council enquiring about Paul Vulpius, the author of the comedy *Hau-ruck*, who they assumed was Jewish. The Theatre Council replied that Vulpius' solicitor had declared that the author was 'of Aryan descent'. The 'German Stage' sent another letter in April 1934 though, in which they declared their 'final' decision on Vulpius. They had consulted the expert on 'Race Research' in the Home Office, who had found that Vulpius was a 'non-Aryan' (see BArch, R56 I/64, pp. 55–6 and 14). In any

case Vulpius' comedy was produced successfully in Münster and received twenty-three performances during 1933–4 – more than any other play during that season. Another example of the regime's ambiguity is a letter by the widow of the playwright Rudolf Presber whose comedy *The Blessed Excellency* she wanted to see performed in Berlin because she was in desperate need of royalties. The 'problem' was that the co-author of the play was 'the Jew Stein' and that according to official policy a performance was impossible. Still, Schlösser's bottom line was that although he did not want to see the play produced in Berlin a production in the provinces was certainly something he would be willing to consider (see BArch, R56 I/11, p. 51).

71 Authors whose works were burnt and immediately forbidden include Bertolt Brecht, Carl Zuckmayer, Arthur Schnitzler, Erich Kästner, Franz Werfel, Fritz von Unruh, and Heinrich and Thomas Mann.

72 Residents only knew that Berend's contract would not be renewed, but no plans for the next season had been published (see *MA*, 23 July 1933).

73 See Apfelstaedt, Max. 'Theater-Tradition in Münster.' *Theater-Tageblatt* 7 (1935): no.1607. See also article series in *WL* in August 1933.

74 Commentators were anxious to stress the relationship between the design of the new curtain, which depicted motifs from Westphalian peasant life, and the regime. They linked the symbolism of this 'exemplary' work to the 'Blood and Soil' propaganda of peasant life and healthy *Volkstum* (see Kaiser, Friedhelm. 'Joos Jaspert über seinen Blaudruck-Vorhang.' *Blätter des Stadttheaters Münster 1933/34*, programme no. 11).

75 See, for example, *Düsseldorfer Nachrichten*, 29 August 1933, in which Münster was praised as a positive example for other cities.

76 As an example of countless other articles and speeches see Ohle's *Theater und Bürgerschaft* (see *MA*, 24 September 1933). The Nazis seized the term *Volkstheater*, which had been associated first with Lessing and then with the socialist free 'People's Theatre' movement a hundred years later. It had now acquired another, profoundly *völkisch*, meaning.

77 In 1932–3 there had been 1,322 season ticket holders, in 1931–2 only 915 (see StdAMS. *Statistischer Bericht der Provinzialhauptstadt Münster/Westfalen 1933*. p. 91). Other cities experienced similar successes with their season ticket after the take-over (for Gelsenkirchen's case see Schmidt, Christoph. *Nationalsozialistische Kulturpolitik im Gau Westfalen-Nord. Regionale Strukturen und lokale Milieus (1933–1945)*. Paderborn: Schöningh, 2006. p. 152. For Detmold see ibid., p. 388).

78 See *Westfälisches Volksblatt*. 12 October 1933.

79 In view of the success, however, officials got carried away on occasions. At one point they wanted to build a 2,000 seat open-air theatre to turn Münster into the 'Salzburg of northern Germany' (*WK*, 16 August 1933).

80 See Ohle, Ernst. 'Neues Theater im neuen Staat.' *Das schöne Münster* 5 (1933). pp. 256–61. Some of Ohle's claims are hugely exaggerated, others are simply wrong:

1. 'Fabulous sums' had never been paid to the theatre during the 1920s (see above). The subsidies paid before 1933 were easily topped by the sums awarded after 1939. The municipal subsidy rose from RM 371,000 in 1932 to RM 1,261,000 in 1940 (see StdAMS, *Verwaltungsbericht 1926–1945*, p. 141).

2. The 'cheap sensational hits' of the 1920s remained in the programmes after 1933.

3. The audience figures had not 'constantly declined' during the Weimar years. If we compare the figures of 1929–30 – before the Studio opened – with the years of the late 1930s we cannot substantiate any quantitative changes. During the 1929–30 season 184,378 people visited the theatre, during 1938–9 it was 182,199.

81 Hans Brockmann, the theatre's publicity officer, claimed that the new theatre replaced the 'chaotic theatre of recent years' (*MA*, 12 July 1933). And *Gauleiter* Meyer asserted the 'National Socialist revolution had found the German theatre in a state of ultimate disintegration' (*Blätter des Stadttheaters Münster 1933/34*, programme no. 1).

82 See Schütze, *Annalen*, p. 52.

83 The changes effected can even be gathered by seemingly banal incidents like the supply of *völkisch* publications to Bielefeld's theatre library, which stocked up on appropriate literature such as Hitler's *Mein Kampf*, Dietrich's *Mit Hitler* and Rosenberg's *Mythus*, all in nice hardback editions for between RM 3.50 and RM 6. The theatre also treated itself to a luxury copy of *The World's Anti-Semitism in Words and Pictures* for a steep RM 23.50 (see StdABI, *Städtische Bühnen und Orchester*, no. 1672).

84 See StdABI. Stadt Bielefeld. Bielefelder Theatergesellschaft. Prot 0064. Protokollbuch 1926–33.

85 See *Vorschau auf die Spielzeit 1934/35 und zum 30 jährigen Jubiläum des Theaters*, leaflet published 24 September 1934 (StdABI, *Städtische Bühnen und Orchester*, no. 1702).

86 The production was praised by the press for its 'colourful, moving, exotic-oriental' atmosphere (*DZ*, 11 January 1933). See also comments by Hans Georg von Borries celebrating the drama as 'one of the most brilliant confessions of true humanity and freedom of thinking' ('Gotthold Ephraim Lessing und *Nathan der Weise*'. *Stadttheater Dortmund 1932/33*: programme no. 7. pp. 51–4).

87 See Stadttheater Dortmund, *Spielzeit 1932/33*, programme no. 11. Inlay between pp. 83 and 84.

88 Together with Gsell six 'non-Aryan' personnel were 'retired', too (see Högl, Günther. 'Das Dortmunder Stadttheater unterm Hakenkreuz. Verfolgung jüdischer Künstler und nationalsozialistische "Gleichschaltung".' *Heimat Dortmund 2/2004*. pp. 31–2).

89 In an interesting (and not unusual) move after a few years the Nazis attributed the Social Democrat magistrate with the decision to close the playhouse. In

1937 Dortmund's mayor 'remembered' the 'evil times of 1932 when it was seriously considered to close the theatre down completely or to surrender it to a private director' (quoted *DZ*, 24 September 1937).

90   In 1934, for example, a high-powered meeting discussed how to pool resources to finance improvements to the theatre (see *WL*, 14 November 1934).

91   See StdABO, D St 15, pp. 20–2.

92   See letter of the *Stadttheater AG* to the regional authorities, 13 April 1933 (StdAHA, Ha1/9230).

93   See StdAHA, Ha 1/9300.

94   Unfortunately, the files do not specify why (see StdAHA, Ha1/10846 and Ha 1/9300).

95   The report was part of an envisaged publication by the Nazi administration to celebrate their 'progress' after the take-over. Despite being asked to be as positive as possible, however, most departments honestly stated the problems they faced. The contributions, therefore, underwent a long reviewing process and the publication was postponed. Only theatre manager Bender complied with the requirements and wrote a glowing review – so glowing in fact that it had to be toned down and never appeared in its original form (see StdAHA, Ha1/8890, Arbeitsbericht Stadttheater Hagen 1933–6).

96   See *MA*, 24 September 1933.

97   See *MA*, 4 June 1933. For a similarly successful public appeal in Gelsenkirchen in 1935 see Schmidt, *NS-Kulturpolitik*, p. 135.

98   *Intendant* Leutheiser from the Prussian Theatre Council, who came to Münster on one of his 'control' visits in early 1934, only found praise for the *Städtische Bühnen*. In his report he especially mentioned the production of *Arabella* conducted by Berend (see BArch, R56 I/54, pp. 79–80).

99   The 'consecration' ceremony ended with a vow to Hitler's government (see *WK*, 4 October 1933).

100 See introductory article by Liebscher (*Blätter des Stadttheaters Münster 1933/34*, programme no. 1).

101 See Figures 4.2 and 4.3.

102 The reason for this, however, does not necessarily have to be the fact that Münster's residents were anti-Nazi and deliberately stayed away as a form of resistance. More likely is the assumption that it was the appalling quality of most of the *völkisch* plays which kept them away.

103 See Liebscher, Otto. 'Gefordertes – Erreichtes – Erstrebtes'. *Blätter des Stadttheaters Münster 1933/34*, programme no. 13.

104 The official statement only mentions a 'proposed restructuring of the theatre in Münster' and speaks of a 'mutual agreement' between himself, the city authorities and the Prussian Theatre Council. The statement seems to imply that Liebscher handed in the notice himself, but leaves us with some scope for interpretation (see *Theater-Tageblatt* 6 (1934): no. 1409/10).

105 Apparently Liebscher was not offered another management position after he

had left Münster but took an administrative post. In 1936 his name appeared on a newsletter of the national employment agency for people working in theatre as the director of the Berlin office (see BArch, R56 I/49, p. 97).

106 See Dussel, *Heroisches Theater*, who looked at the theatres in Karlsruhe, Ingoldstadt, Coburg, Dortmund and Bielefeld. For an overview of the programmes at all German theatres see Eicher, *Spielplanstrukturen*, pp. 279–486.

107 Liebscher was available because he had left his post as manager of the Lübeck theatre in March 1933 (see StdAMS, *Vernekohl bequest*, folder 150).

108 On the occasion of the presentation to the public of the theatre's ensemble (see *MA*, 10 September 1933).

109 Commentators criticised that season ticket holders were regularly treated to second-rate repetitions of first productions. The press openly criticised the lacking quality of orchestra and soloists in a performance of the operetta *Die Försterchristel* (see *MZ*, 20 September 1933). These comments are remarkable especially for their timing. The season had only just started, enthusiasm must still have been high and criticism was certainly not welcome. Generally, commentators criticised Liebscher for not producing a sufficient number of operettas (see *MA*, 12 April 1934). See also *Nationalzeitung* [*NZ*], 21 February 1934.

110 Even the national press criticised Jochum for lacking leadership qualities and mediocre musical interpretations (see *Düsseldorfer Nachrichten*, 11 May 1934; *Allgemeine Musikzeitung*, 4 June 1937).

111 See *WL*, 18 April 1934.

112 In his report to the Prussian's Theatre Council, Leutheiser mentioned that the authorities had already agreed on Liebscher's salary and an increased municipal subsidy to enable him to enter into negotiations with singers and actors for the coming season (see BArch, R56 I/54, p. 79).

113 See BArch, R56 I/54, p. 73. Liebscher himself took the initiative and complained at the *Bühnenverein* (the stage union) about his dismissal.

114 The first press release regarding Liebscher's departure appeared on 5 April 1934 in the *MZ* (see also *MA*, 6 April 1934 and *MA*, 12 April 1934). The fact that Münster's authorities felt they were in a position to overrule a decision by the Prussian Theatre Council is worth taking note of. Firstly it indicates the diminishing power of the Theatre Council, which had lost most of its influence to Goebbels by the end of 1933. Secondly it proves that it was indeed possible to rush a decision through against the will of the national authorities – especially during the first years of Nazi rule.

115 See Liebscher, Otto. 'Die neue Spielzeit des Theaters der Stadt Münster.' *Das schöne Münster* 5 (1933). p. 256. At the end of the season Liebscher had to admit that the activities of the 'German Stage' had not achieved 'the desired results' (Liebscher, Otto. 'Gefordertes – Erreichtes – Erstrebtes.' *Blätter des Stadttheaters Münster 1933/34*, programme no. 13).

116 See BArch, R56/I 54, pp. 79–80.

117 Following an enquiry by Hagen's theatre into the activities of the 'National Socialist Culture Association' (NSKG), the successor organisation of the 'German Stage', many playhouses in the region replied and complained about financial demands and lacking co-operation (see StdAHA, Ha 1/9224).

118 See BArch, R56 I/58, pp. 72–9 for Göttingen, R56/50, p. 81 for Rheine, R56 I/53, 96 for Koblenz and pp. 102–3 for Cologne.

119 See BArch, R56 I/56, p. 36. Leutheiser concluded that Bergmann had to go – but made it clear that the magistrate should see to his being 'looked after', e.g. offering him the position of director of the municipal music school (ibid.).

120 See note by Hans Hinkel, one of the leading cultural functionaries in the Propaganda Ministry who also presided over the Theatre Council, from 4 April 1934. BArch, R56/I 62, p. 1. Still, Bergmann reappeared on the list of managers confirmed by Göring for 1934–5 (ibid., p. 5).

121 See Mämpel, Arthur. *Die Dortmunder Theaterleitung. Aus der Geschichte der Intendanz 1904–1934.* p. 4 (unpublished manuscript). StdADO, *Mämpel bequest*, Bestand 481, no. 105).

122 Uthoff, Kurt. 'Ein halbes Jahrhundert.' Städtische Bühnen Bielefeld, ed. *50 Jahre Stadttheater Bielefeld*. Bielefeld: Sievert & Sieveking, 1954. p. 9.

123 See *Westfälische Zeitung* [*WZ*], 30 June 1934. Reviews of the following season did not improve either (see *Westfälische Neueste Nachrichten* [*WNN*], 27 April 1935; *WZ*, 1 May 1935).

124 The theatre administration tried to counter criticism by referring to the audience figures since 1932, which had been continually rising – but not in any way comparable to the large increase at Münster, for example. Figures rose from 138,104 in 1932–3 to 158,056 in 1933–4 and 170,965 in 1934–5. At the same time, the membership of the 'German Stage' (which was important in view of season tickets) more than halved from 2,400 in 1934–5 to 1,100 in 1935–6 (see Fordemann, Wolfgang. 'Die wirtschaftliche Bilanz des Stadttheaters in den Jahren nach der Machtergreifung.' *Stadttheater Bielefeld 1935/36*: programme no. 18. pp. 141–2). The press, on the other hand, made it clear that they expected the theatre to perform better especially in view of the subsidies which rose from RM 153,000 in 1932–3 to over RM 240,000 in 1934–5 – an increase of 57 per cent (see *WZ*, 2 March 1935).

125 See *Blätter des Stadttheaters Bielefeld 1934/35*: programme no. 12. pp. 89–93.

126 The applications make interesting reading. In March 1935 the city applied for RM 41,500 in view of the rising deficit, which so far had been covered by municipal funds but had risen exponentially after 1933. It is interesting to note, however, that the Propaganda Ministry was not entirely prepared to cover for what seemed to be bad management. Although the Ministry agreed to pay RM 22,000 this time it turned subsequent applications down (see BArch, R55/20314, pp. 11–30).

127 See StdABI. Stadt Bielefeld. Beirat Theater und Orchester. Prot 0065. Protokollbuch 1936–8. Minutes of the meeting held on 9 January 1936.

128 After the last performance of the season Geer, together with his wife, went

in front of the curtain and said good-bye to the audience. Although Geer had quite obviously failed, his career continued as he became manager at Augsburg's theatre. Commentators attributed this 'falling up the ladder' to Geer's political allegiances (see Brinkmann, Fritz. *45 Jahre Theaterbeleuchter. Erfahrungen und Erinnerungen eines Lebens im Theater und für das Theater.* Unpublished handwritten manuscript, 1958–60. StdABI, HGB. pp. 166–4).

129 See *WZ*, 16 May 1936.

130 See *Leipziger Neueste Nachrichten*, 3 August 1933.

131 See Bender's original (but unpublished) review and his business report of the 1933–4 season. On the plus side Bender claimed to have attracted 4,717 season ticket holders (StdAHA, Ha1/8890, Arbeitsbericht Stadttheater Hagen 1933–6).

132 Metzger, Hans-Ulrich. *25 Jahre Stadttheater Bochum.* Unpublished manuscript. Bochum, 1943. p. 40.

133 *Thing* plays were massive shows produced in open-air arenas on an enormous scale. From the beginning the plays suffered from their deficient theatricality. After a short period of public enthusiasm the static displays of hundreds of extras, slow movement, declamatory speeches and lengthy plots, the presentation of ideas rather than characters and the predictable outcome of the plays increasingly bored audiences and seem to have been a major reason for their final failure. Another problem was that political spectacles, parades, marching ups and rallies equally fulfilled the demands made on cultic theatre – which, interestingly, was already recognised by contemporary commentators in relation to the march to the Munich *Feldherrnhalle*, for example (Stumpfl, Robert. 'Vom neuen deutschen Drama.' *Das Innere Reich* 4 (1937–8): p. 956). See also Niven, William. 'The birth of Nazi drama?: Thing plays.' London, *Theatre under the Nazis*, pp. 54–95.

134 The *Thing* movement also reached Westphalia. In Münster plans for an open-air theatre were endorsed by Hanke and a first draft was submitted in 1934. The project never materialised (see *Das Schöne Münster* 6 (1934): p. 126). Gelsenkirchen had even grander plans to build a massive *Thing* arena, until the traditional *Stadttheater* concept eventually won through.

135 As a condition for the money being paid out theatre managements and city authorities had to agree to consult the Propaganda Ministry before appointing any senior positions and to submit a draft repertoire to the National Dramaturge for his approval before the start of each season (see, for example, the case of Hagen, StdAHA, Ha 1/9278).

136 See BArch R55/20349, pp. 171, 188–9, 213, 280, 290, 332 and 359; BArch R55/20314, p. 18.

137 See Schmidt, *NS-Kulturpolitik*, pp. 125–37.

138 After 134,270 visitors in 1933–4, the theatre recorded 181,823 visits in 1934–5, 204,896 in 1935–6, 212,041 in 1936–7 and 211,183 in 1937–8 (see StdAMS, *Verwaltungsbericht 1926–1945*, p. 138. See also *Statistischer Bericht 1937*, p. 58 [StdAMS *Statistische Jahrbücher der Provinzialhauptstadt Münster*

1935–1938]). Although these statistical reports were published and open to everyone, the Nazis tried to exaggerate immensely – and got away with it (for the Nazi figures see Stampfer, Oskar, ed. *Münster 165%*. Münster n.p., n.d. The booklet was published at the beginning of the 1938–9 season.). It is interesting to note that the figures of the Nazi propaganda safely survived the war. Joseph Prinz, for example, copied them and claimed that attendance figures rose to over 300,000 (Prinz, *Geschichte des münsterschen Theaters*, p. 65).

139   A study published by the Council of German Cities stated that every citizen patronised the theatre at least one and a half times every year (see Stampfer, *Münster 165%*). In 1936 Münster had about 130,000 inhabitants.

140   See *Monatsstatistik* 19 February 1938. StdAMS, Stadtregistratur Z.B. no. 135, Bd. V.

141   This was a national and widely reported trend. Generally, theatres in 1934–5 employed more people and played longer seasons than two years earlier (see *Deutsche Allgemeine Zeitung*, 31 January 1935).

142   The 'German Stage' placed big adverts in the local press to recruit patrons for their season ticket (see *MA*, 16 April 1934) and even claimed that they had taken over the entire advertising campaign on behalf of the theatre (see StdAMS, Stadtregistratur Z.B. no.135, Bd. IV, box 13, no.70, p. 261a). As in other cities, however, these claims were far fetched as existing season tickets remained in place (for Gelsenkirchen's case see Schmidt, *NS-Kulturpolitik*, p. 158).

143   See StdAMS, Statistische Jahrbücher der Provinzialhauptstadt Münster 1935–8 and StdAMS, Statistische Berichte der Provinzialhauptstadt Münster/Westfalen 1938–48.

144   See StdAMS, Stadtregistratur Z.B. no.135, Bd. IV, box 13, no.70, p. 259.

145   Hanke's reputation even reached Berlin. In 1935 the *Theater-Tageblatt* devoted a whole issue to Münster and was full of praise. The 'overall impression ... is excellent, indeed so good as at hardly any other stage of similar size' (*Theater-Tageblatt* 7 (1935): no. 1607).

146   Naturally, there was not just praise. Vernekohl in a note, which was obviously only intended for private use, compared Hanke's repertoire of the first four months with Liebscher's regarding the production of works not previously produced in Münster. He concluded that both regarding quantity as well as quality Liebscher had performed better (see StdAMS, *Vernekohl bequest*, folder 102).

147   Some issues were devoted to special topics or single dramatists or composers. During the season 1934–5, for example, one issue concentrated on Beethoven, one on Kleist, and another on Verdi.

148   See *Blätter des Stadttheaters Münster* 11 (1934/35): programme no. 2.

149   Hanke even came to Goebbels' attention. The minister wrote that Hanke had made 'a great impression' on him (see Goebbels, *Tagebücher*, vol. 4, entry 19 November 1940, pp. 303–4). Hanke, however, did not leave the advancement of his career entirely to others. Over several years he tried to obtain the

prestigious title of *Generalintendant* (general manager) with remarkable persistence. In 1938 Münster's *Gauleiter* Meyer applied on Hanke's behalf for the promotion but the Propaganda Ministry declined stating that Hanke had not yet achieved the required artistic level. But Hanke did not give up. In 1940 Nürnberg's mayor Liebel applied on his behalf. This time it was Goebbels himself who declined as Hitler had ordered that there were to be no promotions during the war for the time being and, therefore, he could not endorse Liebel's application. Again Hanke was unperturbed. In 1941 Liebel wrote yet again apparently arguing that in view of recent promotions in Vienna and Cologne exceptions from the rule should apply to Nürnberg just as well. Goebbels' Director of Programmes Hadamovsky approached the Reich Chancery but received a negative reply from Hitler's personal adjutant Schaub, who claimed that 'the cases of Vienna and Cologne have been extraordinary exceptions'. Hadamovsky asked Liebel to shelve any future applications 'until after the war'. Hanke, however, did not take 'no' as an answer. In late 1941 he started another initiative, this time via the *Gau* propaganda office Franken, who joined forces with yet another request by Liebel. Liebel literally insisted on Hanke's promotion in view of similar promotions – and started to get on the Propaganda Ministry's nerves. An oral representation before Hitler now appeared as the last chance as the *Führer* was getting increasingly strict. Eventually, however, Hanke received the longed-for official document in September 1943 (see BArch, R55/72, pp. 198–212, 231, 234 and 256).

150 In many respects Pabst was, therefore, a typical example of a German artist in the first half of the twentieth century, willing to change sides according to the dominant political atmosphere. The majority of these artists claimed after the war that they had regarded themselves as unpolitical and that they had only wanted to serve art (see also BArch, R43 II/887b, pp. 1–100; BArch, R43 II/895, pp. 101 and 102).

151 At the beginning of the 1939–40 season, for example, Pabst wrote in glowing praise of Hitler and as 'one of the chosen ones in a profession to which the Führer has given most honourable status' (*Stadttheater und Kammerspiele Münster* 16 (1939/40): programme no. 1).

152 See Hanke's own account about the first three years of his management in 1937 (StdAMS, *Vernekohl bequest*, folder 106).

153 See review of the 'Low German Stage's' repertoire during the 1940–1 season (*MA*, 15 June 1941). During the same season the 'Low German Stage' embarked on a tour of the Low Countries and Belgium which was used for propaganda purposes. The 'Reports from the Reich' praised their performances as they contributed to 'strengthen the Germanic feeling of solidarity among the Flemish' (quoted in Kuropka, Joachim, comp. *Meldungen aus Münster 1924–1944. Geheime und vertrauliche Berichte von Polizei, Gestapo, NSDAP und ihren Gliederungen, staatlicher Verwaltung, Gerichtsbarkeit und Wehrmacht über die politische und gesellschaftliche Situation in*

Münster. Münster: Regensberg, 1992. p. 210).

154 The 'Leisure Time Society', which was part of 'Strength Through Joy', for example, offered an organised theatre visit in different programmes for 1938–9. Programmes A to D were open to everyone and consisted of nine shows, programmes E and F only offered performances in the Studio, programme G featured talks, and programme H was reserved for the armed forces (see StdAMS, *Vernekohl bequest*, folder 108). The high importance of these closed performances for a regional theatre may be gathered from a list drawn up by Bielefeld's Alfred Kruchen for the Propaganda Ministry. He stated that during the 1942–3 season 81 out of a total of 393 performances had been given as closed performances, more than half of which had been booked by 'Strength Through Joy' (see BArch, R55/20314, pp. 52–64).

155 This fact has to be borne in mind when judging the success of certain plays with respect to high attendances. It is also worth noting that the different organisations, which booked closed performances, all had their own agendas. Whereas Rosenberg's NSKG worked towards a *völkisch* repertoire, Ley's 'Strength Through Joy' was concerned with its massive presence in the bourgeois theatre.

156 Typical topics concerned the foundation of the theatre and the nineteenth-century principal Vagedes and his connections with the famous Düsseldorf manager Immermann (see, for example, *Stadttheater und Kammerspiele Münster 1939/40*, programme nos. 3, 10 and 20. See also Kordt, Walter. '165 Jahre Münstersches Theater'. Pabst, Erich, ed. *Jahrbuch 1940–41 der Städtischen Bühnen Münster*. Münster: n.p., 1940. pp. 7–22). This phenomenon continued in the later war years. Almost every issue of the programme notes featured articles about Münster's theatrical past and poems by Westphalian writers such as Droste-Hülshoff, Anton Sprickmann and Johann Schlüter.

157 This strategy was not confined to the theatre but appeared in all aspects of cultural life from the mid-1930s. In music the Nazis drew back on Bach, Beethoven and Mozart, Nazi art was clearly modelled on the Romantics, and the officially supported architecture could not deny its Greek, Roman and Renaissance roots. Put in perspective, this development links in with the general change in political atmosphere mentioned above. To quieten criticism and gain the essential support, for example, from the industry and the army, the revolutionary image of the NSDAP was abandoned and an ultra-conservative and evolutionary conception was adopted instead.

158 See, for example, Hartmann's demand on the newly appointed members of the company to do everything they could to 'raise the artistic level in a national socialist sense' (see *WL*, 2 September 1936).

159 Hoenselaars declared that he intended to closely 'follow the line mapped out by the *Führer* in artistic and political terms' (*Stadttheater Dortmund 1936/37*: programme no. 12).

160 This title was certainly unusual not only with regard to the importance of

Dortmund's *Stadttheater* in the national theatre landscape but also concerning a city dominated by the working class. In 1933 the city administration in a letter to the Prussian Theatre Council had explained that it did not want to use the title *Operndirektor* because they were anxious not to hurt the feelings of the working-class population. In a circular from the same year by the Propaganda Ministry Hinkel himself had declared that pompous titles should be avoided. Only four years later the conferment of one of these 'pompous titles' to Hoenselaars, however, seemed entirely appropriate (BArch, R56 I/56, p. 73).

161 See *DZ*, 24 September 1937. The press even claimed that it was due to the new regime that the theatre was saved without any mention that it had been the Nazi magistrate who had wanted to close the *Stadttheater* in May 1933.

162 See report on the Bochum theatre budget, written 27 February 1940. StdABO, BO 20/234.

163 In a list drawn up by the Reich Culture Chamber in October 1933 Dortmund's theatre deficit is put at nearly RM 875,000, which is a third greater than the more prestigious playhouse in Bochum and double the amount Münster's theatre received (see BArch, R56 I/60, pp. 43–5). The report also lists other theatres in the region (required subsidies in brackets): Osnabrück: population 89,079 (RM 207,769), Münster: population 106,418 (RM 482,126), Bielefeld: population 86,062 (RM 126,014), Dortmund: population 525,837 (RM 874,636), Bochum: population 313,554 (RM 589,849), Hagen: population 143,701 (RM 455,003), Essen: population 629,564 (RM 1,207,381), Düsseldorf: population 464,543 (RM 997,765), Wuppertal: population 405,515 (RM 512,106), Cologne: population 700,222 (RM 1,885,170).

164 The amount of money Dortmund received over the years is extraordinary as annual payments reached up to RM 80,000. Still the holes in Dortmund's budget remained considerable. In his application for the 1935–6 season dated 27 February 1935 mayor Kaiser stated that out of the theatre's total budget of RM 1,256,100 the deficit would reach RM 869,700. The city could only pay RM 725,500 and, therefore, he applied for a payment of RM 100,000. He did not explain, however, why the amount he applied for had risen by a third within only two years. In any case, the Ministry paid 'only' RM 70,000. Despite these large sums, however, the city officials remained unhappy – and tried their luck again. After they had received an extra payment of RM 80,000 for 1936–7 the city applied for RM 150,000 for the next season (see BArch, R55/20349, pp. 169–75, 188–9, 213, 244–5, 280, 290, 332 and 359).

165 Despite the initial negative reply Dortmund's theatre received another RM 50,000 for 1938–9 (see BArch, R55/20349, pp. 287–90). Dortmund complained again the next year and literally demanded another RM 80,000 for 1939–40, but this time the Propaganda Ministry stood firm (see ibid., pp. 357–9 and 363).

166 Like Hanke, Kruchen avoided open propaganda in the programme notes and

relied on seemingly un-political information.

167 See Schütze, *Annalen*, p. 53.

168 Mayor Budde declined the theatre council's application to raise the annual subsidy from RM 278,000 in 1936 to RM 324,000 in 1937. He decided that unless audiences got considerably larger, payments would 'for the time being' be frozen at RM 311,000 (see StdABI, *Beirat Theater und Orchester 1936–1938*, meeting 29 December 1936).

169 Councillor Schulz proudly remarked that the rise in ticket sales during the 1937–8 season made a rise in subsidy more likely – the theatre council duly applied for a RM 39,000 increase taking the subsidy up to RM 350,000. The council also asked for additions to the municipal orchestra. Judging from the wish list the orchestra must have been in a pretty poor state as it asked for a principal cellist, four 'very good' violinists, one oboist and one clarinettist as a 'minimum' to bring the ensemble up to standard (see StdABI, *Beirat Theater und Orchester 1936–1938*, meeting 14 February 1938).

170 On what can only be described as a control visit to all theatres planning to take part in the 1936 Grabbe Festival Herr Scherler of the Propaganda Ministry applauded Kruchen's work on Grabbe's comedy *Scherz, Satire, Ironie und tiefere Bedeutung* in a letter to Schlösser (see BArch, R55/20451, pp. 147–50).

171 In 1940 the theatre even performed *Lohengrin* at Detmold – certainly a courageous choice for a relatively small regional theatre but again illustrating Kruchen's ambitions.

172 In 1937, for example, the theatre hosted a week-long festival of 'Dramatists of the Hitler Youth' (see programme *Dramatiker der HJ. Bochum 1937. Die Veranstaltungen der Woche der Dramatiker der HJ und der Reichstheatertagung der HJ vom 11. bis 18. April 1937*. Bochum, n.d. [1937]).

173 Bochum was the first German theatre to perform at the Vienna *Burgtheater* in 1941. The *Comédie Française* had been the only other foreign theatre to receive this honour (see Schmidt, *Bochumer Theater*, p. 118). The theatre also regularly took part in the Grabbe Festivals.

174 Subsidies reached RM 804,000 in 1938 und RM 945,000 in 1939. After having remained at an average of 150,000 for several years attendances grew from 169,000 (1934) to 190,000 (1935), but declined again after that to 173,000 (1936), 178,000 (1937), 153,000 (1938) and 110,000 (1939) (see report on theatre budget, 27 February 1940. StdABO, BO 20/234).

175 In a letter to the regional Nazi party headquarters Bochum's mayor Piclum defended Schmitt against allegations that he did not support the regime. Schmitt had always fought against Weimar decadence, Piclum stated (see letter dated 9 November 1937. StdABO, OB Pi 10, file without pagination).

176 During the 1926–7 season 153,000 people had visited the theatre, in contrast to 142,000 in 1938–9 (see Rischbieter, *NS-Theaterpolitik*, p. 128). See also StdAHA, Ha 1/9278.

177 See StdAHA, Ha 1/9275; Ha1/9327. The playhouse became a full municipal

theatre again in 1934.

178 See StdAHA, Ha 1/9277. Despite these problems Bender even gave tickets away. For a performance of the *völkisch* drama *Wittekind* in early 1935 Bender presented two SA units with 220 tickets. He justified this decision, after Hagen's mayor had complained about this practice, with the fact that he was a convinced National Socialist. Besides, without the SA men the auditorium would have been half empty (see StdAHA, Ha1/9327).

179 Between 1933–4 and 1939–40 revenue only increased from RM 206,000 to RM 212,000 (see StdAHA, Ha1/9326).

180 In February 1939 the treasurer stated that the theatre only very rarely reached the required average revenue of RM 780 per performance. Opera and drama sometimes only managed to make half this sum. The head of the city's theatre council added that the number of season ticket holders had been equally disappointing with a decline from 4,717 in 1933–4 to 1,840 in 1938–9 (see StdAHA, Ha1/9326).

181 See various letters from early 1938 StdAHA, Ha 1/9300.

182 According to Bender, between 1934–5 and 1935–6 the number of performances rose from 315 to 337 and attendances grew by 20,000 (see Bender's 1936 report, StdAHA, Ha1/8890).

183 See Rowntree, *Poverty and Progress*, pp. 414–15.

184 The telex from Hamburg's *Gauleiter* hours after war had begun enquiring about the closure of theatres was a rare exception. Within 23 minutes the *Gauleiter* had a reply by the furious National Dramaturge who made it clear that 'the closure of theatres is out of the question' (see BArch, R55/20258, pp. 214–15).

185 See Göring's November 1939 circular to all theatre managers, in which he made it clear that all places of entertainment would remain open during the war. He added that these venues were important places for propaganda and essential for upholding public morale. Apart from that he warned against underestimating the psychological importance of entertainment during the war (see BArch, R55/20111, pp. 128–31).

186 Enthusiasm to fight another war was low in September 1939 – in clear contrast to 1914. Although public opinion changed after the *Blitzkrieg* victories of the German *Wehrmacht*, the Russian campaign never became popular and turned into horror after the defeat at Stalingrad.

187 It is interesting to note though that the arguments for keeping places of entertainment open during the war were in fact not too different in Germany and Britain.

188 The shortage of raw materials, for example, forced theatres to reduce the size of the programme notes, postpone building projects and to abandon lavish set designs.

189 The press featured countless articles about these shows. A typical example is an evening with entertaining music for soldiers and workers of the armaments industry (see *MA*, 20 September 1942. See also 'Was wir für die Truppen

spielen!' *Stadttheater und Kammerspiele Münster 1939/40*, programme no. 7). At the outbreak of the war Pabst indicated that it was an honour for him to organise events for the forces and that he could put on shows immediately (see BArch, R55/20261, p. 147). During 1941–2 the theatre organised 30 variety performances for soldiers and four shows for workers – so-called *Werkpausenveranstaltungen* (see Pabst, Erich. *Bericht über die Spielzeit 1941/42*. StdAMS, Stadtregistratur Z.B. no.232 Bd. II, box 13, no. 556a).

190 At the end of the war 61 per cent of Münster's buildings were destroyed, the city had suffered from a total of 1,128 air raid alarms which lasted for 1,532 hours. The Allies had dropped 32,000 high-explosive, 640,000 incendiary and 8,100 phosphorus bombs. 1,314 people had died during the raids and most of the historic buildings were destroyed (see Kuropka, *Münster in der Nationalsozialistischen Zeit*, pp. 324–6).

191 As in Münster from November 1943, and Bochum from early 1944.

192 After the war Münster was at pains to rebuild the theatre, but in contrast to its reconstruction policy on the Prinzipalmarkt, where the grand houses were restored to their original splendour, the theatre received a different architectural treatment in 1954. Although the new building integrated those parts of the façade of the old *Lortzing-Theater* which had survived the war, its architectural design was essentially modern. It was also Münster's first major building project after the war – proof of the public affection and support for their theatre (see Jakobi, Franz-Josef, ed. *'Theater tut not'. Zum kulturellen Neubeginn in Münster 1945–1956*. Münster: Münstersche Zeitung, 1996).

193 In 1933 subsidies stood at RM 398,000, in 1935 they were raised to RM 525,000 and in 1937 the theatre received RM 724,000 (see StdAMS, *Verwaltungsbericht 1926–1945*, p. 141). This means that already by 1937 the most 'expensive' season of the Weimar years had been outstripped. In 1928–9 the theatre had received RM 706,000 (see StdAMS, *Verwaltungsbericht 1926–1945*, p. 133). The 'fabulous sums', which according to Nazi officials had been paid during the Weimar years, really only materialised at the end of the 1930s.

194 Pabst praised the German soldiers who 'fought the greatest battles of history and who pinned victories over victories to their flags' and dedicated the book to the 'man who created our army, who led our battles, who fought our enemies, who watched over and protected our homeland, who gave our lives reason and strength, our art aim and glory, our Führer Adolf Hitler' (Pabst, *Jahrbuch 1940–41*, p. 5).

195 The *Gaukulturwoche* was held annually from 1936, and for the first two years it only featured cities from the *Gau* Northern Westphalia. In 1939 a big festival with over 1,000 events combined with the 'Days of Low German Culture' was organised in Münster (see Viehoff, Helmuth, ed. *Gaukulturwoche 1939 Westfalen-Nord*. Münster: Buschmann, 1939). As the festival aimed to stress the 'close relations of the Wehrmacht to the home front' the participation of as many soldiers as possible was one of the chief

goals (see *Amtliche Mitteilungen* no. 16/1940. StdAMS, Stadtregistratur Z.B. no. 285, vol. I). Fittingly, the 1942 *Gaukulturwoche* opened with a 'concert of pieces by composers in uniform' (see StdAMS, *Vernekohl bequest*, folder 111). The Detmold *Grabbe Festival* turned into a major showcase of artistic quality and propaganda ability of the theatres taking part. The festival was chiefly organised to commemorate Christian Dietrich Grabbe, who was celebrated as a heroic nationalist playwright, enjoyed Goebbels' patronage from 1936 and was taken incredibly seriously by the Propaganda Ministry (see BArch, R55/20451, R55/20451a, R55/20452 and R55/20452a). In 1941 and 1942, for example, Goebbels agreed to pay special subsidies (RM 30,000 and RM 35,000) to the festival (see BArch, R55/20452, p. 65; R55/20452a, p. 316).

196 There were several plans about how to resume theatrical activity after the raid, but the authorities in Berlin stopped all projects because of their high costs. In a report to the city administration written in summer 1942, Erich Pabst described the catastrophic circumstances under which the theatre functioned after the raid. There were only a few typewriters and telephones, no heating and leaks in the roof (see Pabst, *Spielzeit 1941/42*). To improve the situation, however, the stage of the Studio was enlarged in summer/autumn 1942 (see BArch, R55/20700, pp. 90–1).

197 The problems Münster had to face after the air raid were reported in detail to the Propaganda Ministry by the *Gau* propaganda office in November 1942 especially due to the fact that the main house had been destroyed. The small number of opera and operetta performances were not sufficient and sold out quickly (see ibid.)

198 See Pabst, *Spielzeit 1941/42*.

199 In February 1944 the municipal orchestra's first solo flautist was called up. As the assistant principal flautist had already joined the forces in 1942, his French replacement was reported missing after a heavy air raid in 1943 and the remaining flautist was sixty-six years old and unfit for solo parts, the chief musical director Heinz Dressel approached the authorities in Berlin to ask for a replacement. The orchestra officer of the Reich Music Chamber in his negative reply proposed to employ musicians on a temporary basis. Dressel, however, became increasingly unnerving and even threatened to stop performing if the musician was not sent. As an aside it is interesting to note that the tone of his letters was far from polite – quite the contrary. And in the end he succeeded: after a few months of waiting the vacancy could be filled with a flautist from Linz (see BArch, R56 II/4, pp. 306–20).

200 See *MA*, 1 July 1944.

201 At Gelsenkirchen audiences almost doubled within a few years from 155,000 in 1935–6 to 294,000 in 1942–3, and municipal subsidies increased even more from RM 177,000 in 1936 to over RM 700,000 in 1943 (see Schmidt, *NS-Kulturpolitik*, pp. 151 and 153). In Münster the subsidies rose from RM 371,000 in 1932 to RM 1,020,000 in 1939 and peaked in 1940 at RM 1,261,000 (see StdAMS, *Verwaltungsbericht 1926–1945*, p. 141).

202 After the early stages of the war, however, this eagerness soon petered out – possibly because performances solely reserved for soldiers did not generate sufficient revenue. In any case, the monthly reports by the *Gau* propaganda office Southern Westphalia show that the number of *Wehrmachtsabende* steadily declined in Dortmund, Hagen and Bochum during the first half of 1940 (see BArch, R55/20261, pp. 348, 379 and 426). Regarding rising audience figures, see BArch, R55/20259, pp. 90–1 and 121–2.

203 After one particularly lavish production at the Grabbe Festival Bielefeld struggled to stage others during 1942–3 as its quota had already been used up. In these cases, however, it was possible to apply for additional funds from the Propaganda Ministry (see BArch, R55/20259, pp. 90–1).

In their internal reports the regional propaganda offices did not hold back in their criticism. In a report from November 1942 the *Gau* propaganda office Southern Westphalia, for example, criticised Dortmund for producing Rino Alessi's *Lost Souls* because of its 'weak dialogue', and a production of Schiller's *Maria Stuart* was 'mediocre' – even though it had been supported by guest actors. Hagen's theatre received its fair share, too. In view of the small size of its company the theatre should never have tackled Schiller's *Bride of Messina*, and the quality of its production of Billinger's *The Giant* was poor. Hagen was particularly criticised for the fact that some parts had been given to pupils from local schools in view of staff shortages (see BArch, R55/20259, pp. 106–7).

204 Audience figures rose from 186,900 in 1940–1, to 236,741 in 1941–2, 296,356 in 1942–3 and 293,458 in 1943–4. The number of performances equally rose from 310 in 1940–1 to 385 in 1942–3 (see Seydel, Jochen. *Das Stadttheater Bielefeld. Kriegsjahre und Neubeginn 1939–1947.* n. pl. n. publ., 1947. pp. 10, 13, 18 and 22 [type-written manuscript held at StdABI]).

205 The Bielefeld City Archives hold complete sets of contracts with all theatre staff during the war years. A typical monthly salary for an actor in 1941–2 was RM 365. By 1944 this had risen to RM 430 (see StdABI, *Städtische Bühnen und Orchester*, no. 1678).

206 See StdABI, *Städtische Bühnen und Orchester*, no. 1462. Soon an average of one performance a week had to be stopped due to air raid alarms (see Schütze, *Annalen*, p. 55).

207 In June 1943 Kruchen sent a review of the 1942–3 season 'for the attention of' National Dramaturge Schlösser. He stressed how successfully the theatre had fared not only with regard to attendance and performance figures but also concerning its active part in the war effort with soldiers representing the majority of audiences now. Kruchen praised his work as 'an example of a soldierly sense of duty and utmost commitment' on the home front. He did not fail to make the desired impression on Schlösser who promised to keep him in mind for 'greater tasks' after the war (see BArch, R55/20314, pp. 50–65).

208 See BArch, R55/20349, pp. 2, 5 and 153.

209 See BArch, R55/20349, pp. 18–27.

210 See Dörnemann, Kurt. *Theater im Krieg. Bochum 1939–1944*. Bochum: Stadt Bochum, 1990. p. 5.

211 After having received the title of professor in 1938 the Propaganda Ministry in late 1942 thought about ways in which to honour Schmitt's upcoming twenty-fifth stage jubilee and asked Bochum's mayor for ideas. The National Dramaturge supported the idea of awarding Schmitt the title *Generalintendant*, the city suggested the prestigious Goethe medal, a Goethe bust and a 'bibliophile nicety'. In the end, however, the Propaganda Ministry only sent a telegram (see StdABO, D St 15, pp. 90 and 96).

212 See report on the Bochum theatre budget, written 27 February 1940. StdABO, BO 20/234.

213 This was up from RM 170,000 in 1935–6. Again, however, these figures had been higher during the mid-1920s when the theatre made RM 320,000 from tickets sold (see StdAHA, Ha1/9272).

214 See StdAHA, Ha1/9272. In a letter to the mayor staff still asked for a rise in salaries in December 1942 (see ibid.).

215 See StAMS *Oberpräsidium no. 5501*, pp. 64–261. In 1931–2 Münster's ensemble gave performances in Gelsenkirchen in an obvious attempt to generate additional income, but was criticised for lacking quality (see Schmidt, *NS-Kulturpolitik*, p. 125).

216 After the 1941 raid the Reich Culture Chamber awarded Münster's theatre RM 500,000 to buy new costumes (see StdAMS, *Theatergeschichtliche Sammlung Edith Lippold*, folder 2). The Gau Weser-Ems profited from an emergency programme for the arts inaugurated by the Propaganda Ministry in 1942. From these funds, which totalled RM 800,000, Osnabrück received RM 50,000 (see BArch, R55/20263, pp. 65–9). In 1944 the emergency plan was extended and funds in the sum of RM 500,000 were distributed. The two Westphalian *Gaue* each received RM 20,000, Weser-Ems RM 30,000 and Essen even RM 50,000 (see BArch, R55/20249, pp. 115–17 and 122).

217 See StdAMS, Stadtregistratur Z.B. no. 232 Bd. II, box 13, no. 556a.

218 After the war, however, most *Intendanten* continued their careers unharmed. As in many other areas of public life the year 1945 did not prove a break, the image of 'zero hour' can hardly be sustained. Although Bielefeld's *Intendant* Alfred Kruchen was an exception in that he was interned for two years by the British forces, he returned to theatre management in 1949 (to Oberhausen, where he worked until his retirement in 1959 (see Schütze, *Annalen*, p. 56)).

CHAPTER THREE

Theatre Repertoires in Yorkshire

All good theatres must function commercially.
Harcourt Williams[1]

The study of regional repertoires in Yorkshire seems to reflect the supposition formulated above, with the differences between the two countries outweighing by far the similarities. Theatre in Britain was regarded as a commercial enterprise, artistic considerations did not play a significant role in the day-to-day business, and even Shakespeare was only viable when produced with an array of stars and opulent settings.[2] Theatre managers had no qualms about presenting circus shows and boxing fights as long as they paid the bills. Even if they had wanted to present a different repertoire, the manner in which regional theatre was organised until the 1930s would have made it almost impossible. Many theatres were part of chains owned by businessmen, who controlled personnel, finances and repertoire. British regional theatres were subject to a much stronger influence from the capital than German playhouses. There was a constant flow of new productions, which went on provincial tours after their West End runs.[3] This inter-dependence between the West End and the provinces makes the examination of repertoires in Yorkshire all the more interesting as they reflected national trends. Yorkshire's programmes are, therefore, in many ways typical of British regional theatres in general.

It seems as if the decade between 1920 and 1930 especially highlights the fundamental differences. Whereas the large majority of German regional theatres became fully subsidised after the First World War with their own drama, opera and sometimes even dance ensembles and (relative) financial security, British managers did not receive any subsidies and in particular struggled against the competition from the cinema. Whereas German regional theatres played in so-called 'continental repertory' with a different piece every night, British managers normally booked companies for one week who presented one piece. In order to keep their loyal following, managements not only had to ensure a regular change of programme, but also the presentation of novelties and recent successes.[4] Even more important, however, was the attribute 'London', and a 'London Success' was always especially announced.[5] They were even more popular when performed by the original London company, although casts were regularly changed when they went on tour and often criticised as 'second rate'. The greatest honour a production could receive was the accompanying note 'as performed before Her/His Majesty Queen Mary/the King'. During the 1930s a visit by Queen Mary was 'regarded as the augury of a long run for a play'.[6] Irrespective of the actual originality of the play, this note had an immediate effect on box office receipts. Regional theatre managers felt compelled to follow the London lead. They tended to rely on mediocre but successful plays rather than on brilliant but unknown pieces.[7] By contrast, on German regional stages a 'Berlin success' certainly aroused interest, but a hit from Munich or Hamburg could do equally well. Although Berlin was the undisputed theatre capital, plays which had been successful there were often regarded as experimental or, even worse, 'socialist'. The effect, therefore, was often counter-productive in conservative provincial towns. Regarding the novelty of a play, too, German regional repertories seemed to differ from Britain as they always consisted of a large proportion of classical pieces. Goethe, Schiller and Shakespeare were regarded as essential parts of the theatre programmes, perhaps even the pillars of a respectable repertoire. In this respect their age was not regarded as a hindrance but as an asset. What became important were questions of interpretation and translation.[8] By contrast, in Britain the production of Elizabethan drama was not only far less frequent, but it was also regarded as a somewhat exotic experience. A production did not have to prove that the play was still relevant – an important quality at German theatres – it was explicitly consumed as a 'dated' piece. The fact that audiences did not expect to read productions as offering some sort of universal truth, deeper meaning or otherwise critical approach is also illustrated by the fact that they largely despised modern interpretations and preferred period productions in magnificent costumes instead.[9] In fact, the attitude towards the theatrical past was not only critical of modern interpretations, it bordered on outright rejection. During the 1920s and early 1930s Shakespeare was 'considered a guarantee of empty houses'.[10] Commentators even claimed that 'to sell intelligent drama to the British public is a work for a superman'.[11] It seems logical to expect, therefore, that apart from some obviously rather rare encounters with 'high culture' Yorkshire's audiences were presented with what German patrons would have branded 'cheap entertainment'.

FEATURES OF YORKSHIRE'S REPERTOIRES DURING THE 1920S AND 1930S

A first look at the Yorkshire repertoires seems to support such an interpretation. Apart from some productions of classical plays, touring opera and contemporary drama, managers mainly relied on comedies, thrillers and farces.[12] We have to note, however, that even prestigious touring companies rarely changed their repertoire on their annual visits and more or less presented the same fare every year.[13] It seems fair to assume, therefore, that they hardly ever tried out new interpretations either. Apart from that we have to bear in mind that during those weeks of classical or operatic repertoire, no piece was performed more than twice and hardly ever for a whole week. But even this basic provision – in comparison to Westphalia – did not last at many places. In York, for example, patrons were not treated to classical drama or opera any more after 1927. The chief reason for this development was to keep costs down, as the prestigious touring companies often demanded guaranteed salaries irrespective of the theatre's takings. This could be risky if takings were dire, which was often the case with productions considered too 'high-brow'.[14] Instead, regional theatres increasingly relied on lesser-known companies which played for several weeks in repertory. These seasons proved very popular – and cheap.

A typical season

The 1931 season at York's Theatre Royal illustrates some of these points. There were no longer any visits by Shakespearean or opera companies, but instead a four-month season of repertory presented by the Percy Hutchison Players. The only opera produced was Gilbert and Sullivan's *The Mikado*, although the production by the York Amateur Operatic and Dramatic Society seems to have been rather mediocre.[15] Other visiting attractions included a dance performance by the Russian dancer Lydia Kyasht and a recital by Jan Kubelik, the famous Czech violinist. As 'special attractions' Hutchison presented several plays 'prior to production in London' and appeared in his signature comedy *Brewster's Millions* by Winchell Smith and Byron Ongley. Apart from four contemporary dramas, which dealt with more or less serious topics such as education, prostitution or medical issues, the bill was dominated by contemporary comedies, which reached a share in the programme of over 86 per cent.[16] In a repertoire mirrored at regional theatres all over Britain, York presented comedies and melodramas by A.A. Milne, Charles Cochran, Noel Coward and Frederick Lonsdale, mystery plays and thrillers by Arnold Ridley, Dion Titheradge and Owen Davies, farces by Avery Hopwood and Fred Duprez, musical comedies such as *Nippy*, *Mr Cinders* and *Lilac Time*, and, of course, a pantomime at Christmas.[17]

Foreign repertoire

Yorkshire's theatre programmes indicate that claims by some commentators that British theatre remained largely uninterested in foreign plays needs to be readjusted.[18] A closer look at the repertoires not only reveals that foreign plays did indeed find their way on to regional stages, it also shows that repertoires underwent remarkable changes. In the course of the 1920s interest in French drama declined and gave rise to an increasing focus on American plays.[19] Only a few years earlier French plays or adaptations of French plays and novels were hugely popular – especially in connection with the First World War.[20] The first American plays reached Yorkshire just after the war (many theatres staged Hopwood's *Fair and Warmer* in 1919), but the new trend really took off with performances in the mid-1920s of Lula Vollmer's *Sun-Up*, Avery Hopwood's *The Best People*, comedies such as *Broadway Jones*, *Broadway* or *A Yankee at the Court of King Arthur*, and especially the popular musicals by Oscar Hammerstein and Otto Harbach.[21] Additionally, pieces by British dramatists started to be set in the States, especially in New York, and dealt with 'modern topics' such as the 'Flapper'. The growing influence of American playwriting – and, indeed, American culture – became a reason for concern.[22] Yorkshire's press regularly claimed that the American plays were inferior in quality, superficial and vulgar.[23] Yet this American influence became even stronger during the Second World War, which saw many American and Canadian soldiers stationed on different air bases around Yorkshire.[24]

For obvious reasons, interest in German drama was virtually non-existent after the First World War, all the more so since anti-German propaganda plays had played such an important role on British stages.[25] The overall share of such fare in the repertoire of York's Theatre Royal, for example, reached 18 per cent in 1917 and 15 per cent in 1918. A search for Goethe and Schiller, Kaiser and Sternheim, Hauptmann and Brecht is to no avail.[26] A more detailed look at Yorkshire's programmes, however, reveals that the German contribution was far from insignificant. It also shows that the focus needs to be adjusted. We are mistaken if we expect to find typical examples of Germany's established theatrical canon on Yorkshire's stages. Parallel to a general trend towards contemporary comedies, thrillers and musical plays, interest in German tragedies, serious drama and political plays was low. Schiller and Brecht were, therefore, not matters of vital interest.[27] This phenomenon corresponds to the general perception of theatre and its purpose, which seems to have been fundamentally different in Britain and Germany. As mentioned earlier, Schiller's concept of theatre as a moral institution was widely accepted in Germany and the notion of the educational value of theatre never really questioned. In Britain, by contrast, theatre was supposed to be entertaining, funny and diverting, and many patrons avoided serious drama and 'high-brow' plays. For the German repertoire this means that Yorkshire's audiences would not have been interested in 'high culture' of the Goethe variety but in German comedies. And, these they increasingly received from the mid-1920s onwards. Yorkshire's theatres presented plays by Hermann Sudermann (*Magda*) and Siegfried Geyer (*By Candle Light*), operettas by Franz Lehár (*The Merry Widow*), Leo Fall (*Madame Pompadour*) and Rudolph Schanzer (*The Lady of the Rose*), musical comedies by Rudolf Friml (*Katinka*), Hugo Hirsch (*Toni*), Jean Gilbert (*Katja, the Dancer*), Oscar Straus (*The Last Waltz* and *My Son John*), and Sigmund Romberg (*The Desert Song*), as well as all-time favourites such as *The Student Prince*,

Romberg's musical based on Wilhelm Meyer-Förster's play, and *Lilac Time*, the musical play about Schubert's life.[28] The importance of adaptations to suit British tastes is illustrated by Oscar Straus' musical comedy *The Chocolate Soldier*, which was written by Leopold Jacobson and Rudolf Bernauer and presented in an English version by Stanislaus Stange, and Austin Melford's adaptation of Franz Arnold and Ernst Bach's comedy *It's a Boy* called *Oh! Daddy*. Plays were set in German speaking countries, musical comedies made use of music by German-composers, and the musical programme performed in the intervals often featured Mendelssohn, Wagner and Schubert. It was not only German drama and music, however, which met with increasing interest, but also the country's theatre system as a whole became the subject of admiration.[29] It is interesting to note that this trend was mirrored in the cinema, too. The film *All Quiet on the Western Front*, which was based on Erich Maria Remarque's anti-war novel, appeared in 1931,[30] and two years later Yorkshire's cinemas screened Leontine Sagan's *Mädchen in Uniform* entirely in German with only brief English captions.

It might seem surprising that even after 1933 the interest in drama and music from German-speaking countries continuously increased despite the Nazi terror and an increasing number of refugees in Britain. Plays were set in Heidelberg and Berlin, Innsbruck and Vienna, in Bavaria and in the Alps, and even in areas such as stage design Germany functioned as a role model. Commentators praised Don Marquis' *The Dark Hours*, for example, because it used 'a Germanic form of stagecraft ... with a special platform projecting into the auditorium'.[31] Dodie Smith's *Autumn Crocus* was equally applauded for its use of German as a stage language, which was a 'pleasant change from stage French, even if one does not understand it'.[32] As late as 1940, eight per cent of all the productions in York were German pieces, German adaptations, or plays set in Germany. The *Theatre World*'s Eric Johns praised the working conditions at German theatres and claimed that 'the English actor would be only too pleased to change places with his German fellow-artist, who has a much easier and happier existence'.[33] York actress Elizabeth Scott, therefore, seemed to echo a widespread sentiment when stating that the 'sense of a unified nation and the obvious hero-worship of Hitler, particularly on the part of young people of about her own age, [made her] so strongly pro-Nazi'.[34] Outside the theatre leading politicians expressed a similar admiration for Nazi Germany. After a visit to the country Lloyd George admitted that 'Hitler is one of the greatest of the many great men I have ever met'.[35] The British ambassador in Berlin, Neville Henderson, demanded that the British public 'paid more attention to the great social experiment which was being tried out in Germany' as there were 'many things in the Nazi organisation and social institutions ... which we might study and adapt to our own use with great profit'.[36] The Foreign Secretary Lord Halifax liked Goebbels and enjoyed Göring's 'picturesque and arresting figure',[37] and even the Labour MP Stafford Cripps declared that although defeat by Germany would be a disaster for capitalists it would be no 'bad thing for the British working classes'.[38]

COMPARATIVE ASPECTS

The general look of Yorkshire's repertoires became increasingly different from the Westphalian fare from the early 1930s. Contemporary comedies reigned supreme with an average share in the programmes of around 80 per cent. Classical drama and modern classics had all but disappeared from the bill and in some places even touring opera companies ceased their visits. Additionally, the financial situation of many theatres became increasingly difficult, in view of the competition from the highly popular cinema.[39] An indication of the problems is the decrease of the overall number of theatre productions, which at York sank from over seventy in the mid-1920s to below forty in 1933.[40] It is interesting to note that even with theatres, which more closely resembled central European municipal playhouses, such as the repertory theatres in Sheffield, Hull and York, the differences only increased during the 1930s. Although York's non-profit-making Citizens' Theatre in some way mirrored the perception of municipal theatres in Germany, it clearly differed in its repertoire. During the 1937 season, for example, forty-seven out of forty-eight productions were contemporary comedies including musical comedies, thrillers and farces. And in 1938, apart from two exceptions, none of the works produced in York were ever staged at any theatre in Westphalia.[41] At the end of the 1930s contemporary comedies reached a share of over 90 per cent in the repertoire with the comedy-thriller the 'most popular category of all'.[42]

There are, however, also some points of contact. A growing pride in regional and local identity found increasing representation in repertoires.[43] Plays set in the region and/or comedies in the vernacular were successful in both countries. Priestley's Yorkshire comedies, for example, enjoyed a similar popularity to the Westphalian dialect plays which the 'Low German Stage' performed in Münster.

PROGRAMME NOTES

It was not only with regard to their repertoires, however, that Yorkshire's theatres increasingly differed from Westphalia's; a brief look at the everyday running of the playhouses illustrates other differences also. It has already been mentioned that British regional theatres – much more than their German counterparts – were forced to position themselves in the highly competitive 'entertainment market' and define their particular niche. One way of establishing this niche and projecting a certain image was through the programme notes, which, therefore, had a quality that went beyond their function in Germany.[44] They developed into well-presented booklets profiting from an improved printing quality and better paper, increasingly artistic layouts and photos, bigger formats and an extended number of pages. The receiving theatres in Bradford, Sheffield and Leeds aimed to extend the plush and gilt of their exclusive 'dream palaces' to the pages of their programme notes. And the notes of the repertory theatres, too, became increasingly upmarket in order to correspond to exclusive claims and to distinguish themselves from other venues.[45] In line with this agenda their programme notes featured articles on local and regional theatre history, informed about recent debates and gossip within the industry, and included special features introducing new plays and actors. At the end of the 1930s the programme notes of Yorkshire's repertory theatres offered more information, became less provincial without concentrating on London attractions, and increasingly covered developments at other regional theatres in Britain, on the continent, in America and even the Soviet Union.

REPERTORY SYSTEM

The British repertory system fundamentally differed from 'continental' repertory as each production was only given for one week. This resulted in a strict routine. Normally, shows received 12 performances (there were twice-nightly performances from Monday to Saturday at most playhouses), each performance lasted on average two hours, and 'there are approximately four hours daily for four days a week spent in rehearsal of the next week's production, while the dress rehearsal on a Monday takes nearly all day'.[46] That was also the reason why Monday audiences were usually smaller than later in the week as this first performance of a new play regularly lacked quality.[47] This would not have been a problem had ensembles been bigger than the ten to fifteen actors they normally consisted of. There were sometimes extra artists engaged on a temporary basis, the small casts meant that actors had to appear on stage almost constantly and time for rehearsals was short. The salary in 'rep' was not bad,[48] but holidays were rare, which meant an additional strain, given the fact that a year normally featured forty-eight weeks of productions.[49]

Detailed statistical information regarding attendance figures is only rarely available. In York attendances of 10,000 people a week were considered a great success.[50] Taking into account the normal run of 12 performances, this means that an average of 833 people visited the theatre in a good week, which is a utilisation of 62 per cent.[51] However, it is difficult to project these figures on the whole season as attendances clearly differed. The figure of 1.5 million patrons, who had allegedly visited the theatre between September 1935 and the end of December 1938, simply arose out of a multiplication of the above figure of 10,000 visits per week.[52] Still, attendances were so good that claims that 'the more popular productions are so well attended that it looks as if they could run for longer than a week'[53] seemed well founded. This, in fact, would have been a huge relief, not only for the stressed actors but also in financial terms.

CHANGES AFTER 1939

Music

It seems as if the musical repertoire in particular highlighted the fundamental differences between Yorkshire and Westphalia. In both the use of music in the theatre and the sheer scale of resources – in other words regarding quality as well as quantity – British and German regional playhouses seemed to play in different leagues, and increasingly so with the foundation of fully subsidised municipal orchestras in Germany after 1918. Corresponding to a different attitude towards the arts, Yorkshire's 'theatre orchestras' performed light as well as classical music as an integral part of every performance, both before the show and during the interval. Limited financial resources, however, meant that these 'orchestras' rarely featured more than six to eight musicians. By comparison, Münster's municipal orchestra employed forty-eight full-time musicians and played its own concert series alongside opera and operetta in the theatre. To make matters worse, the economic problems of the early 1930s resulted in the unpopular move to scrap the orchestra altogether in favour of a gramophone at many places.[54] For Yorkshire's cities to have their own fully funded municipal orchestras and opera companies was beyond anyone's wildest dreams. The fact that Wagner's complete 'Ring' cycle was produced in Münster as early as 1913 would certainly have raised more than a few eyebrows in Yorkshire.

Before the war opera had only featured as a rare and rather expensive entertainment for a well-to-do minority mainly based in London. Operas given at Covent Garden were sung in their original language, with foreign singers engaged for the occasion from abroad. Opera had no permanent home, no subsidies, no continuity of tradition.[55] In fact many regarded it as a rather un-British exercise. Training for opera singers was virtually non-existent and, therefore, their acting 'distressingly bad'.[56] It is certainly no coincidence, therefore, that before the war, Sadler's Wells failed to achieve a standard anywhere near the one maintained in the opera houses of other great capitals, or even in the smaller municipal theatres on the continent.[57] Against this background it is astonishing how quickly things changed after 1939. Within a few years Sadler's Wells opera company had established itself as the country's leading ensemble, opera was as popular as ever and played to packed houses and most of the standard operas had been translated and were now available in 'good, lively English which is both actable and singable'.[58] Most of the members of the Sadler's Wells opera company, too, were British now and formed a permanent troupe.[59] Suddenly, there were even plans by CEMA to reclaim the Royal Opera House, Covent Garden, as the national centre for opera and ballet.[60]

Yorkshire's audiences immediately profited from this development and celebrated the return of opera enthusiastically – a surprising reaction given audiences' previous reservations.[61] When Thomas

Figure 3.1 Theatre Royal York, visit by Sadler's Wells opera company, *Yorkshire Evening Press*, 21 December 1943

Beecham conducted an opera by Bradford-born composer Frederick Delius in 1935, for example, the Alhambra remained half empty, which prompted Beecham to remark that if he ever came to Bradford again 'I shall require some very serious evidence in advance that the public will support the operas'.[62] After having been absent from many stages for years opera returned to the provinces in 1942 with companies backed by CEMA – Sadler's Wells gave its debut at many places.[63]

Audiences especially welcomed the English translations,[64] and Sadler's Wells' production of *The Marriage of Figaro* in 1943, for example, featured a new libretto by E. J. Dent. The case of Mozart is especially interesting because as much as the Nazis tried to present Mozart as a German composer, British and American commentators laid stress on the fact that he should not be seen as such.[65] Mozart was not the only composer, however, whose works were used for propaganda purposes. With Gilbert and Sullivan's 'Japanese' opera *The Mikado* commentators were quick to praise English audiences for their ability to appreciate a comic opera set in an enemy country.[66] The same could be claimed for the continuing popularity of the music by German and Austrian composers, which remained at the heart of the musical repertoire. The most popular pieces of the lunchtime concerts in London's National Gallery, for example, were works by Beethoven, Bach and Mozart.[67]

Apart from the introduction of subsidies, the classical music scene in Britain also profited considerably from the influx of high-profile émigré composers and musicians from Nazi occupied Europe.[68] And, again, the provinces enjoyed their fair share of this development. In July 1944 the German-born musician Paul Steinitz conducted Beethoven's fifth symphony and Brahms' *German Requiem* in front of a large audience at York's Theatre Royal.[69] But the most striking example is probably the above-mentioned performance of Mozart's *The Marriage of Figaro*, which was presented in a new production by Kurt Jooss.

Ballet

Probably the biggest difference between pre-war and post-war repertoires is linked to Jooss, too: dance and ballet. Whereas Yorkshire audiences had been treated to the odd week of dance during the 1920s – mostly presented by the Russian dancer Lydia Kyasht – provincial audiences now experienced serious ballet performed on a regular basis.[70] Sadler's Wells Ballet Company, which was soon regarded as Britain's national ballet company, performed its London programme with its London company (including their stars Margot Fonteyn and Robert Helpmann) and took Yorkshire by storm.[71] It is hardly imaginable that 'arty' and elitist ballet would have found an audience before the war – now it played to capacity houses. Having completely bypassed the city before, ballet now came to Hull at least twice annually. At York ballet even appeared in repertoire for two weeks after Christmas 1944. This prestigious slot especially shows how much had changed. The shift in attitude of both audiences and managements also illustrates a change of perception: theatre developed from a place of amusement into a cultural institution.[72] This attitude and the fact that until the end of the war most Yorkshire theatres provided substantial slots for both opera and ballet is an interesting parallel to Westphalian theatres.

Classical drama

The revival of 'high culture' was by no means limited to opera and ballet. Classical drama and modern classics received a similar upsurge after they had been virtually neglected during the preceding decades. Between the wars the only production of serious continental drama in the West End was Ibsen's *A Doll's House* at the Playhouse.[73] One of the greatest stars of his time, Gerald du Maurier, answered the question on why he would not play Richard III with the remark that 'my audience would find my appearance in such a play embarrassing'.[74] The 'gentlemen actors' of the 1920s were not expected to 'inflict' anything intellectual on their loyal followers.[75] Although the situation changed slightly from the mid-1930s and especially Shakespeare received increased attention, this trend was largely limited to Lilian Baylis' Old Vic and theatres on the fringe. We also have to note that, despite this renewed interest, the way theatre was organised did not change, as productions still had to make a profit and rehearsal time was exceedingly short.[76] When John Gielgud wanted to establish his own company entirely devoted to a classical repertoire, this was seen as revolutionary and unrealistic. The general feeling in the 1930s was that 'this kind of highbrow thing was best left to occasional London visits by the *Comédie Française*'.[77] The Shakespeare Memorial Theatre struggled, too. After it had burned down it took six years to rebuild it, and despite a grand reopening in 1932 the theatre incurred losses.[78] Yorkshire's theatres reflected this trend perfectly. Shakespeare only 'made but infrequent appearances on the York stage',[79] and in 1934 Cecil Chisholm summed up the general mood in the provinces when stating that 'Shakespeare is always a difficulty'.[80]

The general attitude towards the classics changed radically after the outbreak of the Second World War. Suddenly it was felt that they could mark a return to Britain's great theatrical past, make people aware of their national heritage and, therefore, play an important role in the war effort. In contrast to the First World War, which, as many claimed, had been characterised by cheap entertainment and pointless farces, commentators were relieved to see dramatic standards at the highest possible level now.[81] In 1940 in London Donald Wolfit presented a series of highly popular lunchtime performances of Shakespeare, and the Old Vic company played *King Lear* and *The Tempest* to capacity houses.[82] Suddenly, even rarely performed Restoration plays received glittering revivals. The 1943 Festival of English Comedy proved to be one of the highlights of the season, and William Congreve's *Love for Love* was one of the biggest overall successes of wartime theatre.[83] Plays which had been regarded as dated and out of step with contemporary taste returned to the stages in numbers now.

Again, Yorkshire's theatres reflected the national trend towards educational and 'uplifting' repertoires. At York, no Shakespearean play had been performed after 1930, and the resident repertory company had not produced any classical drama since its inception. Similarly, Sheffield's Repertory Company tackled one single Shakespearean drama in the first eleven years of its existence and so did Hull. In a scenario mirrored at regional theatres in general the 'great national poet' returned in 1941 and from then on appeared at least once a year. Hull and Bradford welcomed Wolfit's Shakespearean tours,[84] and Leeds experienced additional visits by John Gielgud and his company. York's company produced *Romeo and Juliet* in November 1942 and *The Taming of the Shrew* less than half a year later, and the reaction was enthusiastic.[85] The increasing importance attributed to Shakespeare became even more obvious in the following two productions. In December 1943 York's repertory company produced *Hamlet* in a two-weeks' special, which 'held spellbound the large audiences'.[86] The press covered the event with several articles including a preview – an interest never encountered before.[87] The first-night audience included the civic heads, the archbishop, and the General Officer Commanding-in-Chief, Northern Command, and was presented to 1,300 schoolchildren in a special matinee, which underlined the new educational mission of theatre. The company even received 'civic thanks' and were entertained by the Lord Mayor and the Sheriff – an honour hardly imaginable before the war. It is interesting to note that at this point the new function of the theatre as a quasi-municipal playhouse coincided with its morale-boosting purpose in the war. *Othello*, performed for 'the closing fortnight of our very successful 1944 season', became another 'outstanding success'.[88] This fortnight's run stands in contrast to the Shakespearean repertories of the 1920s when during one week Frank Benson or Charles Doran produced six or seven different plays to guarantee diversion.[89] The fact that the Theatre Royal produced one Shakespearean tragedy for two weeks at a time normally reserved for money-spinning pantomime shows the enormous importance now attached to classical drama.[90]

In short, Yorkshire's theatres put into practice what the *Manchester Guardian* had demanded as early as 1940, namely that 'no better National Service can be given at the present time, than to present Shakespearean Repertory'.[91]

Contemporary comedies

National morale was not only fostered through classical drama but also via comedies, farces and revues, whose enormous success made them a perfect vehicle. Their seemingly non-political and escapist character acquired a distinct political quality in wartimes. Comedies proved useful to make people forget not only about the hardships of war, but also about continuing social inequalities. In doing so they boosted morale, which was of central concern, for in war 'the thing that counts is national morale'.[92] Yorkshire's theatres, therefore, not only continued to stage 'harmless' comedies but also presented entertaining patriotic shows, many of them in support of one of the various war funds. As part of the 'York Warship Week', for example, the repertory company produced Arthur Jagger's 'burlesque' *Arms and the Maid*, and the evening ended with a 'tableau' entitled *Rule Britannia*.

Typical comedies of the war years include Lynne Dexter's *Other People's Houses*, which is set in the country home of a war widow,[93] du Garde Peach's *You Never Know*,[94] and the famous variety show *The Hulbert Follies*, 'a slick, non-stop show, a pot pourri of fun, dancing, music and song'. This show, however, also contained a serious piece entitled *How Britain Fights* by Eric Maschwitz, a 'dramatic interlude depicting incidents in the lives of unsung heroes of the *blitzes*' including a bus driver, a typist and a roof spotter.[95] This piece indicates

Figure 3.2 'Entertainments' in York, *Yorkshire Evening Press*, 8 November 1943

the importance of plays which dealt with the war in more realistic terms or dramatised wider issues.

Contemporary (non-commercial) drama

Research so far has failed to recognise that changes in wartime repertoires were much more profound than previously thought. They did not only affect the attitudes towards certain genres, but the whole perception of theatre. This phenomenon marked a fundamental difference from the theatre programmes of the First World War and becomes especially obvious in the rise of contemporary non-commercial drama. Playwrights addressed not only issues corresponding to the war itself, an increasing number of them also raised questions about the future thereafter. Topics like the uncertainty of this future, the need for social reforms and the question of what this war was being fought for, came on to the agenda.

In terms of propaganda, theatres quickly reflected changes in public opinion. They ceased to produce plays *from* Germany and instead started to stage plays *about* Germany and the Germans. As mentioned above, however, even the 1940 season still featured plays with a positive image of Germany, exemplified by the romance *Autumn Crocus* with its German dialogue.[96] After that there was a clear break and from 1941 such fare was no longer staged. It was, however, neither the Nazi ideology nor Hitler's war in Europe which radically changed both public opinion and theatre programmes – it was the immediate fear of being invaded after the fall of France. The production of propagandistic anti-German plays did not commence in 1939 but in 1941.[97] Then, however, spy comedies, war drama and variety shows, plays about Nazi agents entering Britain, French resistance against the Germans and the expected invasion arrived on Yorkshire's stage in numbers.[98] Geoffrey Kerr's *Cottage to Let*, for example, was hailed as 'the first spy drama of the present war'[99] and coincided with propaganda initiatives by the Ministry of Information.[100] Other examples of this genre include Mary Hayley Bell's drama *Men in Shadow* about the plotting of anti-Nazi saboteurs headed by a British pilot in France, Edward Wooll's court drama *Libel* about a baronet supposedly killed after an escape from a German prison camp, Joan Brampton's *The Portrait*, which deals with a Polish refugee who flees to England to escape the Nazis, Henry Marshall's 'stirring melodrama of the Armada' *Drake's Drum*,[101] John Steinbeck's *The Moon Is Down*, presenting a 'microcosm of the resistance movement in Europe, revealed through the medium of a small mining town in Norway',[102] Chetham Strode's smugglers' play *Strangers' Road* about 'a period of English history similar in many ways to our own [with] Buonaparte across the Channel awaiting an opportunity to invade this country',[103] and Lionel Brown's *This Land of Ours* about life on a Shropshire farm during the war. One of the most successful war plays, Lilian Hellman's *Watch on the Rhine*, developed the topic of spies and fifth columnists even further.[104]

At the same time, plays like J.B. Priestley's *Desert Highway* addressed uncertainties about positive war aims and thereby reflected a general mood in the British public, who expected substantial social reforms after the end of the war. The play is also a perfect illustration of how close theatre and government had become. It was specially written for and about the army, it was jointly produced by CEMA and ABCA and was presented by a cast entirely drawn from the army in July 1944.[105] Similar plays include Robert Sherwood's *The Queen's Husband*, which deals with the question of dictatorship[106] and Cary and Thompson's visionary drama *Burning Gold*, which 'radiates the vision with which young Britons went to war in 1939'[107] and whose main theme is 'the striving of the younger generation for a plan which will make "England's green and pleasant land" something more than a phrase'.[108] A number of similar plays contributed to a significant rise of this genre, which at York reached a 20 per cent share in the 1945 season.[109] Corresponding to this idea of a 'fresh start' Leeds' Grand organised a week-long victory festival called 'Youth Marches On' in June 1945.[110]

This rise also hints at one of the lasting effects of the war. Although the establishment of the theatre world intended to return to business as usual in 1945 – and effectively did so for the following years – the success of Osborne's *Look Back in Anger* and the 'Kitchen Sink' drama of the late 1950s is hardly imaginable without this drama of social relevance at the end of the war. In reflecting wishes and hopes for the future repertoires became platforms for the discussion of social problems. And again we find a direct link to political developments. The landslide victory of the Labour Party in 1945 clearly corresponded to the working classes' call for a greater share in England's 'green and pleasant land'.

Comparative aspects

In view of the comparative perspective of this study it is interesting to note that the outlook of Yorkshire's repertoire towards the end of the war became increasingly similar to the one at Westphalian playhouses. The high share of contemporary comedies declined to about 40 per cent, the share of classical opera and ballet rose, the classics received elaborate two-week productions and contemporary plays dramatised social questions. This repertoire exemplified a new function of regional theatre similar to German municipal playhouses. This is, in fact, a finding which runs counter to research so far, but can be clearly substantiated through a close study of the repertoire.

One could argue, however, that such changes in theatre programmes are nothing unusual and that the representation of war or a stronger link between politics and theatre becomes apparent in every military conflict. And, indeed, a look at past repertoires shows that this link has had a long tradition. During the Napoleonic Wars, for example, Yorkshire's theatres featured patriotic plays, songs and addresses, 'military hornpipes', and the pantomime *Harlequin's Invasion* with a 'Representation of a Sea Fight between the French and the English'.[111] During the Boer War we find a similar picture with plays such as *Death or Glory Boys*, *The Victoria Cross*, *Bootle's Baby – A Story of the Scarlet Lancers* and *Soldiers of the Queen*. The immediate impact of the First World War on the programmes has already been mentioned – more than ever before was the theatre eager to contribute to the national cause. Against the background of this obvious total commitment, many commentators have claimed that repertoires during the Second World War were notably free of propaganda and war plays.[112] Although, however, this fare did not feature as prominently as during the First World War, its share was still considerable.[113]

What constituted the new quality of the Second World War, however, was the sudden and increasing involvement of the government in matters theatrical. This new policy had an immediate impact on regional stages. Suddenly, audiences enjoyed performances with West End stars and, of course, the Old Vic and Sadler's Wells companies on their regular tours.[114] More importantly, the repertoire at those theatres which produced their own shows in particular (Sheffield, York, Hull, partly Bradford's Prince's Theatre) not only became increasingly nationalistic but also – corresponding to the changed attitude of the government – more educational, with a strong emphasis laid on Britain's dramatic heritage. Elizabethan drama and Restoration comedies, revivals of Sheridan, Jonson and Vanbrugh, and modern classics by Pinero, Wilde and Shaw were performed alongside old favourites such as *1066 And All That*. Suddenly, Yorkshire's playhouses even presented the same modern European classics which would have guaranteed an empty house in the 1930s.[115] The productions of plays by Ibsen and Pirandello clearly have to be seen as part of this new educational concept. And it is interesting to note that this new concept worked perfectly. Ibsen's *Hedda Gabler*, which received its first production in York in April 1944, for example, was the best-seller of that season.

Wartime repertoires also illustrate how quickly theatres reacted to changes in the general political climate, highlighted in particular by the sudden interest in Soviet drama. After Germany had attacked Russia in June 1941 a wave of public support ran through Britain and plays such as Valentin Katayev's *Squaring the Circle*, Afinogenev's *Distant Point* and the musical *Sorotchinski Fair* were produced in the West End.[116] Two years later the Old Vic produced Konstantin Simonov's *The Russians* and contemporary Soviet drama reached Yorkshire stages.[117] At this point the comparative aspect of this study becomes particularly interesting as German regional theatres showed a similar sensitivity to political developments. For a brief period between autumn 1939 and spring 1941 Russian plays received a revival due to the Hitler–Stalin pact. This example also illustrates, however, one of the fundamental differences between the two countries. Whereas Nazi propaganda continuously reminded the public in general and theatre managers in particular of their national duty, the British government did nothing of the sort. Although the political atmosphere towards theatre had changed markedly, there are no examples of direct intervention regarding particular programmes at individual theatres, and even official statements regarding repertoire questions appeared only rarely.[118]

Theatre and state

This does not mean, however, that the government was not aware of the possible dangers of an excessively critical programme. On the contrary, the British government passed far-reaching legislation which meant that, for the first time, theatre repertoires could not only be affected by the Lord Chamberlain's decisions or by the police in case of safety problems, but also from March 1942 the Home Secretary had the right to interfere directly if a certain play was deemed detrimental to the war effort – a fact which, crucially, has been overlooked by research so far.

Censorship

Theatrical censorship in Britain had a long tradition. The Lord Chamberlain, directly appointed by the monarch, carried out his duty as a member of the Royal Household. He was not accountable to the government or Parliament and was, in fact, 'outside the law'.[119] It is important to note in this context, however, that the Lord Chamberlain did not pursue any active theatre politics. Also, the outbreak of the war did not affect the fundamental principles on which censorship was based. The five reasons for which a play could be banned remained the same: on religious grounds, for depiction of the Royal Family, for dealing with 'recent events', for political and diplomatic reasons, and for causing 'moral turpitude'.[120] There was also an invisible censorship at work as many playwrights learnt to live with the censor's decisions and tried to avoid writing plays which were likely to be banned.[121] Although a public outcry could sometimes change the censor's mind, in other cases the objections were so acute that even the play's international status could not save it.[122]

Regarding anti-Nazi plays, the Foreign Office tried to enforce a strict ban, which the Lord Chamberlain was happy to apply, claiming it corresponded to one of the central ideas of British theatrical censorship: the protection of foreign heads of state. Although neither the Foreign Secretary nor the Lord Chamberlain could be accused of being pro-Nazi, Goebbels was certainly pleased with the way British censorship worked. When Shaw, for example, asked to apply some changes to his satire *Geneva*, notably to rename 'Battler' into 'Hitler' and let him appear in Nazi uniform, the censor refused permission.[123] German officials applauded the decision because it meant that Battler would not be played 'in the mask of the Führer'.[124] They noted with satisfaction that the Lord Chamberlain was careful not to offend German sensibilities in any way – even after the war had started. The censor, however, went even further. He not only regularly consulted the German embassy before awarding a licence but also acted according to their wishes regarding adapting or banning a play.[125] Even small comic turns in obscure revues produced in the provinces were noted by the Germans and complained about – and the Foreign Office duly sprang into action.[126]

Subsidies, intervention and control

Where the Lord Chamberlain carried out his duty during the war mainly as he had done before, the government became increasingly interested in exerting an influence over the theatre. In summer 1940, for example, the government 'feared' a quiet war winter 1940–1. To counteract the expected loss of morale, entertainment for the forces and the civilian population became top of the agenda. At the same time, officials like Kenneth Clark, stressed the fact that they did not just want any kind of entertainment 'of the film or music hall order, but something to occupy people's minds'. He explicitly demanded that the government ought 'to take some active part in stimulating activities of this sort'.[127] This active part soon began to take shape in the question of the Sunday opening of theatres, which found increasing support not only in the theatre world but also among the general public.[128] Suddenly, in February 1941, the government agreed to allow performances on Sundays for the first time in 300 years and the theatre world subsequently celebrated having 'won the battle'.[129] Although the initiative was defeated in Parliament by a small majority of eight votes, the government had nevertheless proved how much it was willing to sacrifice for theatrical entertainment during the war – the resistance of the church had been especially substantial – and how highly it rated its contribution to the war effort.[130]

Soon, however, Home Secretary Herbert Morrison wanted to take government involvement in the arts to another level and, in effect, carry out active cultural politics (or *Kulturpolitik*) for the first time. In a memorandum on public entertainments in wartime, put before the War Cabinet on 27 February 1942, Morrison asked 'the War Cabinet [to] consider the present position and make a decision on general policy'.[131] Morrison complained that his powers regarding entertainments were restricted to security and safety questions. He claimed that the Home Secretary should have additional powers to prohibit performances if they were detrimental to the war effort. Under point 16 Morrison asserted that it

> therefore appears necessary that the Government should be empowered to prohibit or restrict entertainments on the ground that they are inimical to the war effort, irrespective of the degree of risk to those present, and that the Defence

Regulations should be amended to give control of entertainments in circumstances where the efficient prosecution of the war is in issue.

The cabinet discussed Morrison's far-reaching memorandum in early March 1942, agreed, and only two weeks later the King signed the relevant amendment of the defence regulations.[132] In effect, Morrison had at least in principle gained total power over the performing arts.[133] Although it seems doubtful whether Morrison ever used his new powers of direct control, the importance of the fact that in theory he would have been able to do so, can hardly be overestimated.[134]

'Our great National Poet'

The one genre which corresponded perfectly to governmental concepts of entertainment and morale was classical drama and especially Shakespeare, now hailed as 'our great national poet'.[135] Shakespeare's plays received an increasing number of productions and scored record audiences. After decades of neglect, Shakespearean drama suddenly attracted the country's greatest actors and producers. In August 1942 alone three new Shakespeare productions started their runs in London, with Gielgud's *Macbeth*, the Old Vic's *Othello* and Robert Atkins' open-air productions in Regent's Park.[136] And in 1944 the Old Vic at the New Theatre as well as Gielgud at the Haymarket established their classical repertory. These ventures more than anything else appeared to contemporaries as the dramatic highlight of the war, the quintessence of what Britain was fighting for.[137]

This sudden revival was no coincidence but was closely linked to the war. Although the use of Shakespeare for political purposes was not new, the scale and quality of his revival is unparalleled in British history.[138] The 1916 tercentenary of Shakespeare's death, for example, failed to attract enough support to found the National Theatre, for which an influential pressure group had been fighting for decades. In the early 1940s, however, their idea not only returned to the political agenda, it quickly became reality, with a prestigious site for the project and generous funding. Contemporary commentators clearly saw the connection between this interest and the increased importance of Shakespeare during the war.[139] Shakespeare was used to establish a

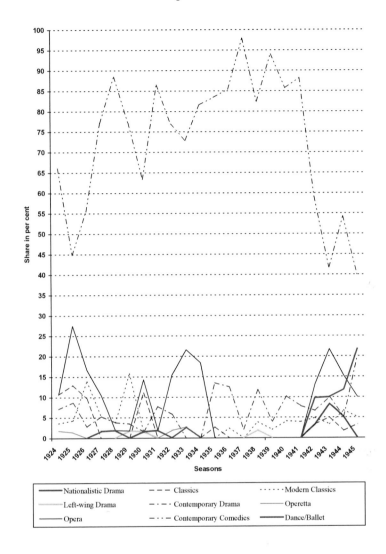

Figure 3.3 Share of genres in productions at York Theatre Royal

link to Elizabethan times with a clear view of constructing a parallel between Hitler's threat of invasion and the defeat of the Armada.[140] Another similar parallel concerned the Napoleonic Wars and led to headlines such as 'Appreciation of Shakespeare Unparalleled Since Waterloo'.[141] It was made clear that to produce Shakespeare at this particular time was a service to the nation as, although Britain faced invasion in summer 1940, her 'spirit is undimmed and her speech …

is still the speech of Shakespeare'.[142] Especially remarkable is the way in which the government used Shakespeare to portray a positive image of wartime Britain to the world outside. This approach corresponded to pre-war ideas, which stressed the importance of projecting a positive image of Britain. As a national institution, Shakespeare was regarded as a perfect carrier of such positive ideas.[143] During the conflict publications such as the *Bulletin from Britain* served exactly this purpose. Shakespeare's name appeared again and again and gave 'a reflection of the new spirit in England'.[144]

It was not only the sheer presence of Shakespearean drama on stage, however, which seemed important, but also a particular interpretation of his plays. Commentators praised the Old Vic's 1941 production of *King John* for the topical reading and its 'consistent war-like atmosphere'.[145] Sybil Thorndike was congratulated on her apparent presentation of Macbeth as Hitler on her Welsh tour, and a particularly strong anti-Nazi message must have been sent out by the performance of Shylock by the émigré Frederick Valk in *The Merchant of Venice* in 1943.[146]

NOTES

1 Harcourt Williams on Gielgud's departure from the Old Vic in 1930 (quoted Morley, *John G.*, p. 79).

2 It remains important today especially with opera productions to stress the spectacular effects they may feature. Recent announcements of the Ukrainian National Opera Odessa, for example, promised an 'exquisite Japanese water garden, waterfalls and stunning aquariums filled with golden fish' in Puccini's *Madam Butterfly*, and the appearance of 'hunting dogs, hawks and lavish sets' in Verdi's *Rigoletto* (see *The Guide North*, 23–29 August 2003. *The Guardian* 23 August 2003. p. 2).

3 By contrast, the Berlin influence on German provincial theatres was not only weaker it was also less desirable as it stood for decadence and artistic experiments, none of which one wanted to be exposed to. For German actors, however, Berlin was as desirable as London was for their British counterparts, although a job in Munich, Hamburg or Frankfurt was certainly more attractive than a position in Manchester, Birmingham or Glasgow in Britain.

4 The high number of productions corresponds to these demands. York's Theatre Royal, for example, presented an annual total of some sixty-five productions during the 1920s. This figure was considerably lower in Münster where it sank below forty during the late 1920s. In terms of novelties local commentators complained if the fare presented was not recent enough. In

York, 'Curtain-Raiser' calculated that 'only six plays older than two years were performed in the first season, while during the Summer season fourteen plays of greater than two years' existence were presented. The season so far has seen fifteen plays presented, of which only five are two years or younger, while five are ten years old or more' (*YEP*, 25 November 1936).

5   It is important to note, however, that 'recent' and 'London' could not be separated in their supposed magic spell over audiences. A play, which only reached Yorkshire's stage a few years after it had been successful in London, seemed likely to be branded 'dated'. And a recent success from Birmingham was certainly far less attractive than its London counterpart. With exceptionally successful plays managements informed patrons about the overall number of performances they had had in London. Additions such as 'has just completed its 762nd Performance on Monday, November 25th' were common.

6   Hutchison, *Masquerade*, 1936, p. 123. By comparison a visit by Reich President Ebert to a certain play might have even had a counter-effect on the production, in particular as regards the right-wing press and its clientele.

7   See Marshall, *Other Theatre*, p. 162. Marshall states that even the provincial revival of classics often coincided with West End revivals of the same plays.

8   During the Weimar years supporters of different schools of Shakespeare interpretation engaged in heated debates. Productions, which either seemed too radical or too conservative or too ordinary, could cause storms of protest (see Hortmann, Wilhelm. *Shakespeare und das deutsche Theater im 20. Jahrhundert*. Berlin: Henschel, 2001. pp. 66–70). The question of translation, too, was regarded as vital.

9   It was not until 1925 that Barry Jackson produced a modern-dress *Hamlet* at the Birmingham Repertory Theatre (see Cochrane, Claire. *Shakespeare and the Birmingham Repertory Theatre 1913–1929*. London: The Society for Theatre Research, 1993. pp. 120–147).

10   See Hobson, *Theatre in Britain*, p. 9.

11   Chisholm, *Repertory*, p. 194.

12   Regular guests at Yorkshire's theatres included the Charles Doran and Frank Benson companies in Shakespeare repertoire, the Royal Carl Rosa, D'Oyly Carte and O'Mara opera companies and J.A.E. Malone with continental operetta.

13   The repertoire of the Royal Carl Rosa Opera Company, for example, always presented six or seven operas during one week, chosen from a small array of established works. On their provincial tours in the 1920s, for example, the programme almost always featured Offenbach's *Tales of Hoffmann*, Bizet's *Carmen*, and Puccini's *Madam Butterfly*. In general Yorkshire's audiences had no chance to become familiar with contemporary opera. The regular appearance of D'Oyly Carte's staple Gilbert and Sullivan bill serves as a perfect example of this lack of variety.

14 The detailed Books of Receipts of Bradford's Alhambra are an excellent source in particular as they list gross takings, artists' salaries and net receipts for every production and even detail any individual arrangements with particular ensembles or artists in variety programmes (West Yorkshire Archive Service, Bradford. 11D82/B/1/a/3/52 and /53). Elsewhere in Yorkshire, letters-to-the-editor were proof of the fact that plays considered too 'demanding' failed to attract substantial audiences. In York readers claimed that 'if in future Mr Percy Hutchison gives them a surfeit of spineless musical comedy, they have only themselves to thank' (*YH*, 7 April 1923). Hutchison himself admitted the poor audiences but assured residents that 'rather than be compelled to present a surfeit of "spineless musical comedies" I would resign my management of the Theatre' (*YH*, 13 April 1923).

15 During previous years the Amateurs had regularly attracted biting comments regarding the poor quality of their productions (see, for example, *YEP*, 8 March 1927 and *YEP*, 7 March 1933).

16 York's Theatre Royal featured four contemporary dramas during the 1931 season. *Cynara* by H.M. Harwood and Gore Brown was branded a 'provocative play' because of its 'moral: have a good time with the shop-girls, gents, and then get back to your wife in time for supper' (*YEP*, 30 June 1931). Robert McLaughlin's *The Eternal Magdalene* dealt with the life of a prostitute, Dorothy Brandon's *The Outsider* was a medical drama and John van Druten's *After All* 'unfolds the eternal conflict of thought between parents and children' (*YEP*, 5 December 1931).

17 Like today, the annual Pantomime was hugely popular and the biggest single financial asset of the theatre. In 1924, for example, *Robinson Crusoe* was seen by nearly 8,000 people in its first four days (see Rosenfeld, *York Theatre*, p. 322). The Pantomimes were also the only productions which regularly ran for more than a week. York's Theatre Royal Panto usually ran for two weeks, Wakefield's Opera House Panto for seven and Francis Laidler's production at Bradford's Alhambra even ran for nine. Their financial importance is illustrated by an example from Huddersfield's Theatre Royal where normal gross takings for a decent week in 1930 amounted to about £200. The same year's Panto *Cinderella*, however, took more than £600 in one week (see West Yorkshire Archives Huddersfield. Theatre Royal Records 1901–36. B/HTR/as/11. pp. 38 and 42).

18 See, for example, Nicholson, Steve. 'Unnecessary Plays: European Drama and the British Censor in the 1920s.' *Theatre Research International* 20.1 (1995): pp. 30–6.

19 One of the last French plays to appear in York is an interesting case. Jacques Duval's romantic comedy *Tovarich* was produced in a translation by Robert Sherwood in 1937 and again in 1945. It represents one of the few examples of direct contact between Yorkshire and Westphalia regarding a play from a country foreign to both. In Germany Duval's play appeared as *Towarisch* in an adaptation by Curt Goetz.

20 For the decisive influence of French literature on British regional stages see Bargna, Katya and Whittaker, John. 'Translation and the British Stage; Or, How to Deform Esmeralda.' Unpublished article of the Performance and Translation Centre. University of Hull, 2001. In 1918–19 alone examples of French plays on the York stage include *Sleeping Partners* in an English adaptation by Seymour Hicks, the musical comedy *High Jinks* adapted by Frederick Lonsdale from the French play by Paul Bilhaud, the 'romantic play' *Henry of Navarre* by William Devereux, the 'great naval play' *In the Night Watch* adapted by Michael Morton, and the revue *As You Were* by Arthur Wimperis in an adaptation from Rip's *Plus ça Change*.

21 The American cultural influence had become so strong during the 1920s and 1930s that 'mid-Atlantic accents had become almost obligatory for popular singers, encroaching more and more on the raucous Cockney and fruity Lancashire of the old music hall' (see Calder, *People's War*, p. 311).

22 Commentators expressed their fear that England was overrun by thousands of American tourists arriving on hundreds of ocean-liners in the summer. A central point of concern was that American youths might bring with them a degenerate language and informal manners, which would endanger the decency of English girls. Even 'the problem of the theatre latecomer' was attributed to US influence (see *YH*, 19 May 1923).

23 The American musical comedy *Irene* by Leslie Henson was commended as it contained 'music that at times, when it forgets the American idiom, is very attractive' (*YEP*, 26 November 1929). The British musical comedy *Lady Mary* was praised as it 'comes as a relaxation and a restful relief from the pronounced jazz type of musical play so common nowadays' (*YEP*, 19 February 1929). Correspondingly, John Drinkwater's comedy *Bird in Hand* was admired as it was 'typically English, and probably that is why the play is so popular, quite a change from these American plays' (*YEP*, 31 August 1929).

24 The American influence on the stage was also blamed for the rise of 'indecent' striptease shows on theatre stages.

25 Examples include plays like *General Post* by Harold Terry and Lechmere Worrall, the 'powerful French military play' *Under two Flags*, *The Better 'Ole (A Gas Attack)* by Bruce Bairnsfather and Arthur Eliot – with acts entitled 'Explosion 1' and 'Explosion 2' – the 'greatest of all spy plays' *Inside the Lines* by Earl Derr Biggers, the 'latest and most intense military play' *A Spy in the Ranks* by Mrs Kimberley, the 'new spy play with naval interest' *The Luck of the Navy* by Clifford Mills, and the 'successful royalty spy play' *The Man Who Stayed at Home* by Worrall and Terry, in which an obscure 'Fraulein Schroeder' spied for the Germans on the east coast.

26 Commentators lamented that whereas in Germany Shakespeare and Shaw were regularly performed, British audiences knew hardly anything about German drama (see Theilkuhl, Wolfgang. *Deutsches Land und Deutsches Leben*. London: Methuen, 5th ed. 1944. pp. 119–20). The fact that by 1934 no decent translation of Hauptmann's dramatic works existed indicates the low

level of interest (see Chisholm, *Repertory*, p. 116).

27 Ernst Toller enjoyed some kind of cult status with the British workers' theatre movement, especially with his play *Masses and Men*. Outside this clientele, however, his plays were virtually unknown (see Samuel, Raphael, MacColl, Ewan and Cosgrove, Stuart. *Theatres of the Left 1880–1935. Workers' Theatre Movements in Britain and America*. London: Routledge & Kegan Paul, 1985. p. 22). When Birmingham's Repertory Company produced Georg Kaiser's *Gas* its 'population of 919,000 rolled up to the extent of forty-seven to ninety persons per night' (Chisholm, *Repertory*, p. 193). We also have to keep in mind that many of the German left-wing or avant-garde plays would have been banned by the Lord Chamberlain anyway. According to the Examiner in 1925, the Lord Chamberlain prohibited plays 'the performance of which would have been a real scandal'. The corresponding list of banned plays included works by Schnitzler, Leonhard Frank, Toller, Bruckner, Emil Ludwig and Wedekind (see Findlater, Richard. *Banned! A Review of Theatrical Censorship in Britain*. London: Panther, 1968. p. 155).

28 In 1924 the share of plays with some kind of German connection – written or composed by a German, using a German setting or the German language – in the overall repertoire at York's Theatre Royal, for example, reached 13 per cent (in the following years and until the late 1930s the 'German share' was between four and ten per cent). Musical pieces such as Lehár's *The Merry Widow* and *Gypsy Love* as well as Wagner's *Lohengrin* and *Tannhäuser* in general quickly regained their places in British repertoires. The fact that these works had been popular before the war obviously contributed to a feeling of not regarding them as German but as part of an international cultural heritage. Popular favourites were especially the waltzes from Vienna or Budapest. Pieces like Lehár's *The Count of Luxembourg* and *Gypsy Love*, Jacobi's *The Marriage Market* and Fall's *The Dollar Princess* had literally 'created a vogue' before 1914 (see Disher, Willson M. 'Jubilee Years in the Theatre.' *Theatre World* May 1935: p. 202).

29 When York's Theatre Royal produced Sherriff's *Journey's End* it is interesting to note that as part of the advertising campaign the management felt it was useful to state that the play had been 'accepted for production in no less than forty-eight theatres in different parts of Germany, a record which no other play has ever achieved' (*YEP*, 1 February 1930).

30 Another proof for the popularity of Remarque's novel is a variety show entitled *All Right on the Western Front*, a burlesque depicting 'the lighter side of life in war time', which York's Empire staged in November 1930.

31 *YEP*, 13 April 1935.

32 *YEP*, 12 January 1932.

33 Johns, Eric. 'The Actor in Germany.' *Theatre World* November 1936: p. 227. Johns praised a system in which 'the actor, instead of being beaten down to the lowest possible salary by an independent manager, becomes almost a Civil Servant ... at a fixed salary.' This also meant that German actors 'are not faced

with possible unemployment five or six times a year' like their English colleagues. Johns was equally impressed by the German pension system 'which pays out regular pensions on retirement'.

34 Scott claimed that 'much is going on in Germany which other nations might well copy' (see *YEP*, 9 September 1936). Scott's remarks caused a great deal of correspondence. The reaction of the majority of the readers, however, was not a criticism of her opinions but a general appreciation of the 'achievements' of the Third Reich. Commentators claimed that prior to the Nazi take-over 'the provincial shows and, to a large extent, the Berlin ones also, were of the lowest and most suggestive type' and that Hitler had 'cleaned up many demoralising and immoral institutions' (*YEP*, 16 September 1936). Others added that 'in the years succeeding the war, the moral tone of the German theatre was distinctly bad. Not only was pornography and obscenity the order of the day on the stage, but literature was debased and the standards of the gutter were set ... I have the greatest admiration for Adolf Hitler and the Nazi regime' (*YEP*, 16 September 1936; similarly *YEP*, 11 September 1936). These comments were no exception. The 'social experiment', the reduction of unemployment, the creation of a political euphoria and people's solidarity, the compulsory work service and the building of the motorways generally received positive assessments from British tourists visiting Nazi Germany (see Schwarz, Angela. *Die Reise ins Dritte Reich. Britische Augenzeugenberichte im nationalsozialistischen Deutschland (1933–1939)*. Göttingen: Vandenhoeck & Ruprecht, 1993. pp. 189–261). Home Intelligence reports show that anti-Semitism, too, was wide-spread and increased during the war (see PRO. Ministry of Information. INF 1/292 (part 3). Home Intelligence Daily Reports. 6 May 1943). It seems that public opinion concerning Nazi Germany did not change until autumn 1940. After the Italian declaration of war in June 1940 it was Italy rather than Germany which earned the anger of the British. Ian McLaine argues that 'not until September 1940 were there any reports of bitterness against the Germans, and even then they were said to have been aroused not by Nazi ideology or German victories in Europe but by direct air attacks on Britain' (McLaine, Ian. *Ministry of Morale. Home Front Morale and the Ministry of Information in World War II*. London: Allen & Unwin, 1979. p. 143. See also Reid, Gannon Franklin. *The British Press and Germany 1936–1939*. Oxford: Clarendon, 1971).

35 After having met Hitler in Germany Lloyd George claimed that 'I have never seen a happier people than the Germans' and reassured Britons that 'Hitler does not want war' (*YEP*, 21 September 1936).

36 Henderson, Neville. *Failure of a Mission. Berlin 1937–1939*. London: Hodder and Stoughton, 1940. pp. 23–4. As an example of the regime's 'achievements' Henderson quoted the labour camps, which 'serve none but useful purposes. In them not only are there no class distinctions, but there is, on the contrary, an opportunity for better understanding between the classes'. Although he

recognised the loss of personal liberty, Henderson concluded that 'some sort of an operation had been necessary' and acknowledged the 'amazing power of organisation, thoroughness, and discipline of the German nation' – thanks 'to Hitler's own personal inspiration' (ibid., pp. 39–40).

37 Lord Birkenhead as quoted in Brendon, Piers. *The Dark Valley. A Panorama of the 1930s*. London: Cape, 2000. p. 525. For similar pro-Nazi attitudes among the British elite see Kershaw, Ian. *Making Friends with Hitler. Lord Londonderry and Britain's Road to War*. London: Allen Lane, 2004.

38 *The Times*, 15 November 1936.

39 In 1936 York had an average weekly cinema attendance of 45,000. Ticket prices ranged from 6d to 1/6d (see Borthwick Institute, *Rowntree Papers PP/21*, 31). This price structure meant that a visit to the Theatre Royal could be cheaper than a cinema visit as a seat in the gallery cost only 4d. from 1935.

40 Other theatres in the region experienced similar difficulties. At Huddersfield's Theatre Royal, for example, only 40 per cent of the productions showed a profit at the end of the 1920s. In 1931–2 the overall profit for the whole year amounted to £262 (see West Yorkshire Archives Huddersfield. Theatre Royal Records 1901–36. B/HTR/af/1–17). The town's other major theatre, the Hippodrome, was turned into a cinema in 1930 (see Chadwick, Stanley. *Jubilee Presentation. Hippodrome Stage-1905–1955-Tudor Screen*. Huddersfield: *Huddersfield Gazette*, 1955. p. 40).

41 The exceptions are Wilde's *The Importance of Being Earnest* and Shaw's *Mrs Warren's Profession*.

42 York programme notes, 18 September 1939. One incident, which more than others sums up the differences between British and German regional theatres, is the biggest event of 1937: the 'Coronation Week' in May. The fact that with *Yellow Sands* a well-known comedy was chosen for the celebrations and not Shakespeare would have met with disbelief in Germany. To mark the accession to the throne of Wilhelm II, for example, with anything other than a classical drama or a Wagner opera would have been unimaginable.

43 Local plays such as *Without the Prince* by the Harrogate author Philip King in 1939 regularly became favourites with York audiences. Other such successes included *Murder at the Ministry* by the Harrogate authors Falkland Carey and A. Thompson in 1943, and *Burning Gold* by the same playwrights in 1944.

44 Westphalian theatres mainly used the programme notes to provide information. They did not have to distinguish themselves too much from the cinema as they were generally regarded as two different art forms. The public discourse in Westphalia in the 1920s and 1930s, therefore, never featured discussions about the danger of the 'talkies' on a similar scale to that in Yorkshire.

45 From 1922 the cover of York's programme notes featured high-quality photos of characteristic views of the city. In 1925 a picture of Percy Hutchison in smart naval uniform was added and, to distinguish itself even further, the

theatre introduced an elaborate Art Deco layout in 1928.

46 See *YEP*, 18 December 1935.

47 The press regularly commented on how much a certain performance relied on the prompter. In late 1944, for example, the *Yorkshire Gazette* praised York's company for their performance of *Close Quarters*, because 'on the opening night there was not a single prompt' (*YG*, 1 December 1944).

48 We have no reliable information about salary at Yorkshire's theatres but Somerset Maugham's novel gives some interesting hints. After she earned £12 a week in a touring company Julia Lambert's salary drops to £8 in weekly rep. On her renewal of the contract, however, Julia manages to get £15 a week (see Maugham, *Theatre*, pp. 21–3 and 48). This pay compared favourably to the average weekly wages in the 1930s, which reached £2.95 in 1938. The majority of British households had an average weekly income of less than £5 (see Bowden, Sue. 'The New Consumerism.' Johnson, Paul, ed. *Twentieth Century Britain. Economic, Social and Cultural Change.* London: Longman, 1994. pp. 255–6).

49 In contrast to German theatres, where seasons normally started in autumn and ended in spring/summer of the following year, seasons at British theatres normally lasted for six months. In 1939 at York, for example, the company returned from their Christmas holidays on 16 January and performed until 16 July. After a three-week holiday they resumed playing on 7 August and were on stage until 31 December.

50 However, many theatres kept records regarding their takings (such as Bradford's Alhambra, Huddersfield's Theatre Royal and Leeds' Grand Theatre). York's high attendances aroused the interest of the *Theatre World*, which stated in 1937 that 12 per cent of the overall population (90,000 at that time) went to see *Sweet Aloes* as the theatre had increased its 'audiences week by week' (Fearon, George. 'It's a Way They Have in Repertory!' *Theatre World* September 1937: p. 108). The theatre seems to have been successful in retaining these attendances over the following years (see Rowntree, Seebohm. 'The Municipal Theatre *Can* Be a Success.' *Local Government Service* 22 (1943): p. 452. See also Rowntree, *Poverty and Progress*, pp. 414–15; Borthwick Institute, *Rowntree Papers PP/21*, Folder 'Social Survey of York. Leisure-time Activities. Interim Report for the Trustees of the J.R.V.T. May 1 1936'. p. 32).

51 The theatre seated 1,340 people.

52 As claimed by the *Yorkshire Evening Press* in late December 1938 (see *Collection Nellie Woodhouse*, vol. III 1938/39, pp. 143–4).

53 See *Yorkshire Post*, 14 June 1943.

54 As happened in York, although only for a brief time. The management reinstated the band, because live music was so popular, and from 1936 the Repertory Trio entertained audiences with three or four different tunes a night. The band was extended over the following years and became the Repertory Sextette in 1939. Despite the enlargement of the band, however,

musical comedies remained difficult to stage, a fact patrons continuously complained about.

55 See Berghaus, Günter. 'The Émigrés from Nazi Germany and their Contribution to the British Theatrical Scene.' Mosse, Werner, et al., eds. *Second Chance. Two Centuries of German-Speaking Jews in the United Kingdom.* Tübingen: Mohr, 1991. pp. 297–314.

56 See Marshall, *Other Theatre*, p. 208. As a result opera singers mostly looked like 'oratorio singers in fancy dress'. See also Levi, Erik. 'Carl Ebert, Glyndebourne and the Regeneration of British Opera.' Berghaus, Günter, ed. *Theatre and Film in Exile. German Artists in Britain, 1933–1945.* Oxford: Berg, 1989. p. 180.

57 See Marshall, *Other Theatre*, p. 209.

58 Ibid. See also Dent, Edward J. *A Theatre for Everybody. The Story of the Old Vic and Sadler's Wells.* London: Boardman, 1945.

59 See Myers, *Music Since 1939*, pp. 117–18.

60 See CEMA, *Fifth Year*, pp. 5–6 and 9.

61 In 1942 the York press praised Sadler's Wells for 'a memorable operatic week, with the theatre deservedly crowded at all performances' (*YG*, 23 January 1942). A year later D'Oyly Carte were 'received by crowded houses' (*YG*, 5 February 1943). See Fig 3.3.

62 Quoted in Holdsworth, *Domes of Delight*, p. 52.

63 Even Huddersfield – claimed by many to be an un-theatrical town – was visited by D'Oyly Carte again in 1941 after 'a lapse of fifteen years'. Sadler's Wells came, too, as did the Anglo-Polish Ballet (see Chadwick, Stanley. *Theatre Royal. The Romance of the Huddersfield Stage.* Huddersfield: Advertiser Press, 1941. p. 37).

64 See *YG*, 22 January 1943.

65 Commentators urged audiences not to regard *The Marriage of Figaro* as a German piece, as 'this German opera by the Austrian Mozart was composed to a libretto by a Venetian Jew ... Lorenzo da Ponte. Da Ponte's source for the libretto was the most French of comedies – Beaumarchais' *Barbier de Seville*, and the locale was Spain' (*Theatre Arts* 24 (1940): p. 228).

66 'An amazing race, the English. While Hitler and his gang feed "offending literature" to the flames, we are rational enough to sit back comfortably in our theatres and see depicted on the screen and stage dramas and comic operas of the very enemy we are fighting in this war. But we enjoyed Gilbert and Sullivan's *The Mikado* long before the war, and although it has to do with "those nasty little men", we can still reel in its jollity' (*YEP*, 2 February 1943).

67 See Myers, *Music Since 1939*, p. 116. The government was well aware of the propaganda value of Myra Hess's concerts in the National Gallery. In a letter from May 1941 the Gallery asked the Treasury whether they were prepared to pay £160 to make the place safer and thereby enable the concerts to continue. Apart from having the support of the Minister of Home Security, the Gallery's best argument was that 'Miss Hess makes a great point of the

propaganda value of the concerts … One argument is that they are the main instance of cultural activities continuing unbroken in wartime London and another, that this fact being known in America produces considerable effect over there' (PRO. Home Office. HO 186 Air Raid Precautions. HO 186/466 Entertainment (1941). Letter by D.L.M. (National Gallery) to H.B. Usher (Treasury Chambers). 2 May 1941). The money was granted a few days later and work started immediately. It was also covered for a Ministry of Information film (see ibid. Letter by M.W. Bennitt of H.M. Office of Works to P. Hayman in the Ministry of Home Security. 15 May 1941).

68 The foundation of the Glyndebourne Festival Theatre by Fritz Busch and Carl Ebert, for example, was an important contribution and immensely influential. The inauguration of the Edinburgh Festival in 1949, too, was linked to the influence of German émigrés (see Berghaus, *Émigrés*, pp. 311–13).

69 See *YEP*, 6 July 1944. Steinitz also played an organ recital in York Minster.

70 In contrast to the ballet performances presented during the war Kyasht's dance shows of the late 1920s entitled *Gala Nights* or *Piccadilly Cabaret* had been characterised by a note of light entertainment.

71 See Williamson, Audrey. 'Vic-Wells: The English National Ballet?' *Theatre World* December 1942: pp. 30 and 33. See also Manchester, P.W. *Vic-Wells: A Ballet in Progress*. London: Gollancz, 1946. Regarding the company's immense popular success in Yorkshire see, for example, *YEP*, 3 January 1945; *YH*, 6 January 1945; *YH*, 24 February 1945; *Hull Daily Mail* [HDM], 5 December 1939. See Fig 3.3.

72 A change which, according to the government, was an important phenomenon of the war. Commentators claimed that present audiences 'from the theatre at its best … seek something of deeper significance' (*Bulletin from Britain*. no. 26. 26 February 1941. p. 1).

73 See Marshall, *Other Theatre*, p. 12.

74 Quoted in Morley, *John G*, p. 49.

75 Interesting insights into common attitudes regarding Shakespeare can also be gathered from Maugham's *Theatre* novel. Michael Gosselyn, husband of the protagonist Julia Lambert, toured in Benson's Shakespearean company but came to the conclusion 'that Shakespeare would get him nowhere … if he wanted to become a leading actor' (see Maugham, *Theatre*, pp. 14–15). The ignorance towards Shakespeare also becomes obvious in Julia's future plans. Despite her lack of experience she contemplates playing Hamlet as 'Siddons and Sarah Bernhardt played him. I've got better legs than any of the men I've seen in the part'. The only problem was, of course, 'that bloody blank verse' (ibid., p. 263).

76 When Gielgud, for example, produced his hugely successful 1934 *Hamlet* he was offered the 'generous' rehearsal period of four weeks (see Morley, *John G.*, p. 111).

77 Ibid., p. 151.

78 The theatre only made profits again from 1941 when attendances rose sharply (see Marshall, *Other Theatre*, pp. 182–3).

79 Rosenfeld, *York Stage*, p. 312.

80 Chisholm, *Repertory*, pp. 126 and 129. Percy Hutchison admitted that Shakespeare's 'commercial possibilities' were low and only 'few managers seem to have the courage … to present Shakespeare on the stage' (Hutchison, *Masquerade*, p. 141). Other regional theatres were similarly cautious (see Wyndham Goldie, Grace. *The Liverpool Repertory Theatre 1911–1934*. Liverpool: Liverpool University Press, 1935. pp. 135–89 and 270–1; Seed, *Sheffield Repertory Theatre*, p. 91; Dyas, Aubrey. *Adventure in Repertory. Northampton Repertory Theatre 1927-48*. Northampton: Northampton Repertory Players, 1948. pp. 192–216; Gillett, *History of Hull*, p. 436). Chisholm stated that, above all, 'the British playgoer likes an hilarious farce which will make him laugh all night' (see Chisholm, *Repertory*, p. 119).

81 Speaight claimed that the mistakes of the First World War were not being repeated in the Second (see Speaight, *Drama Since 1939*, p. 29).

82 Although the dressing-rooms were bombed and the costumes in them destroyed, Wolfit's company continued to play one-hour excerpts from Shakespeare for more than a hundred performances to an average audience of four hundred people a day (see Marshall, *Other Theatre*, p. 133). The Old Vic productions featured many stars who were 'appearing for next to nothing at the Old Vic because they realize that the battle of the Old Vic is one we cannot afford to lose' (Farjeon, Herbert. *The Shakespearean Stage. Dramatic Criticisms*. London: Hutchinson, 1948. pp. 161–2). Commentators praised the Old Vic's productions as 'these great artists have served the cause of culture in this country with unremitting energy and self-sacrifice. It is an amazing story, and one that will live in the annals of the English theatre for all time' ('War-time Story of the Old Vic and Sadler's Wells Companies.' *Theatre World* November 1941: p. 41).

83 The acclaimed Festival of English Comedy also coincided with the Arts Theatre's most successful year, which saw its membership rise to 10,000 (see Trewin, Wendy and J.C. *The Arts Theatre, London. 1927-1981*. London: The Society for Theatre Research, 1986. pp. 16–17).

84 See *HDM*, 2 September 1941, 29 September 1942.

85 The press celebrated the 'Repertory Success in Shakespeare' and claimed that the company 'reached heights of cleverness that would have satisfied Stratford's exacting audiences' (*YEP*, 13 April 1943). Commentators noted that 'not for months have the company received the kind of ovation they got after the opening performance on Monday night' (*Malton Gazette*, 16 April 1943).

86 *YH*, 8 December 1943. The play was advertised as the highlight of the season. Commentators celebrated the production as 'well dressed, but not overdone in spectacle and background' (*YEP*, 8 December 1943). This praise stands in some contrast to the lavish touring productions of Shakespearean plays in the

1920s. Corresponding to new ideals of austerity, the 1943 *Hamlet* was explicitly praised for the absence of any splendour and spectacle.

87 See *YEP*, 7 December 1943.

88 *YEP*, 6 December 1944. The production was staged between 5–17 December 1944.

89 This qualitative difference is not mirrored in Fig 3.3. The 1926 season, for example, shows a ten per cent share of the classics in the programme because of the seven Shakespearean plays, which Frank Benson presented. By contrast, the 1944 classical share of two per cent relates to the fact that the theatre 'only' performed *Othello*. The two-week run of that production, however, is double the time of Benson's stay, which is not reflected in the diagram as I only counted the number of productions as runs of more than one week occurred only rarely. In qualitative terms the *Othello* production should rank higher than Benson's week of Shakespearean repertory.

90 Harrogate's Shakespearean Festival Society had some 250 members and its successful productions enjoyed a strong backing in the community (see 'Amateur Stage. Notes and Topics.' *Theatre World* June 1944: p. 31). In Wakefield the first visit of a state-sponsored company in September 1942 was a grand civic event and in Huddersfield the outbreak of the war resulted in a flood of publications regarding its 'great' theatrical history. This interest is surprising as some years earlier local commentators had admitted that Huddersfield was 'not a good theatre town' and that companies only reluctantly paid a visit (see *Huddersfield Weekly Examiner* [*HWE*], 6 June 1936).

91 Quoted in Fuller, Rosalinde. 'A Shakespeare Tour in Wartime.' *Theatre Arts* 24 (1940): p. 181.

92 Hobson, *Theatre in Britain*, p. 80.

93 'The fun begins with the arrival of brusque Mrs. Short, an evacuee from Brixton and her daughter Saffron. There are sudden complications when the Sheldon's find themselves with new neighbours, the husband "next door" becoming infatuated with coy and glamorous Saffron, and the wife finding herself quite innocently accused of endeavouring to steal the affections of the RAF fiancé of one of Mrs. Sheldon's daughters' (Theatre Royal Programme Notes, 14 September 1942).

94 The play was set in a Dales bar 'at a date when the invasion of this country was a live issue'. The inevitable Nazi spy gets spotted due to the 'inquisitiveness of the village gossip' (*YG*, 13 February 1944).

95 *YG*, 13 June 1941.

96 Similar productions included the Tyrolean play *Oh, Leo!* with lyrics by Howard Dietz and music by Arthur Schwartz, which was produced in London in early 1940 (see *Theatre World* February 1940: p. 36).

97 Until the war came closer Britons made a distinction between the Germans and the Nazis. Home Intelligence reports from 1940 show that bitterness against the Germans only became substantial after the first direct air attacks

(see PRO. Ministry of Information. INF 1/264. Home Intelligence Daily Reports. 4, 5, 13 and 19 September 1940).

98 In York these plays made up 14 per cent of the entire repertoire in 1944. Although plays with anti-German sentiments had already appeared in 1941, their share was much lower than during the First World War. Out of fifty-three performances in 1941 only six per cent were in some way directed against Nazi Germany, and for 1942 the share remained the same. In 1943 it rose slightly to seven per cent before reaching its peak in 1944 with 14 per cent. In 1945 five per cent of all performances could be deemed anti-German. See Fig 3.3.

99 The play is set in a village on the English coast in September 1939 and depicts a famous scientist who is engaged in experiments, which prove of great value to the government. 'Certain enemy agents' become interested in his invention and 'try to kidnap the scientist and convey him to Germany in a U-boat' (*YG*, 13 February 1942). There were a few plays with a similar pattern, for example the above-mentioned *Murder at the Ministry* by Carey and Thompson, which dramatised the 'tragedy of Sir James Reid, working at the Ministry of Protection on a secret weapon' (*YEP*, 19 October 1943).

100 Examples include leaflets explaining what to do 'If the Invader Comes' and the poster series 'Careless Talk Costs Lives'.

101 The press stressed that it was 'not without parallel since 1939 in Europe' (*YEP*, 14 March 1944) as Drake and his companions 'protect the noble Elizabeth of England from the treacherous "Quislings" of the period' (*NEWS*, 10 March 1944).

102 *Leeds Mercury*, 15 August 1944.

103 *NEWS*, 1 September 1944.

104 The play, hailed as 'one of the great plays, probably the greatest, of the war' (*YG*, 15 January 1943), was set in spring 1940 and concerned an anti-Nazi German who brings his American wife back to her mother's home near Washington, together with their three children. The story 'shows how the serenity and security of this home seemingly so remote from the European conflict, is shattered by the far reaching influence of the Gestapo' (*YG*, 8 January 1943).

105 See Noble, *British Theatre*, pp. 95–6.

106 See *YEP*, 30 March 1940.

107 *YEP*, 2 May 1944.

108 *NEWS*, 28 April 1944.

109 Other examples of noteworthy contemporary drama include Karel Capek's vision of a de-humanised robot future in *R.U.R.* (*Rossum's Universal Robots*) and John Priestley's *They Came to a City*.

110 See Joy, David and Lennon, Patricia. *Grand Memories. The Life and Times of the Grand Theatre and Opera House, Leeds*. Ilkley: Great Northern, 2006. pp. 31–5.

111 See Fitzsimmons, *Theatre Royal*, p. 180.

112 See, for example, Noble, *British Theatre*, pp. 169–73. Instead the theatre was praised for the fact that it 'withstood the shock of events even better than it had done in 1914' (Hobson, *Theatre in Britain*, p. 117).

113 Commentators noted that war plays 'were all the rage in the autumn of 1942' (see Shellard, Dominic. *Harold Hobson: Witness and Judge. The Theatre Criticism of Harold Hobson*. Keele: Keele University Press, 1995. pp. 54–5). Out of thirty London shows running in October 1942 six were war plays (see *Theatre Arts* 26 (1942): p. 670).

114 Yorkshire audiences immediately realised that to see such an array of stars on their local stages was the chance of a lifetime, which resulted in 'full houses all the week' (*YG*, 5 January 1940).

115 During the 1920s and early 1930s 'the hatred of Manchester, Birmingham and Liverpool audiences for Hauptmann's genius was positively rabid' (Chisholm, *Repertory*, p. 97).

116 See, for example, the minutes of CEMA's tenth meeting on 1 July 1941 (AAD, EL 1/6 Minutes Meetings 1-20).

117 See Noble, *British Theatre*, pp. 20–1. *The Russians* was a propaganda play about partisan warfare against the *Wehrmacht* set in occupied Russia.

118 One of the rare examples are some remarks from Kenneth Lindsay, Parliamentary Secretary of the Board of Education. As 'it is not often that a Government spokesman offers his views on current theatrical fare' the *Theatre World* was quick to publish them as they 'must not be lost'. Lindsay himself offered a damning judgement as 'apart from the classics there is hardly a play worth seeing in London at the present time. The trouble is that new drama can only be born out of a live people, and we have been moderately dead for the last 20 years [but] I hope that out of the present war there will be born some fresh artists' (*Theatre World* April 1940, p. 94).

119 Findlater, *Theatrical Censorship*, p. 9. Only music halls and private theatres were outside the censor's jurisdiction. In greater detail see Nicholson, Steve. *The Censorship of British Drama 1900–1968*. Volumes I and II cover the years 1900 to 1952 (Exeter: University of Exeter Press, 2003 and 2005).

120 The censor was obsessed with the protection of the Bible. This prompted the veto of several plays from abroad, for example Hauptmann's *Hannele*, in which the character of 'the Stranger' had to be clean shaven in order not to resemble Jesus (see Findlater, *Theatrical Censorship*, p. 97). Wedekind's plays clearly offended the Lord Chamberlain's canon of decency and were banned on 'moral' grounds (see ibid., pp. 162–4). In the tense atmosphere of the late 1930s the slightest hint of political satire could see a play banned for political reasons, especially if it appeared to be disrespectful of Mussolini and Hitler, and would thus offend the foreign heads of state. Rattigan's *Follow My Leader* was only licensed after the outbreak of the war and so was Rice's *Judgement Day*, which dramatised the Reichstag Trial. Sherwood's *Idiot's Delight*, which was set in Mussolini's Italy, was not allowed to contain any direct reference to Italy or Mussolini. Revues, too, were carefully watched for indiscriminate

suggestions that Hitler and Mussolini were figures of fun. As late as 1939, a Herbert Farjeon lyric was banned because it began with 'Even Hitler had a mother, Even Musso had a ma' (see ibid., p. 161). Interestingly, censorship in Nazi Germany shows some similarities to Britain. Neither recent political events, like the 1918–19 revolution, nor actors in German uniform were permissible according to a circular from July 1939 (see BArch, R55/20111, p. 101).

121 See Nicholson, *Unnecessary Plays*, p. 30. This hidden censorship, however, only worked with some playwrights and Shaw could not be intimidated. He was the one playwright who suffered most from the censor. It took Shaw's *Mrs Warren's Profession* thirty-three years to be publicly produced (see Findlater, *Theatrical Censorship*, pp. 103–5).

122 *Miss Julie*, for example, was only passed for public performance in 1939 (see ibid., pp. 31–4).

123 As quoted in the Stockholm newspaper *Aftonbladet* on 28 September 1939 (for the German translation see BArch, R55/20217, p. 8). At about the same time Shaw also intended to change the Italian part of *Geneva*. In a letter to the Foreign Office Major Gordon of the Lord Chamberlain's Office enquired whether the changes proposed by Shaw would meet with government approval. In their reply the Foreign Office made it clear that 'we do not at all like the direct reference to Italy's betrayal of the Axis. It is not yet absolutely certain that Signor Mussolini will definitely betray his ally', and suggested concrete changes (see PRO. Foreign Office. FO 371/23829 Political-Southern-Italy 1939. pp. 285–8).

124 Letter written by Herr von Selzam of the German embassy in The Hague on 11 November 1939. With a similar excitement Selzam quoted the *Daily Telegraph* who had reported that Elmar Rice's *Judgement Day*, which dramatised the Reichstag trial, had been prohibited as well (BArch, R55/20217, p. 24).

125 See Selzam letter quoted above (ibid.).

126 A typical example of a complaint was a letter by Fritz Randolph of the German embassy from January 1938 about a satirical scene in a variety programme at Shepherd's Bush Variety Theatre, in which Henry Hall's 'Fun Racqueteers' ridiculed the Hitler salute by comparing it to a dog lifting his leg (see PRO. Foreign Office. FO 371/21701 Political-Central-Germany 1938. Anti-Nazi Plays. pp. 1–3). Only from early 1940 did the theatres enjoy more freedom to produce shows such as *Who's Taking Liberty*, which was staged at the Whitehall Theatre. It was a variation of the Cinderella theme, brought into line with the European situation, and featured as the Ugly Governesses Gretchen Hitler and Katinka Stalin (see Fairweather, David. 'Over the Footlights.' *Theatre World* January 1940: p. 7).

127 See PRO. Ministry of Information. INF 1/260. Home Morale and Education During the Winter 1940–1. Above quotes from page 14 of the file (Extract from Minutes of Policy Committee, 26 July 1940).

128 Members of the Theatrical Managers' Association, the Society of West End Theatre Managers, British Actors' Equity, the Variety Artists' Federation and the Theatrical Trade Unions vigorously fought for Sunday openings 'in the National interest'. They made representations to the Home Secretary and expressed their view that 'entertainment is essential in helping to maintain the good spirits of the military and civil population' (letter from Horace Collins, the secretary of the Theatrical Managers' Association to Harold Butler, Regional Commissioner, Southern Region, Reading, 11 December 1940. PRO. Home Office. HO 186 Air Raid Precautions. HO 186/1894 Entertainment). See also *Theatre World* November 1940: p. 101, and similar articles in the December 1940 and February 1941 issues.

129 'Over the Footlights.' *Theatre World* March 1941: p. 51.

130 Opinion polls carried out during the war show that a majority supported Sunday openings. In summer 1943 58 per cent of those asked 'Would you approve or disapprove of theatres being allowed to open on Sundays, just as they do on other days?' gave a positive answer, 33 per cent disapproved and nine per cent did not know (see PRO. Ministry of Information. INF 1/292 (Part 3). Home Intelligence Reports, July 1942–August 1943. pp. 213–14. Appendix to a public opinion survey compiled by the British Institute of Public Opinion, presented on 24 January 1943).

131 See PRO. Home Office. HO 186 Air Raid Precautions. HO 186/742 Entertainment (1942). p. 3.

132 Statutory Rules and Orders. 1942 no. 502. Emergency Powers (Defence). General Regulations. The amendment enabled Morrison to 'prohibit or restrict ... the use of premises ... for the purposes of any entertainment, exhibition, performance, amusement, game or sport to which members of the public are admitted, in so far as such prohibition or restriction appears ... to be necessary or expedient for any of the purposes enumerated in subsection (1) of section one of the Emergency Powers (Defence) Act, 1939' (PRO. Home Office. HO 186 Air Raid Precautions. HO 186/742 Entertainment (1942).

133 Officials were quick to stress that the government did not intend to stop entertainments as wartime policy so far 'has been to permit them to continue on a restricted basis in the belief, that, within reason, popular entertainments act as lubricant rather than a brake on the war machine' (PRO. Home Office. HO 186 Air Raid Precautions. HO 186/1894 Entertainment (1944). Statement made by the Minister of Home Security in the House of Commons on 12 March 1942 (enclosure to H.S. Circular no. 74/1942).

134 The reason for his refraining from any direct intervention was almost certainly twofold. Firstly, the vast majority of theatres did not offer him any opportunity for intervention, because their programmes hardly left anything to be desired. Secondly, the military situation for the Allies improved considerably in the course of 1942 and there was hardly any reason for critical remarks from the stage. In general, Home Intelligence Reports regularly

showed how popular Churchill was as a military leader and how overwhelmingly the British supported the present war.

135 This quote from Noble, *British Theatre*, p. 98.

136 See *Theatre World* August 1942: p. 5. Gielgud's *Macbeth* was presented 'by arrangement with CEMA' and featured incidental music by William Walton (see *Theatre World* September 1942: p. 9).

137 Officials claimed that these two ventures 'gave proof of the vigorous quality of the national theatre, its tenacity in preparation and its brilliance in achievement' (CEMA, *The Fifth Year*, p. 5). Commentators made it clear that 'it is a long time since two Shakespearean productions of such stature as the *Hamlet* at the Haymarket and *Richard III* at the New could be seen in London at the same time' (Stephens, Frances. 'Over the Footlights.' *Theatre World* November 1944: p. 5).

138 From the mid-nineteenth century left-wing politicians and Chartists referred to the Bard in their struggle for social justice. The 1864 Tercentenary especially provided an opportunity to reclaim Shakespeare for popular culture, an attempt which was in fact 'typical of many similar ceremonies honouring national poets and dramatists throughout Europe at this time' – e.g. the Schiller 1859 centenary in Germany 'which sought to elevate national traditions, whilst creating an icon of transcendent genius with which all Germans could identify' (Taylor, Antony. 'Shakespeare and Radicalism: The Uses and Abuses of Shakespeare in Nineteenth-Century Popular Politics.' *The Historical Journal* 45 (2002): p. 373. See also Foulkes, Richard. *The Shakespeare Tercentenary 1864*. London: The Society for Theatre Research, 1984). During the 1930s it was especially the Russian émigré Komisarjevsky who 'was palpably aware of the connection between the theatre and the new ideologies' (Howard, Tony. 'Blood and the Bright Young Things: Shakespeare in the 1930s.' Barker, Clive and Gale, Maggie B. eds. *The British Theatre between the Wars 1918–1939*. Cambridge: Cambridge University Press, 2000. p. 152).

139 Whitworth, *National Theatre*, p. 144.

140 Commentators stressed that after the defeat of the Armada 'England was no longer to be subservient to continental influence … but, … must function as unity, as herself. Immediately a new excitement, a new life, was felt, and that life speaks to us to-day in the words of Shakespeare. To those words England must always return in times of peril' (Wilson Knight, G. *This Sceptred Isle. Shakespeare's Message for England at War*. Oxford: Blackwell, 1940. p. 1).

141 Headline to Harold Hobson's article reviewing Olivier's *Richard II* at the New, which had by then already attracted record audiences of 37,000 people, in *Christian Science Monitor*, 29 November 1944.

Knight claimed that England from time to time 'has to hurl back invaders from "less happier lands": in Shakespeare's time the Spanish Armada; in Nelson's, the armies of Napoleon; and in ours, the embattled legions of Hitler. Today the test is sterner than ever, the seas more vast and turbulent, and, as London itself, like a great ocean liner, weathers the storm and lightning of aerial bombardment, one can feel the soul of England buffetted [*sic*], swaying, but undeflected' (Knight, *Sceptred Isle*, p. 35).

142 See *Theatre Arts* 24 (1940): p. 767.

143 See, for example, Tallents, Stephen. *The Projection of England*. London: Faber, 1932. p. 14.

144 The *Bulletin* claimed that people 'have grown tired of the society comedies and of realistic dramas that deal with the external trivialities of life'. They were looking for a 'deeper significance' (*Bulletin from Britain*. no. 26, week ending 26 February 1941: p. 1).

145 See 'New Plays in Town.' *Theatre World* July 1941: p. 4.

146 See Farjeon, *Shakespearean Stage*, pp. 55–6. Regarding Thorndike see Fawkes, Richard. *Fighting for a Laugh. Entertaining the British and American Forces 1939–1946*. London: Macdonald & Jane, 1978. p. 71. Although this study is not concerned with cinema it should be noted that Shakespeare also inspired wartime propaganda films such as *Henry V* (1944), which reminded audiences of Britain's historic successes in invading the continent. Another example is *Richard II*, which provided no fewer than three film titles alone: *This England* (1941), *The Demi-Paradise* (1943) and *This Happy Breed* (1944) (see Taylor, Philip M. *Munitions of the Mind. War Propaganda from the Ancient World to the Nuclear Age*. Wellingborough: Stephens, 1990. p. 143. See also Aldgate, Anthony and Richards, Jeffrey. *Britain Can Take It. The British Cinema in the Second World War*. Oxford: Blackwell, 1986; Chapman, James. *The British at War. Cinema, State and Propaganda, 1939–1945*. London: Tauris, 1998; and Taylor, Philip M. *Britain and the Cinema in the Second World War*. London: Macmillan, 1988).

CHAPTER FOUR

Theatre Repertoires in Westphalia

The character of the repertoire determines the nature of theatre.
Hermann Christian Mettin[1]

According to the above axiom we should expect German repertoires to mirror the idea of theatre as an educational institution, with programmes dominated by the classics and modern drama alongside contemporary political and avant-garde plays and some civilised comedies. Musical theatre, certainly, with works by Wagner and Verdi, but no musical comedies, revues or farces. In addition, given the distinct identities projected by the cities in question, we should expect repertoires characterised by differing emphases on particular genres.[2] However, although the theatres tried to distinguish themselves from one another, their repertoires were surprisingly similar. Dortmund's mainly working-class and Protestant population wanted to see classical drama represented on the local stage, just as Münster's largely middle-class and Catholic residents did.[3] And although Bochum was a city dominated by heavy industry, *Intendant* Saladin Schmitt produced an ambitious programme of classical drama. Civic authorities and largely bourgeois audiences generated demands on the theatres which were very similar in the different cities: the canon required was to be worthy of a 'representative' theatre with grand opera and uplifting drama. These demands, therefore, cast the first doubt on the assumption formulated above, regarding avant-garde and political drama. And, indeed, a first look at the programmes immediately shows that repertoires were conservative rather than revolutionary, conventional rather than experimental – even during the Weimar Republic and in contrast to claims by many scholars who make no distinction between avant-garde experiments in Berlin and the often rather anti-modernist attitudes in the provinces.[4] But what about the other assumptions? How far do Westphalian playhouses fulfil their claim to be institutions of high culture, education and edification? Corresponding to the focus of this study, it will also be especially interesting to see to what extent the political changes in 1933 and 1939 affected the repertoire.

THE WEIMAR YEARS

As a theatre of average size, Münster's *Städtische Bühnen* employed an average of twenty actors, five producers, twenty-four singers (soloists for opera and operetta), ten ballet dancers, a chorus plus an additional amateur choir of forty-eight persons, the municipal orchestra, five directors of music, one prompter, two stage managers, one painter, two lighting technicians, one set designer and one costume designer.[5] A typical season's programme consisted of about fifty productions. Normally, plays made up more than half of the productions, with opera and operetta each occupying between a fifth and a quarter of the repertoire. The number of performances reached around 500 each season, which normally lasted from September to May or June the following year.

Immediately after the First World War had ended, Westphalia's theatres were eager to live up to the expectation of them as institutions of high culture. During 1918–19 Münster staged an impressive thirty-nine plays, twenty-one operas and ten operettas, including three first productions.[6] Bochum started equally ambitious. Saladin Schmitt presented an average of thirty new productions each season during his first years – a premiere almost every week.[7] These figures also indicate that audiences demanded a wide variety of plays and managers were anxious to present novelties in order to prevent audiences from feeling compelled to watch the same play twice. In Bielefeld patrons expected at least one new play each week.[8] Their new status as civic theatres only enhanced their cultural claims. Whereas the prime concern of British regional theatres was to distinguish themselves from the glossy cinema as well as the boisterous music halls, the demands on German civic theatres were different. By 1924 all Westphalian playhouses had become municipal endeavours, they had been taken over into public ownership, and everyone working in the theatres had suddenly become a civil servant. Regional playhouses, it seems, had finally arrived at a stage where they were able to fulfil both Lessing's and

Schiller's demands for an educational, uplifting and 'moral' repertoire.

The dramatic repertoire

A close look at these repertoires, however, reveals that the programmes only rarely corresponded with these claims. Classical drama, for example, occupied an important but not a prominent position. As a theatre of typical size, Münster, out of an average total of twenty-five plays produced each season, presented about six classics: one or two plays by Shakespeare, one or two by Schiller, one by Goethe or another German classic (often Hebbel or Kleist), and sometimes Calderón, Goldoni or Molière. The share in the overall productions of about 15 per cent, however, stood in some contrast to the lower share in the number of performances, which sometimes only reached half that figure.

The number of modern classics staged at Westphalian theatres was generally lower and dominated by Naturalist playwrights with nearly always a Scandinavian dramatist featuring alongside Hauptmann and Shaw. The most interesting findings are to be encountered in connection with contemporary political plays. Generally speaking, these plays were more likely to be produced if they were right-wing, and from 1931 *völkisch* plays reached the stage in numbers. By contrast, left-wing and avant-garde drama, often regarded as one of the backbones of Weimar repertoires, only played a marginal role and productions were confined to the years 1929 to 1933.[9] Another surprising finding is the dominant role contemporary comedies played in the repertoire. Comedies, farces, thrillers and other purely amusing pieces gained in popularity and by the end of the 1920s generally made up at least a third of all the productions.[10] This prominent role not only contradicts contemporary as well as recent claims regarding theatre programmes being dominated by 'high culture', but it is also an interesting parallel to Yorkshire. This parallel, however, is not only a question of genre but also of individual plays as Westphalian theatres staged numerous comedies by British dramatists, among them Brandon Thomas, Edgar Wallace, Arnold Ridley, Edward Childs Carpenter, William Somerset Maugham, Frederick Lonsdale, Noel Coward and St John Ervine.[11] During 1930-1 and 1931-2 Münster's *Städtische Bühnen*, for example, produced four British comedies each season.[12] Given these points of contact it even seems fair to assume that, apart from one or two classics and some contemporary dramas, repertoires at Westphalian theatres of the early 1930s would have been a success in Yorkshire, too.[13]

The musical repertoire

These parallels, however, only concern the dramatic repertoire; the musical programme was a different matter. Music had traditionally received substantial attention, and operetta proved especially popular. On the whole, opera and operetta reached higher attendance figures than plays. We have to note, however, that the musical repertoire, too, was traditional and modern 'experiments' were avoided.[14] The interesting results, which can be gained from a differentiation between production and performance figures, are illustrated in the fact that opera evoked much less audience interest than operetta. During the 1931–2 season at Münster, for example, the shares of opera and operetta productions each made up slightly more than 20 per cent in the overall number of productions. Regarding the performances, however, operettas fared much better: their share in all the performances reached 37 per cent in comparison to a meagre 13 per cent share for operas.[15]

On average the operatic repertoire at regional theatres (provided they had an opera ensemble) consisted of twelve operas per season.[16] The pillars of the programme were Wagner, Verdi and Mozart. Aside from that, theatres regularly produced Puccini, Rossini, Bizet, Lortzing and Mascagni/Leoncavallo, and frequently pieces by Gluck, Beethoven, Offenbach, Cornelius, Strauß, Weber, d'Albert, Donizetti and Gounod. Contemporary works were rarely featured and, if they were, their success was minimal. In any case, they only stood a chance of more than one performance if their score was based on late romantic rather than modern music.[17]

The operetta repertoire is particularly interesting because they not only remained favourites with German audiences when they had long lost their appeal to musicals and musical comedies on Anglo-American stages, their popularity even rose. Regular favourites were pieces of the Viennese tradition (Strauß, Lehár, Millöcker, Zeller), the Berlin school (Lincke, Künnecke), and contemporary works by Abraham, Kálmán, Fall, Benatzky and Stolz. These contemporary pieces, however, rarely reflected modern ideas in composing and were based on the tradition of the classical operetta. Operettas and musicals based on truly modern scores with either jazz or atonal 'experiments', such as the works by Krenek, Weill or Dessau, stood little chance of entering regional repertoires.

Context

Westphalian theatres increasingly played in a different 'league' from their Yorkshire counterparts concerning both the quantity and the quality especially of their musical programmes, but theatres in both countries were characterised by largely similar repertoires. Although Münster in the mid-1920s presented long forgotten monumental Händel operas and staged avant-garde dance performances in opulent settings, and Bochum organised its colossal annual *Festwochen*, these productions were the highlights of otherwise quite conventional programmes. Hardly any *Intendant* tried his hand with experimental pieces.[18] The pillars of German regional repertories during the 1920s were not Shakespeare and Brecht but comedies and farces – as in Britain. Throughout a period in German history which experienced some of the most radical artistic developments, both the musical and the dramatic repertoires at Westphalian theatres showed a remarkable stability. Essentially, the Weimar years seem to have generated only two important developments: the appearance of nationalistic and *völkisch* plays and a short period of dramatic experiment around 1930.

Changes in the late 1920s

Right-wing drama entered Westphalian stages before the economic crisis precipitated by the Wall Street Crash. As early as 1927–8, during the 'prosperous' middle years of the Weimar Republic, Westphalian audiences were treated to their first nationalistic play, Alfred Neumann's *Der Patriot*.[19] During the 1931–2 season *völkisch* plays reached the repertoire in numbers, and their share increased further in 1932–3.[20] During this season right-wing drama made up nine per cent of all the productions and generated 12 per cent of the ticket sales in Münster.

Contemporary plays by left-wing playwrights only seem to have stood a chance if they were comedies, or at least this was the case until 1929.[21] Only after that, and just for one or two seasons, did

Westphalian theatres present some avant-garde and left-wing plays. Although it is remarkable that dramatists like Sherriff, Hasenclever, Kaiser, Wedekind and Brecht did eventually reach the stage, it is also telling that both Dortmund's Gsell and Münster's Bernau, for example, originally had far more radical plans.[22] The revised repertoire – although, or perhaps *because*, it did only vaguely correspond to the concept of 'Weimar culture' – was successful with patrons and attendance figures rose.[23] The fear of losing especially the precious season ticket holders was certainly not the only reason for the rather brief encounter with avant-garde plays during the Weimar years, yet this incident nevertheless indicates that audiences had a substantial influence even at subsidised theatres. In any case, after this short period of experiments, Westphalian theatres returned to their established and conventional repertoire for the 1931–2 season.[24]

THE THIRD REICH

The year 1933 did not only mark a change in political terms, it also heralded radical transformations in Germany's cultural life as theatre and drama took centre stage in Nazi propaganda.[25] Supporters as well as critics of the Nazis, therefore, expected the take-over to have massive implications for the theatre, and the regime's protagonists stressed the importance and imminence of radical change. In what way, then, were the repertoires at Westphalian theatres affected by the take-over and the beginning of the 'Thousand Year Reich'?

Take-over

The appointment of the Hitler cabinet came half-way through the 1932–3 season, which, as mentioned earlier, was already featuring a number of nationalistic plays, and it had an immediate effect. The First World War play *Battle on the Marne* by Paul Cremers and *Ostmark*, a drama about 'Germanic Austria', by Berthold Withalm appeared on Westphalian stages, the Nazi 'Stage of the Militant League' started to exercise an increasing influence by producing its own plays as well as by booking whole performances for its members, and the new city administrations organised visits by school parties to some of the nationalistic plays. At the same time, however, Münster's theatre opened an evening with one-act plays by Arthur Schnitzler and Stefan

Zweig on 8 February 1933 and performed it successfully until the end of the season, while Dortmund's playhouse still produced Lessing's *Nathan the Wise*.[26] Equally inconsistent with claims of a radical change in the repertoire is the vast number of quite un-heroic comedies and farces, which were produced after the take-over, and the musical programme, too, remained traditional. In fact, the overall character of the programmes did not change after January 1933 – at least not until the beginning of the new season.[27]

After the new Nazi administrations in Westphalia's cities had settled in and support for the theatres had become top priority, over the summer money poured into renovation programmes and propaganda campaigns (see above). Expectations were high, the Nazis – justifiably, it seemed – claimed the dawning of a new era and the ground was prepared for a truly nationalistic and *völkisch* programme, which the new managers were keen to deliver. They intended to concentrate on plays about symbolic struggles of heroic characters, wanted to 'shape the beliefs' of the audience and promised not to 'torment patrons with problem plays'.[28] The programme notes featured countless ideological articles by representatives of the new regime to demonstrate unanimous support.[29] In obvious accordance with the claim of a total shake-up, the common ground of these articles was their call for a radically new repertoire. If we take all these articles, speeches and announcements at face value it seems fair to assume that Westphalia's theatres were turned into propaganda stages with the start of the 1933–4 season – taken over by Nazi personnel, Nazi ideology, and Nazi drama. To put this assumption to the test it will prove helpful to look at this first season in greater detail.

The first 'National' Season

Regarding changes in personnel, we find that a substantial number of employees left Westphalian theatres at the end of the 1932–3 season. Left-wing and 'non-Aryan' staff were made redundant, most of them immediately after the take-over and often under dubious circumstances. Most of the changes, however, had no political background and were due to people moving on. This was not uncommon at the beginning of a new season and new managers in particular brought members of their old casts with them. Ultimately, however, new appointments could only be made after theatre administrations had made sure that the candidate was politically 'reliable'. In August 1938, for example, the theatre painter Alfred Moritz was appointed to Bielefeld's theatre only after the police and the Nazi district authorities had endorsed his application.[30]

The second aspect of the representation of Nazi ideology concerns the question of dramatic theory. Theorists, practitioners and politicians agreed on the need for radical change and on the decadence of the Weimar years, but, crucially, failed to formulate a positive counter-theory.[31] Agreement was only reached on a few general ideas, chief among them the idea that the new drama should be characterised by a super-elevation of the dramatic action.[32] Otherwise the intense discussions hardly led to any results.[33] Despite numerous attempts, which continued up to the last days of the war, a genuine National Socialist dramatic theory was never formulated.[34] And perhaps even worse for the theorists was the fact that the repertoires hardly reflected their discussions about dramatic theory. This failure made it vital not only for Westphalia's theatre managements but also for the party and municipal authorities to present a repertoire dominated by nationalistic and *völkisch* plays – a genre which at least in some ways reflected aspects of the Nazi ideology.[35] And this is exactly what the new managers did during the 1933–4 season. Münster, for example, produced seven *völkisch* plays, an impressive twenty per cent share in the overall number of productions. *Völkisch* plays received extended press coverage and Nazi organisations took out block bookings.[36] The elaborate propaganda which accompanied the season's start, added to a general feeling of the dawning of a new era.

Without exception, however, Westphalian theatre experienced a fiasco during the 1933–4 season. It not only failed to live up to the high expectations, but also in most cases it did not even compare favourably to the preceding seasons, which had, after all, been portrayed as 'decadent' and against which the new theatre was to stand out. In terms of quantity, no Westphalian theatre was able to raise the number of productions significantly; and in terms of quality the share of purely amusing pieces did not decrease – in fact, it was to the contrary. More importantly, the share of 'uplifting' *völkisch* drama was not in any way substantial enough to claim the beginning of a new era.[37] The assertion that the 'National Revolution' would immediately set free muted creative and innovative powers could not be sustained either – neither during the first season after the take-over nor during any of the following seasons – with most of the *völkisch* plays remaining surprisingly traditional. Parallel to increasing general attempts to place the Nazi movement firmly in the middle-class establishment in order to get rid of its rough image, the majority of the *völkisch* authors dramatised 'safe' historical topics.[38] Worse still, most plays were entirely constructed around theoretical concepts and were characterised by their lack of theatricality. Apart from this, most of the *völkisch* drama produced was not new and had been written long before 1933.[39] Münster is a case in point. Out of the seven nationalistic and *völkisch* plays featured in 1933–4 only three were recent works, three dated from the 1920s and one was written by a Swiss.[40] On top of that, and even more disturbing for the new administration, was the fact that their success was poor. The 20 per cent share of the plays in the overall number of productions marked a strong contrast to the 11 per cent they reached in the performance figures. In fact only Friedrich Förster's nationalistic drama *All Against One, One for All*, which was heavily promoted by the 'German Stage' and other official bodies, reached a satisfactory number of performances.[41] Audiences in general were disappointingly low, the quality of the productions poor, and the standard of the *völkisch* plays appalling. Bielefeld's press criticised the new drama (Forster's *Widukind* and Frenssen's *Geert Brügge*) as unconvincing and un-dramatic.[42] In Hagen in 1936–7 no play generated less audience interest than Burte's *Katte*. For shows, which were not part of the season ticket, the theatre normally sold between 200 and 300 tickets, for popular operettas as many as 900. *Katte* only generated ticket sales of seventy-four. The administration even linked the decline in the number of season ticket holders to the fact that 'the artistic quality – in particular regarding the dramatic repertoire – had been going down'.[43] And following audience protests against Eduard Kiss' *Wittekind* the production was called off after only a few performances.[44]

Looking through the repertoire of the first 'national' season it is interesting to note that contrary to expectations it is characterised by a relative stability rather than by radical changes. The outlook of both the opera and the operetta repertoires are similar to any Weimar season.[45] All the classical works, the modern classics and the comedies could have appeared during the 1920s, too. In fact there are only three more or less significant changes to take effect after 1933. The first is the remarkable increase in the production of *völkisch* pieces, the second is the disappearance of left-wing plays. Put into perspective, however, we realise that these changes did not represent radical breaks with the past. *Völkisch* plays had been produced since the late 1920s and left-wing drama had never played a significant role on regional stages.[46] The third change is subtler and was probably not realised by everyone. It was, however, the most far-reaching development of all. All works by Jewish composers and dramatists were banned immediately after the take-over. In Münster, this prohibition would only have affected four works of the 1932–3 seasons, but it would have banned fourteen pieces of the 1931–2 and fifteen pieces out the 1930-1 seasons – in both years, therefore, around 25 per cent of all the productions.[47] It is in this area that Nazi politics were most effective and left a lasting mark.[48]

Still, the attempts by theatre managers to celebrate the beginning of the 'new era' with an array of *völkisch* plays not only proved highly unpopular and fatal to the further career of some of them, it also remained a singular event. No German theatre dared to repeat the obvious mistakes of the first season and, as a result, the share of *völkisch* plays decreased considerably after that. One could even claim with some justification that the theatres increasingly returned to a repertoire which was not too different from the Weimar years. Goebbels was furious and admitted that the theatrical start into the 'Thousand Year Reich' had been far from satisfactory.[49] It is interesting to note, however, that from the mid-1930s the politicisation of the repertoires did not feature on the regime's agenda any longer. Rainer Schlösser claimed in 1935 that the German classics, the classics of world literature and entertaining plays were the essential ingredients of a successful repertoire; *völkisch* drama was not mentioned any more.[50]

'Normalisation'

As indicated, the regime's focus on the theatre had changed by the mid-1930s and a new type of manager was required to achieve one thing in particular: record attendances. Managers like Münster's Hanke, Bielefeld's Kruchen and Dortmund's Hoenselaars, who took over the respective managements in the mid-1930s, seem to have been prototypes of this new breed of *Intendanten*. They managed to attract these large audiences, however, with a different repertoire.

Nationalistic and *völkisch* drama was still staged but to a much lesser extent. At Münster it hardly ever reached more than five per cent of both the production and the performance figures – a reduction of 75 per cent concerning the former and nearly 50 per cent in the latter in comparison to 1933–4.[51] Dortmund hardly presented any propaganda plays at all after 1933–4 and fared especially well with fairy-tales such as *Brownies*, farces like *Row in the Annexe* and operettas. At the same time, the detailed lists of production and performance figures, which the Dortmund management regularly provided to the Propaganda Ministry, indicate that, ultimately, in a city like Dortmund, the regime was not worried about a popular programme as long as the theatre attracted substantial audiences.[52] The city administration even took it upon themselves to suggest that the theatre better accept that 'on putting together the programme one has to take into consideration that Dortmund's audiences desire a more folksy repertoire'.[53] Similar problems were encountered in Bielefeld, although audiences here differed from working-class Dortmund. In meticulous reports composed for the Propaganda Ministry the theatre management commented on bookings for every production and grudgingly noted that 'good' attendances were more likely to be achieved with comedies and farces than with classical plays, whose audiences were more likely to be 'average'.[54] Although some of the remaining *völkisch* productions were accompanied by massive propaganda, public interest remained meagre.[55]

Changed approaches to propaganda

This does not mean, however, that managers refrained from any propaganda, but they used subtler forms of influencing instead.[56] To achieve this, for example with classical plays, they had different methods at their disposal. First, they could leave out the works of some classical dramatists and concentrate on others. The plays by Goethe, for example, were rarely produced, but Schiller regularly played.[57] Grabbe, whose monumental dramas were deemed heroic, experienced the most remarkable revival.[58] Some theatres even produced Grabbe's fragmentary drama *Marius and Sulla* in combination with Hanns Johst's nationalistic play *The Loner* in order to make the 'new' spirit absolutely clear.[59] Second, managers could work with new translations of Elizabethan drama, Greek tragedies and modern classics. Many produced Ibsen's *Peer Gynt* in the 'free' translation by Dietrich Eckart, who had been Hitler's mentor in the early 1920s.[60] Oscar Wilde's *Lady Windermere's Fan* received a similar treatment. The aim of the new translation by Karl Lerbs was to make the text 'compatible' with the regime.[61] With Shakespeare, however, the question of 'correct' translations became a matter of national importance, given the role the Bard had been playing on the German stage.[62] As a third possibility, managers could leave out certain parts of certain plays or put emphasis on particular scenes or characters. One of the best examples is, of course, Shylock in Shakespeare's *The Merchant of Venice*.[63] Fourth, the choice of works by certain dramatists could make all the difference. Lessing's *Nathan the Wise* was clearly avoided but his *Minna von Barnhelm* often staged.

In this respect the question of interpretation, of staging a play, became crucial. Programme notes frequently featured articles which either commented generally on how to interpret classical plays in a National Socialist sense, or were directly related to actual productions, to ensure that patrons read them in the intended way and understood the underlying message. One of these articles in Münster's programme notes deals with Hebbel's *Agnes Bernauer*. The author stresses the idea

> that the individual, magnificent and great, noble and kind as it may be, under all circumstances has to subordinate itself to society, because in society and in its formal manifestation, the state, all human beings live, whereas in the individual only a small portion of society is able to blossom.[64]

In a quite similar way, the production of Ibsen's *Pillars of Society* is introduced to Münster's audiences as a play which has to be interpreted in the 'spirit of our times':

> The task of the adaptation was to remove the doctrinal socialist ideas in order to put more emphasis on the struggle for social stability with regard to the kind of community socialism, which Ibsen definitely had in mind.[65]

But managers did not only make demands on classical plays, even comedies were used to transport *völkisch* ideas. Alois Johannes Lippl's comedy *Die Pfingstorgel*, for example, would not deal with 'personal' problems but with 'typical' human characters, with farms, villages and rural landscape; and as 'the audience is carefully but deliberately injected with the ideology, one can not escape it, and as the ideology is valuable, the outcome is good and right, too'.[66]

This idea seems to have already been applied in the first 'national' season. The ban on comedies by Jewish dramatists made it vital that replacements (*Ersatzdramatik*) were found. Comedies and farces by dramatists whose political allegiance was beyond doubt were particularly welcome.[67] What mattered was not so much the plot but the ideology behind it. The ultimate consequence of this concept was that any play became a possible carrier of ideas – providing it received the right treatment by a clever director. Some contemporary theorists even claimed that the transmission of ideology worked better with seemingly apolitical comedies because audiences would not expect any attempt to influence them.[68]

These findings, however, should not be generalised. Not all plays were interpreted in a *völkisch* sense. The reasons for this were often quite banal and linked to the production methods at German provincial theatres. Especially with productions which had been in the repertoire for a long time, it is unlikely that casts could rehearse new interpretations quickly. And it had to be quick, due to the repertory system, which demanded the production of a substantial number of plays each season.[69] Additionally, it is doubtful whether the productions actually reflected the ideas mentioned in the articles.[70] It is even possible that these articles were deliberately included in the programme notes to justify the production of seemingly pointless comedies and farces and establish some link to a political agenda.[71]

Stressing continuities

Theatre history and the classics

Some aspects of continuity between the Weimar Republic and the Third Reich regarding the repertoire have already been mentioned. The most important aspect is probably the fact that the Nazis never challenged the role of theatre as a cultural and educational institution. On the contrary, they increasingly stressed this function and tried to profit from a rich theatrical heritage not only in order to establish a feeling of continuity but also to recommend themselves to the establishment as a cultured leadership.[72] The crucial role which was attributed to the theatre and the extent to which it was funded by the state are indeed singular in German history.[73] In line with this official support and the idea of stressing continuing elements rather than revolutionary tendencies, the regime increasingly fostered the production of classical drama, and even more so since the *völkisch* plays had failed so disastrously. Politicians, theorists and practitioners were, therefore, anxious to establish close links to the great classics. They claimed, for example, that Lessing's idea of the National Theatre was only being truly fulfilled in the Third Reich or that Schiller, had he lived in the present, 'would certainly have been the poetic pioneer of our revolution'.[74]

Regional theatres quickly took up these ideas and established links to their own 'glorious' heritage and classical dramatists or composers in order to place their local playhouse in the context of Germany's theatrical tradition as a whole. As mentioned before, the programme notes, too, moved away from the present and avoided references to contemporaries. Instead, a continuity from ancient Greece via Shakespeare and the classics to the present day was stressed and accompanied a similar concentration in the repertoire. Münster's Karl Immermann, for example, not only regularly featured in the programme notes as an important nineteenth-century theatre manager, with which Münster claimed to have had a close connection,[75] the theatre also produced his play *The Prince of Syracuse* – although without much success. Westphalian theatres felt particularly entitled to claim Grabbe's oeuvre because of his Westphalian origin.[76] High importance was attached to their participation in the prestigious Grabbe Festivals, which offered the possibility to stress the connection between Grabbe's 'legacy' and National Socialism.[77] Ultimately, commentators claimed, the commitment to Grabbe was a commitment to the 'German cause'.[78] These demands were no exception as new roles were attributed to many classical dramatists. Schiller played a particularly important role as the 'national poet'. The Propaganda Ministry asked to use the character of Talbot in Schiller's *Joan of Arc*, for example, to present Britain as materialistic and hostile to new ideas.[79]

With regard to the scope of this study, it is especially interesting to examine the role of Shakespeare. It has already been mentioned that productions of Shakespearean drama have a long tradition in Germany. In contrast to the virtual neglect of his works on British stages after the First World War, Shakespeare had always been regarded as an integral part of the canon in Germany.[80] Despite some attempts by radical Nazi theorists to prove his 'un-Germanness', Shakespeare's presence in the repertoire was never really questioned. On the contrary, there were constant efforts to incorporate Shakespeare in the *völkisch* ideology and interpret him as the archetypal Germanic playwright.[81] Even during the war, Shakespeare was still performed all over Germany.[82] Although theatres had to apply for permission from March 1941, this seems to have been regularly granted.[83] The fact that an application had to be written, however, seems to have put many theatres off, as performances of Shakespeare's plays generally declined in the course of the war. Münster did not produce any Shakespeare after 1939–40, and neither Dortmund nor Hagen tackled a Shakespearean play at all during the war. This information, however, has to be seen in context. The theatres in Dortmund and Hagen had never produced much Shakespeare and were hardly affected either by the take-over or the 1941 decree. And the municipal theatre in Bielefeld is a perfect example of the fact that if you wanted to perform Shakespeare you could: apart from 1940–1 the theatre produced Shakespeare in every season until the end of the war. In other ways, too, Westphalian theatres mirrored national trends, in particular regarding the attempts to 'Germanify' him. In 1939–40, for example, Münster produced *A Midsummer Night's Dream* with new music composed by Wolfgang Rössler, as Mendelssohn's famous stage music was now banned.[84] The crucial translation question is mirrored in Münster, too. Both the 1932–3 and 1934–5 productions of *Measure for Measure* and *The Tempest* made use of the controversial Rothe translations, whereas the 1936–7 production of *As You Like It* appeared in the traditional Wolf Graf Baudissin translation – immediately after Goebbels had banned the Rothe translations. Both of these examples clearly illustrate that theatre managers keenly followed official directives; possibilities for disobedience or resistance were not seized.[85]

Demands on modern classics

In line with this approach, the regime also made demands on modern classics like Ibsen, Shaw and Hauptmann, although the situation in this genre was more delicate and the official position subject to change. Despite the theoretical discourse being characterised by a near-unanimous rejection of Naturalism, the regime was anxious to incorporate Naturalist dramatists into their ideology, and many authors, if they were still alive, happily lent their support. As with the classics, however, the choice was crucial. Whereas the oeuvre of Scandinavian authors could easily be interpreted as 'Nordic', the regime felt uneasy with the German Naturalists Hermann Sudermann and Gerhart Hauptmann, especially regarding their early work. Emphasis was laid on uncontroversial plays such as Sudermann's *Saint John's Fire* or Hauptmann's comedy *Beaver Coat*. Both plays were officially supported during the Third Reich, and Sudermann's play was even turned into a film. In producing such fare, therefore, managers did not challenge the party line but moved on safe terrain. Instead of taking risks by choosing plays which did not directly conform to official directives, the vast majority of regional theatre managers played safe. It is interesting to note that other Naturalists such as Hermann Bahr or Max Halbe were less controversial as their plays could be incorporated in the 'Blood and Soil' concept. Additionally, the regime was at pains to reach a *modus vivendi* with Hauptmann, who had received the Nobel Prize for literature in 1912, and whom they needed to supply them with a cultural façade. On the other hand, Hauptmann had been a prominent advocate of the Weimar Republic. A special test case, therefore, was Hauptmann's eightieth birthday in 1942, which the regime celebrated but tried to keep as low key as possible. The Propaganda Ministry made it quite clear that it did not wish to see any productions of Hauptmann's early plays such as *The Weavers, Drayman Henschel* or *Elga*. At the same time the regime was willing to exploit Hauptmann's fame shamelessly. Rainer Schlösser supported the idea of performing Hauptmann's plays all over occupied Europe as this was 'propagandistically fruitful, because on the one hand productions of his plays would contribute to the greater glory of German intellectual spirit, and on the other foreigners would have to agree that they were not subjected to propaganda'.[86] Germany's theatres marked Hauptmann's birthday, but were anxious not to get into conflict with official policy as they avoided his early plays and concentrated on his comedies or other officially sanctioned plays instead.

Westphalia's theatres both reflected these demands and illustrated the continuing inconsistencies. Dortmund, Bielefeld, Hagen and Münster all produced Hauptmann's *Beaver Coat*. On the occasion of his birthday in 1942 Münster's theatre duly honoured Hauptmann with a matinee, but avoided any mention of his pre-1933 fame and even claimed that he had only reached his true stature during the Third Reich.[87] On the other hand, both Bochum and Dortmund staged Hauptmann's *Drayman Henschel* as part of the celebrations, and during the late 1930s both Dortmund and Hagen had presented *Elga* – plays which the Propaganda Ministry had clearly asked theatres to avoid.

Problems, inconsistencies and the foreign repertoire

There were, however, two problems. First, the classics and modern classics never developed into the mainstay of repertoires. The idea of exchanging the failed *völkisch* plays for uplifting classics did not work. Their share in the productions all through the 1930s remained at a level already achieved during the Weimar years, or even below that. Comedies and farces, which in their majority the Nazis could not claim to be morally uplifting, not only remained the dominant fare but also grew increasingly important. The second problem concerned the foreign repertoire and was potentially even more disturbing, especially after the failures of *völkisch* drama and *Thing* plays. The proclaimed concentration on the German dramatic heritage leads to the assumption that – apart from Shakespeare and some 'Nordic' playwrights – the foreign repertoire was completely banned with immediate effect after 1933. Theatres would surely have avoided any works by Wilde, Pinero, and especially Shaw. And, indeed, the lively critical debate leaves no doubt as to the aim of eliminating every 'un-German' influence. Wolf Braumüller asserted that Molière, Sardou and Pailleron were 'dated and fuddy-duddy' and rejected Shaw's plays because they did not even 'possess an antiquarian quality for the contemporary German stage'.[88] Hanns Johst stressed the idea that German authors always ranked higher than foreign dramatists and that the repertoires had to reflect this fact. 'Domination' by foreign works was not acceptable.[89] Claims by Otto Laubinger that the regime would still encourage productions of foreign plays seemed nothing more than half-hearted attempts to appease foreign critics.[90]

Again, however, the discrepancy between demands and reality becomes obvious in a close examination of the actual repertoires, as the share of foreign plays remained substantial. In 1938 Schlösser produced a dossier on the 'foreign infiltration of the Berlin repertoires', which showed that earlier claims of 'purification' had not been fulfilled, and which certainly outraged Goebbels. The dossier stated that one-third of all opera performances had been foreign works, mostly by Italian composers, although Verdi and Puccini would not be a 'problem'. Schlösser complained that 'apart from the *Staatsoper* ... no opera house produces works by contemporary composers'. Although the operetta programme was 'nearly one hundred per cent German', the dramatic repertoire showed a high percentage of foreign pieces (between 35 per cent in April and 75 per cent in October) even if 'dramatists such as Shakespeare, Ibsen and Björnson [were] counted as German'. Popular plays by English-speaking authors included works by Oscar Wilde, Bernard Shaw, Somerset Maugham and Laurence Housman.[91] Apart from this, the positions in the theoretical debate remained far from undivided. Corresponding to other fields in the arts, agreement on which foreign dramatists and composers were acceptable was never reached. Hinkel, for example, regularly disagreed with Schlösser on Meyerbeer and Offenbach whose works the National Dramaturge wanted to ban (apart from *Tales of Hoffmann*, of course). Hinkel, however, defended his different, more liberal, view.

Given the scope of this study, Shaw is an especially interesting case. From the mid-1920s the number of performances of Shavian plays had increased all over Germany. Indeed, he was so popular that the Nazi authorities did not dare to ban his plays although, as a British Socialist openly criticising dictatorial regimes and even Hitler personally, Shaw was certainly not popular with the Nazi elite. Even *Geneva*, however, which openly caricatured Hitler as 'Battler' in a costume of Lohengrin, was never forbidden.[92] During the 1930s the continuing presence of Shavian plays in the repertoire was repeatedly attacked, but Goebbels did not want to risk a public outcry.[93] Instead, the regime presented Shaw either as Irish or as a modern classic or both to justify their decision.[94] This propaganda stunt, however, does not seem to have paid off as internal reports show that the general public continued to regard Shaw as an Englishman.[95] After the German attack on the Soviet Union, and as further critical remarks by Shaw and complaints by officials piled up in the Propaganda Ministry, Hitler himself decided that Shaw's plays should remain in the repertoire.[96] Although their production became subject to special permission by the National Dramaturge from March 1941 (as with Shakespeare) performances were still possible. As late as 1943 Dortmund was told that the National Dramaturge had no objections to either *Pygmalion* or *Candida*.[97] Even the delicate question of royalties was dealt with properly and payments went ahead – they were even raised in June 1939.[98]

It was not only Shaw, however, who remained in the repertoire, but other foreign dramatists enjoyed similar privileges. Westphalian theatres produced Wilde, Scribe and Sardou, and Münster's 1938–9 season alone featured two British modern classics.[99] Equally surprising is the fact that although French works were prohibited from 1939, Bizet's *Carmen* continued to be produced because it was simply too successful.[100] The possible claim that the regime only left all-time classics such as Bizet, Wilde and Shaw in the repertoire, however, does not correspond to reality either. Westphalian theatres produced plays by Ivor Novello, St John Ervine and Somerset Maugham and even obscure comedies by Lawrence Huxley right up to the war.[101] The interest in British drama especially remained a characteristic feature. During the 1930s Edward Stirling's Paris-based 'The English Players' toured Westphalia and produced plays in English.[102] Goebbels eventually used the outbreak of the war to ban all contemporary Polish, French and English plays.[103] This does not mean, however, that foreign plays disappeared altogether. Although the Propaganda Ministry had intended to monitor the situation closely and asked theatres to inform the National Dramaturge about every single foreign play they wanted to produce, Goebbels soon dropped this idea and restricted it to premieres.[104] We can conclude, therefore, that although claims regarding a 'German' repertoire increased over the years and the share of foreign repertoire certainly declined, musical and dramatic pieces from outside Germany continued to play an important role in the repertoires.

Additional problems for theatre managements came with the unpredictable changes in official policy regarding foreign dramatists, which were subject to the general political climate. Anti-Polish plays, for example, which had been successful before and after the take-over, were suddenly forbidden after the German–Polish treaty of 1934. Spanish plays, on the other hand, reached the German stages in the course of the Spanish Civil War and Lope de Vega alongside Calderón experienced celebrated revivals. After the inauguration of the 'Steel Pact' in 1939 Italy was suddenly hailed as the new theatre-land, and

Dortmund's theatre duly organised a 'cycle' of contemporary Italian operas with works by Giordano, Ciléa, Zandonai, Camussi and Pedrollo.[105] For a brief period even Soviet plays were staged in the course of the 1939 agreement between Molotov and Ribbentrop. After the German attack on the Soviet Union the regime endorsed plays from Hitler's allied countries, especially Hungary, Bulgaria and Finland. And eventually Japan, too, became a dramatic treasure trove. These developments were mirrored on Westphalian stages. They produced *Autumn Fire* by the Italian playwright Gherardo Gherardi[106] and presented Ostrowski's *Late Love* during the brief period of appeasement between Germany and the Soviet Union, only to pay tribute a few months later to renewed anti-Soviet sentiments with the production of Reinecker's *The Village near Odessa*.[107] As far as the sudden interest in Japanese drama was concerned, they followed the trend immediately, too. Münster produced the 'ancient Japanese heroic drama' *The 47 Ronin* in the presence of the Japanese ambassador in 1942,[108] and Bielefeld presented 'the ancient Japanese' play *The Golden Dagger*.

Even in this sensitive area, however, Goebbels did struggle to secure total control. In a 1944 circular to thirty-five theatres he requested the production of *Paracelsus* by the Finnish dramatist Mika Waltari. The reasons for the push were clearly of a political nature, with Finland being an important wartime ally. Despite this urgency only five theatres answered the appeal and only two minor theatres thought about producing the piece.[109]

The musical repertoire

The operatic and operetta repertoire at Westphalia's theatres is another example of how little the Nazis achieved in developing genuine aesthetic concepts. At the same time, the strong conservative elements in the musical repertoire proved useful in connection with Nazi claims of fulfilling Germany's great cultural past.

Westphalian theatres produced the established classical repertoire in the opera, interspersed occasionally with some contemporary pieces, which, although not being modernist, can not be branded *völkisch* either – most of the works were simply late romantic.[110] Composers such as Carl Orff and Werner Egk combined their interest in folk melodies with modern connotations, which were often inspired by Stravinsky.[111] Parallel to the demands on classical drama, however, the Nazis tried to incorporate the classic operatic repertoire in their political agenda, too. One of their chief means was to commission new translations and adaptations especially of Mozart operas. Corresponding to the claim that Mozart was a German and not an Austrian composer, his Italian operas were translated into German. Some commentators, however, even criticised works that were already written in German and, for example relating to the production of Mozart's *Magic Flute*, lamented its 'unfortunate libretto'.[112] Siegfried Anheisser, backed by the radical Rosenberg circle, wrote a new 'authoritative' adaptation, which, however, was soon challenged by another version by Georg Schünemann. This had been commissioned by Goebbels, was based on the original autographs and appeared much less ideologically biased.[113] The effect these translations had is nearly impossible to measure. The fact, however, that adaptations were replaced so quickly by one another indicates that their influence was fairly limited. More interesting is the fact that, as with similar decisions at the highest political level, regional theatre managements were anxious to reflect the new demands. Whereas Münster, for example, in 1933–4 performed *Cosi fan Tutte* in Italian, *The Marriage of Figaro* was already produced in Anheisser's new adaptation during the following season,[114] and as soon as the Schünemann versions appeared they quickly replaced any older editions.[115] Despite these examples of allegiance, however, there were other cases where directives were clearly ignored. In a circular by the Reich Theatre Chamber from September 1940, for example, it was made clear that if theatres produced an opera with a libretto by a Jewish writer, they were not allowed to print the name on handouts or programme notes. Münster, however, did exactly that as late as 1944 and printed Lorenzo da Ponte's name alongside the announcement for *The Marriage of Figaro*.[116] Apart from these, the odd contemporary work, and – rarely – the recovery of a 'forgotten' piece, however, the opera repertoire in the provinces remained conventional[117] – and in fact very similar to the Weimar years.[118]

The operetta repertoire, however, was a different story. Many of the successful Weimar composers had been Jewish and after 1933 a search for new names began. Apart from the classic pieces by Johann Strauß and Franz Lehár, who remained the backbone of the programme and whose shares rose considerably, the repertoire changed drastically with an increasing number of works by contemporary composers.[119] In contrast to the *völkisch* plays, however, which audiences failed to support, it is interesting to see how quickly they accepted the new operettas, after the works by Emmerich Kálmán, Paul Abraham, Leo Fall, Jean Gilbert or Oscar Straus had been banned.[120] The new works by Oskar Nedbal and Walter Kollo achieved record attendances, and even pieces by more obscure composers such as Robert Winterberg and Walter Bromme fared reasonably well.[121] For example, 70 per cent of all operettas presented during Münster's 1935–6 season were pieces by contemporary composers.[122] The reason for their quick acceptance almost certainly lies in the fact that they did not differ much from the works they replaced. Music, setting and plot were similar, a happy ending, and a 'good night out' were guaranteed.

By the end of the 1930s, however, – and in many ways similar to the *völkisch* drama a few years earlier – the contemporary operetta became increasingly criticised for its alleged lack of quality and theatres duly returned to the classic Berlin and Vienna operetta of the late nineteenth century, with works by Johann Strauß, Franz von Suppé and Paul Lincke. Commentators now rejected contemporary operettas for their 'erotic and exotic atmosphere' – a clear 'sign of degeneracy'.[123] Contrary to propaganda demands a few years earlier, critics such as Harry Ziems now asserted that 'down to earth topics with traditional subject matter, peasant dances and folk music' were as undesirable as political subjects.[124] In effect, the new operetta of recent years had become rather dull.[125] Although much better than the 'Jewish' pieces five years ago,[126] the new operetta lacked 'music full of sparkling dance rhythms, relaxation, entertainment, laughing high spirits and healthy humour',[127] which would have guaranteed productions of 'clear and clean taste'.[128] Corresponding to other aesthetic debates, however, these comments failed to make any lasting impression, and many managers quickly returned to the established hits of the contemporary operetta with pieces by Franz Lehár, Robert Stolz, Fred Raymond, Paul Burkhard and Peter Igelhoff, as well as older works. Irrespective of these debates, operetta productions remained as popular as ever and, therefore, one of the backbones of the theatres' financial planning.[129]

Entertainment

By the mid-1930s it had become clear that regional theatres could not be turned into *völkisch* propaganda stages. Managers were quick to realise that the only way to claim municipal playhouses for the regime was their success in quantitative terms. And it was in exactly this area that they proved most successful. The number of productions and performances rose continually and seasons were consistently extended.[130] Even the expensive musical programme received massive boosts. In 1933–4 Münster produced nine operas and seven operettas; two seasons later these figures had already risen to thirteen operas and ten operettas. Despite being constantly strapped for cash (and although opera attendances were traditionally lower) Hagen in 1936–7 treated itself to eight opera and seven operetta productions. And Gelsenkirchen's theatre even introduced opera after the war had already started. Managers in general returned to a repertoire which was quite unexceptional: a mixture of classical plays, contemporary comedies, established operas and popular operettas.[131] Their concentration on a largely entertaining dramatic repertoire in particular is worth mentioning in this context. The fare written by authors such as Leo Lenz, Curt Goetz, Rolf Lauckner, Axel Ivers, August Hinrichs and Karl Bunje was hugely popular and did not differ much from the comedies produced during the Weimar years. Folk plays and dialect comedies, detective and crime plays, thrillers and farces, comedies about disguise and deceit, double entendres and mix-ups, love and sex remained as popular as ever. Local references, amateur dramatics and dialect comedies, too, proved successful at Westphalian theatres and could be subsumed under 'Blood and Soil' ideals.[132] Although the production of plays in Low German dialect, for example, was officially endorsed, high hopes regarding their propaganda value rarely materialised. The vast majority of these plays were farcical comedies and it took substantial imagination to read *völkisch* intentions into them.

In 1938 the eminent critic Kurt Fischer lamented that radical changes in the theatre had still not materialised. Fischer complained especially that 'simple' comedies and 'cheap' farces, folk plays and the operetta, with its typical clichés, still dominated the repertoire.[133] The eagerly awaited new contemporary drama simply did not emerge.[134] The fact that *völkisch* drama did not play a decisive role any longer is also illustrated by the official nationwide performance figures. Although Hanns Johst was the most popular *völkisch* dramatist with a total of 1,337 performances between 1933 and 1938, this was but a small achievement.[135] During 1937–8 alone German theatres produced eleven Lehár operettas which received 3,300 performances.[136] And Karl Bunje's farce *Der Etappenhase* (*Base Wallah*) alone was performed 2,837 times the year before.[137]

Context

In view of the comparative aspect of this study, it is interesting to note that the vast majority of these comedies were contemporary pieces – as in Yorkshire. During the 1935–6 season at Münster, for example, 75 per cent of all comedies were contemporary works. In this genre more than anywhere else a play's novelty was vital. Although this factor was certainly more important in Yorkshire, where the production of a London hit while it was still being performed there was a sure winner, the managements of Westphalian theatres, too, looked for recent successes. The only possible political connotations with regard to the quick change of plays concern the increasing number of right-wing playwrights who, obviously in connection with the failure of their attempts with *völkisch* drama, now turned to writing comedies. This *Ersatzdramatik*, as mentioned above, increasingly entered the stages from the mid-1930s and provided some of Westphalian theatres' biggest successes.[138] It is interesting to note, however, that hardly any of these comedies propagated any *völkisch* ideas but presented classical comedy themes – the ménage à trois and similar mishaps.

Equally interesting is the increasing interest at Westphalian theatres in local references. The presence of the 'Low German Stage', for example, is an example of parallel developments in Münster and York. Both the 'Low German Stage' and York's Musical and Dramatic Society were made up of local lay actors who took pride in appearing on the stage of 'their' professional theatre on a regular basis. The success of both groups not only shows the strong links between theatre and community, but they also fostered these links and probably brought a new clientele into the theatre. The attempts by the Nazi regime to incorporate these activities into their propaganda, however, also illustrate the differences between the two theatres.

Figure 4.1 Bielefeld municipal theatre, theatre programme, 4–11 May 1941

War repertoires

It has already been mentioned that the outbreak of the war did not affect Westphalia's theatre to a substantial degree until the early 1940s.[139] The first few war seasons showed more record numbers of productions and performances.[140] The dominant genres in the repertoire remained the classics and, most of all, light entertainment, followed by operas and operettas. Productions of nationalist and *völkisch* drama, however, were few and far between.

At the same time, regional theatres immediately felt drastic changes. Possible niches disappeared, control became tighter and the tie between theatre and state closer. The ban on British dramatists, for example, not only meant that plays by Bridie, Coward and Wilde disappeared, it also signalled the start of the propaganda war against Britain. Britain was presented as a state without any interest in the arts, where the theatre and its actors did not enjoy any support and were left to fight for their bare survival.[141] At home the regime left no doubt as to the function of theatre in war. As an 'intellectual weapon' it had to support the fight at the front, a *l'art pour l'art* attitude was now impossible[142] and the idea of the arts as an island within a sea of war had finally become unacceptable.[143] Westphalian theatres responded not with a rise in *völkisch* productions but with an increase of classical plays. In Münster the share of the classics in the overall programme jumped from 10 to 18 per cent, and performance figures reached a 26 per cent share in 1942–3.[144] Bielefeld's manager Kruchen similarly raised the number of classics in the repertoire, regularly reported sold-out performances (an overall 90 per cent utilisation) and proudly remarked that audiences were 'largely made up of *feldgrau* soldiers' uniforms' – a comment which probably went down well with officials at the Propaganda Ministry to whom these reports were sent.[145]

It is interesting to note that both phenomena, the realisation of theatre as a propaganda tool and the rise of classical drama, are parallel developments in Britain and Germany. The reaction to the outbreak of the war was not primarily a flight into farces and spy comedies as during the First World War, but an awareness of theatre as a cultural institution and a concentration on uplifting classics, on edification rather than entertainment. At the same time, however, and this runs counter to official claims, the number of contemporary comedies at Westphalian theatres rose, too. Although they never completely dominated the repertoires to a similar extent as in Yorkshire, their share in the performance figures rose to over 50 per cent at some playhouses.[146]

More severe changes were instigated by damage caused by the increasing number of air raids from 1942. Apart from the time and resources it took to repair the material damage, they had numerous consequences for the repertoire, too. In some cases new performance venues had to be found, which were often unsuitable for large-scale musical productions, the number of productions and performances dropped drastically, and lack of scenery, costumes, properties and elaborate lighting caused additional problems.[147] At the same time, however, theatres were at pains to uphold the cultural façade. Among an increasing number of air raids as well as rising logistical and technical problems, Westphalia's theatres managed to maintain or even raise the number of productions. In December 1943 Münster's manager Pabst even presented a completely revised version of Mozart's *The Marriage of Figaro* in the city hall.[148]

CONCLUDING REMARKS

In conclusion, we have seen that the regime's high aims regarding the 'new' theatre could not be realised. Westphalia's playhouses were not transformed into Nazi propaganda stages and the general outlook of their repertoires did not change fundamentally. Neither the theatre managers nor the party authorities were able to establish *völkisch* drama on Westphalian stages permanently. The 1933–4 season in particular was a failure and a blow to the ambitions of managers, party and city authorities.

If we change the perspective slightly, however, and ask whether the Nazis were able to make use of the theatre as a cultural institution and if they managed to incorporate Westphalian playhouses in their political agenda, for example by applying their anti-Semitic politics to the theatre, we have to give a positive answer. After the failure of the first season, which remained an exception, managers like Hanke, Kruchen and Hoenselaars performed successfully with a slightly new strategy. Too much overt propaganda on the stage was avoided and substituted by subtle forms of influence. Seemingly harmless comedies and operettas could be useful even if they did not contain any direct political messages. Supposedly, they were even more useful to the Nazis because they stressed ideas of normality and continuity. Although attempts to incorporate Schiller and Hauptmann into the regime's 'hall of fame' must have appeared clumsy, they seem to have paid off. The Nazis had finally found a way to use the theatre for their purposes: instead of radical changes, they made use of the theatre system as it was. Westphalia's *Intendanten* managed to achieve attendance records while deliberately using the established *Stadttheater* as a platform. The concentration on the acclaimed drama of the classics and modern classics also had the advantage of proving

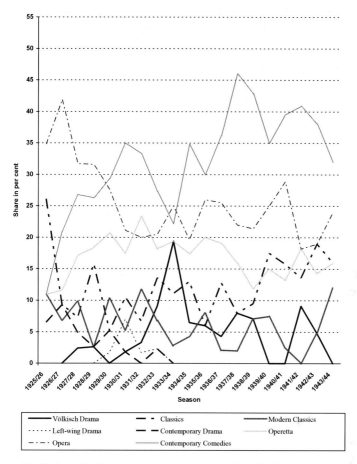

Note: The diagram shows the share in per cent of each single genre in the overall number of productions each
season. It illustrates the intentions of the management concerning the programme rather than the
audience's influence.

Figure 4.2 Share of genres in productions at Münster's *Stadtische Bühnen*

to foreign commentators that Nazi Germany was in fact still a
Kulturnation. In fact we have seen that repertoires became quite similar
to the Weimar years. Most of the musical and dramatic works could
have appeared during the 1920s and, indeed, a lot of them had done
so. Correspondingly, the theoretical discourse about the 'new' theatre
quickly lost its appeal and respective articles disappeared from the
programme notes. Instead, record attendances, entertaining
repertoires and historical reflections moved to the centre of attention.
In doing so, the current situation appeared as the fulfilment of the
promises of Germany's great theatrical past.

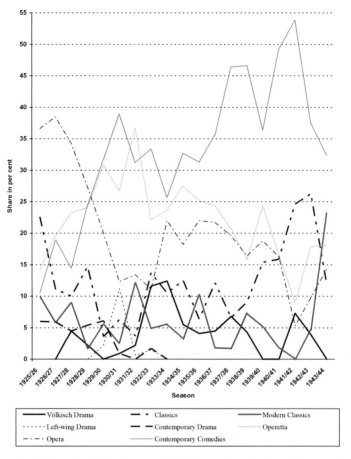

Note: The diagram shows the share in per cent of each single genre in the total number of performances each
season. It illustrates the reaction of the audience to the programme presented to them. When put in relation
to Figure 4.2 it provides answers to questions concerning the success of particular genres or the repertoire
policy on the whole.

Figure 4.3 Share of genres in performances at Münster's *Städtische Bühnen*

In a nutshell, Westphalia's theatres during the Third Reich
reflected how little the Nazis achieved, both with respect to the
development of their own dramatic theory and regarding the
production of *völkisch* plays of decent quality. At the same time,
however, they fitted into the system.[149] Although there would have
been possibilities to express critical ideas, especially through a certain
kind of repertoire, these possibilities were not explored.[150]

NOTES

1   Mettin, *Situation des Theaters*, p. 29.

2   Münster regarded itself as *Provinzialhauptstadt*, Bielefeld as the regional and commercial centre of Eastern Westphalia, Hagen as an important link between the rural *Sauerland* and the urban *Ruhrgebiet*, Dortmund as the biggest city in Westphalia claimed an increasingly dominant role, and Bochum understood itself as the industrial powerhouse of the Ruhr.

3   Indications of attempts to influence the repertoire on religious grounds can only be found in Münster. In the late 1920s the Christian visitors' organisation *Bühnenvolksbund* wrote to Münster's Theatre and Music Council and demanded a permanent seat on its advisory committee on the grounds that they bought 'nearly 2,000' tickets each month for their members (see StdAMS, Stadtregistratur Z.B. 266, box 14, no.56, p. 98). There is only one instance where the influence of Catholic groups led to a repertoire change. In 1946 they complained about a production of Schnitzler's *Liebelei*, which Münster's mayor Zuhorn insisted be withdrawn from the programme, because it supposedly violated Christian beliefs (see Teppe, *Politisches System*, p. 70).

4   The theatrical avant-garde was concentrated almost entirely in Berlin and hardly reached out to the provinces (for a different interpretation see Lacquer, Walter. *Weimar. A Cultural History 1918–1933*. London: Weidenfeld and Nicolson, 1974. pp. 140–54). One example of prevailing conservative attitudes in the provinces affected Brecht's drama, which, apart from some exceptions, was thoroughly avoided. Although Münster produced the *Threepenny Opera* during 1929–30, it failed disastrously and was only performed twice. Generally it was not until the late 1960s that Brecht's plays experienced successful runs in the provinces.

5   See Bernau, Alfred, ed. *Das Theater der Stadt Münster in der Spielzeit 1930/31. Verzeichnis der Mitglieder – Spielpläne – Stammsitzbedingungen*. Münster: Krick, n.d. [1930].

6   See Ockert, Otto, ed. *Rückblick auf die erste Spielzeit 1918/19 des wiedereröffneten Stadttheaters Münster unter der Direktion Otto Ockert*. Münster n.p., n.d.

7   See Ketelsen, Uwe-Karsten. *Ein Theater und seine Stadt. Die Geschichte des Bochumer Schauspielhauses*. Köln: SH-Verlag, 1999. p. 141.

8   See Dussel, *Heroisches Theater*, pp. 14–15.

9   In Münster it was only in 1930–1 that left-wing drama reached a respectable 11 per cent share in the performance figures. During the preceding and the following seasons its share was much lower and only reached three per cent or less (see Fig 4.3). In the wider region only Osnabrück produced another Brecht piece (apart from the *Threepenny Opera*), performing *Lindberghflug* in 1932.

10   The most successful playwrights of this genre during the Weimar years were

Curt Goetz, Carl Laufs, Franz Molnar, Bruno Frank, Ludwig Hirschfeld, Max Bertuch, Laszlo Fodor, Toni Impekoven, Ludwig Fulda, August Hinrichs, Leo Lenz as well as the duos Arnold/Bach and Bernauer/ Oesterreicher.

11   Arnold Ridley's *Ghost Train* was performed in York in 1926 and serves as a good example of the fact that it took British successes at least two years (in this case as long as four) to find their way onto German regional stages.

12   During 1930–1 the theatre produced Ridley's *Ghost Train*, Thomas' *Charley's Aunt*, Maugham's *The Constant Wife*, and *Vater sein dagegen sehr*, an adaptation of a play by Edward Childs Carpenter. They had a share of 20 per cent in all the comedy productions. The sixty-one performances they received resulted in a share of 29 per cent in the overall number of comedy performances. The British plays in 1931–2 were Lonsdale's *The Last of Mrs Cheney*, Coward's *Private Lives* and two productions from the preceding season: *The Constant Wife* and *Charley's Aunt*. During 1932–3 one of the most successful productions was *The first Mrs Selby* by St John Ervine.

13   In 1931–2, for example, the theatre produced four classical dramas (two by Goethe and two by Schiller), which might have been regarded as too 'heavy' in Yorkshire. The two right-wing plays *Warbeck* and *Flieger* might have been equally problematic. The seven modern classics by Ibsen, Hauptmann, Halbe, Schönthan, Meyer-Förster and Schönthan/Kadelburg, however, would certainly have been appreciated by Yorkshire audiences. Meyer-Förster's *Alt-Heidelberg*, after all, had been turned into *The Student Prince*, one of British theatre's biggest popular hits. The twenty comedies would certainly have been equally successful in Yorkshire, and the large musical programme with twelve operas and fourteen operettas would have been admired there. German-style operetta at that time experienced a short-term revival in London, which had its implications for the provinces, too. Especially famous was *White Horse Inn*, which, coincidentally, was staged in Münster in 1931–2 in the original German as *Im Weißen Rößl*.

14   The first production of Richard Hagemann's Die *Tragödie von Arezzo* in 1932 was as much an exception as the performances of Ermanno Wolf-Ferrari's *Sly/Big* during 1929–30. We also have to note that both pieces were composed in a late romantic style.

15   The preceding season 1930–1, too, showed the prominent position operetta enjoyed in the audience's appreciation. Whereas an opera production received an average of six and a play eight performances, the typical operetta ran fifteen times. The operettas' share of 24 per cent in the overall production figures was nearly doubled in the performance figures which reached 40 per cent (see Figs 4.2 and 4.3).

16   Until 1925 Münster regularly produced around twenty operas per season. After the 1941 air raid the number of both opera and operetta productions fell to about four each season.

17   Even in Berlin with its exciting experiments and variety of musical life the

influence of reactionary forces was substantial and opera repertoires were much more traditional and conservative than some commentators have claimed (see Levi, Erik. *Music in the Third Reich*. London: Macmillan, 1994. pp. 1–13).

18 For a typical account see Schlaghecke, Hans. 'Lage des Berufstheaters.' *Almanach 1927. Theater der Stadt Münster*. Intendanz des Theaters, ed. Münster: n.p., 1927. pp. 18–24. Schlaghecke demanded a new spirit, which denied utilitarianism, intellectualism and individualism in order to reach a unified national theatre true to its cultic roots. Experiments had to go as otherwise the theatre was in danger of being excluded from the 'living stream of blood' and would 'degenerate'. It is interesting to see how anti-modernist attitudes mix with proto-Nazi vocabulary in this article. Its incorporation in a book, which was designed to present the quintessence of Münster's theatre renaissance during the mid-1920s, indicates how accepted these views were. In similar articles commentators criticised Max Reinhardt's experimental stage designs (see Bergenthal, Josef. 'Bühne und Publikum.' *Blätter des Theaters* 4 (1927/28): p. 98), expressed their disgust at plays about adultery (see Heising, Wilhelm. 'Die Gesellschaftsstruktur der heutigen Zeit.' Ibid., p. 126), and warned against modernist approaches in general (see Heising, Wilhelm. '"Klassikertod" und Zeittheater.' *Blätter des Theaters* 5 (1928/29): pp. 144–5).

19 Contemporary commentators, however, failed to see the potential danger of these plays and insisted that most of them only dealt with 'problems of the nation' (see, for example in Münster, Hillekamps, Carl H. 'Alfred Neumann und *Der Patriot*.' *Blätter des Theaters* 4 (1927/28): p. 49).

20 Some of the biggest successes of that season at German theatres in general were Kolbenheyer's *The Bridge*, Cremers' *The Battle on the Marne* and especially Schäfer's *18th October*, a play which centres around a Prussian army colonel's inner conflict between the oath of loyalty he gave to Napoleon and his commitment to the 'German cause' (see Schäfer, Walter Erich. 'Der 18. Oktober.' *Theater der Stadt Münster* 9 (1932/33): programme no. 4. For in-depth analysis of this and similar war plays see Fischli, Bruno. *Die Deutschendämmerung. Zur Genealogie des völkisch-faschistischen Dramas (1897–1933)*. Bonn: Bouvier, 1976. pp. 173–97).

21 See, for example, Georg Kaiser's comedy *The Courageous Seafarer*, which was performed at many regional playhouses in 1927–8.

22 In the preview for the 1929–30 season Bernau promised to produce fifty-seven plays, thirty-eight operas and sixteen operettas (in the end only twenty-three plays, fifteen operas and eight operettas materialised), including such avant-garde operas as Hindemith's *Hin und zurück*, Janáček's *Jenufa*, Stravinsky's *Pulcinella*, and Weill's *Der Zar läßt sich photographieren* (see Bernau, Alfred, ed. *Theater der Stadt Münster. Spielzeit 1929/30. Vorteile und Bedingungen der Platzmiete*. Münster: n.p., n.d. [1929]). A similar discrepancy appeared in the following season (see Bernau, Alfred. *Theater der Stadt*

Münster. Zur kommenden Spielzeit 1930/31. Münster: n.p., n.d. [1930]). This choice would have made a real change, and perhaps this was the reason why Bernau did not pursue some of these ideas any further. Still, some of the plays he did produce stood in clear contrast to the prevailing anti-modernist views like, for example, Sherriff's *Journey's End*. The vast majority of war drama, however, was right-wing and revisionist.

23 In 1928–9 Münster's theatre was visited by 140,731 patrons (see StdAMS. *Statistischer Bericht der Provinzialhauptstadt Münster/Westfalen 1929*, p. 58). Bernau managed to raise this figure by 30 per cent to 184,378 within one year (see *Statistischer Bericht 1930*, p. 68). Against the background of an increasingly tight civic budget, however, Bernau was aware that it was not enough to keep his following; he was bound to increase these figures. Especially important were the season ticket holders, who represented the backbone of the theatre's finances. The number of season ticket holders rose from 1,030 in 1927–8 (see *Statistischer Bericht 1928*, p. 29) to 1,133 in 1928–9 (ibid.), 1,240 in 1929–30 (see *Statistischer Bericht 1929*, p. 58) and eventually to 1,473 in 1930–1 (see *Statistischer Bericht 1930*, p. 68). During the 1930–1 season the income generated from season tickets was more than half the annual box-office receipts. Season tickets alone brought in RM 103,340, whereas the overall box-office takings amounted to RM 195,177 (see StAMS, *Oberpräsidium no. 5501*, p. 17). Consequently, the theatre heavily advertised its season ticket (see Bernau, Alfred. 'Vorschau auf die Spielzeit 1930/31.' *Blätter des Theaters der Stadt Münster* 6 (1929/30): p. 210; Bernau, Alfred, ed. *Theater der Stadt Münster in der Spielzeit 1930/31*; Bernau, Alfred. *Theater der Stadt Münster. Spielzeit 1931/32.* Münster: Krick, 1931).

24 From 1930–1 Münster's attendances declined again and fell by almost ten per cent to 167,662. The number of season tickets even decreased by a record 38 per cent and only reached 915 during 1931–2 (see *Statistischer Bericht 1931*, p. 33). In Bochum avant-garde plays never gained a foothold. Conservative Schmitt withstood attempts around this time from commentators who asked for a more modern repertoire (see Schmidt, *Bochumer Theater*, pp. 31–5).

25 Commentators claimed that 'theatre is ideology. National Socialism demands the highest integrity from the theatre; it shall be of exactly the same nature, the same character, the same ideology. What the stage announces, be it overtly or hidden, must eventually concur with what National Socialism regards as its own world of thought.' (Schmid, Eugen. 'Jugend und Theater.' *Theater Tageblatt*, 9 November 1933).

26 Arthur Schnitzler was Jewish, his plays were forbidden immediately after the take-over – as were the plays by Stefan Zweig. Interestingly, the performances were apparently not attacked by the nationalistic press but, instead, received positive reviews from the social-democrat *Volkswille* and the conservative *Münsterischer Anzeiger* (see *VW*, 11 February 1933 and *MA*, 12 February 1933).

27 A different position is put forward by Thomas Eicher who claims that 'after

February 1933 hardly any play by an "unwanted" dramatist made it onto the stages' (Eicher, *Spielplanstrukturen*, p. 484).

28   See Liebscher, Otto. 'Die neue Spielzeit des Theaters der Stadt Münster.' *Das schöne Münster* 5 (1933). p. 256.

29   The notes also featured many articles about the new nationalistic and *völkisch* plays, which flooded the stages now. See *Blätter des Stadttheaters* Münster 10 (1933/34): programmes nos. 3, 5 on Förster, 8 on Kolbenheyer and 11 on Graff.

30   See StdABI. Stadt Bielefeld. Städtische Bühnen und Orchester. no. 1515. Personalangelegenheiten 1938–62. File Alfred Moritz.

31   It is interesting to note that agreement on what the term 'Weimar Culture' meant did not exist either. It was rather a symbol, which subsumed everything the Nazis regarded as inferior or 'un-German' under a common idea. According to leading Nazis it was especially the theatre which had been affected by the 'Weimar spirit' (see Hitler, Adolf. *Mein Kampf.* 434th–443rd ed. München: Eher, 1939. p. 284; Rosenberg, Alfred. *Der Mythus des 20. Jahrhunderts. Eine Wertung der seelisch-geistigen Gestaltenkämpfe unserer Zeit.* 53rd–54th ed. München: Eher, 1935. p. 447).

32   In most theories the choric element played an important role. The aim of the chorus was to symbolise the *Volksgemeinschaft* (national community), for which the hero sacrificed himself. In contrast to Greek drama, however, the function of the chorus was not to reflect and comment upon the action but to shape it together with the antagonists (see Langenbeck, Curt. 'Dürfen wir uns bei dem jetzigen hohen Stand der Schauspielbühne beruhigen?' *Das Innere Reich* 3 (1936): p. 768). It is interesting to note that this revival of the chorus was not a genuine Nazi idea as theorists only continued a discussion which had started long before. Already in the mid-1920s left-wing activists had plans for proletarian choruses modelled on the Greek example (see Schönlank, Bruno. 'Schafft Sprechchöre.' *Junge Menschen* 6 (1925): pp. 159–60). In essence, these theoretical ideas awarded the theatre a quasi-religious function, and the *Thing* plays came closest at fulfilling this demand. Commentators asserted that the shape of the *Thing* sites reminded audiences of Germanic sacrificial altars 'on hills and in holy groves' (see Emmel, Felix. *Theater aus deutschem Wesen.* Berlin: Stilke, 1937. pp. 92–3) and claimed that 'there are no spectators. There are no good seats. There is only a nation and a place' (Euringer, Richard. *Chronik einer deutschen Wandlung 1925–1935.* Hamburg: Hanseatische Verlagsanstalt, 1936. p. 237).

33   For a detailed account of the different theories see Ketelsen, Uwe-Karsten. *Heroisches Theater. Untersuchungen zur Dramentheorie des Dritten Reichs.* Bonn: Bouvier, 1968. pp. 127–208.

34   Already long before 1933 right-wing theorists like Paul Ernst and Dietrich Eckart aimed at a theatre of 'formal neo-classicism' based on 'the word'. Following Ernst, playwrights like Bacmeister, Langenbeck and Möller after 1933 demanded a drama of super-elevated style, the heroic 'tragedy of fate'.

By contrast, Kolbenheyer, Johst and Hymnen aimed at 'symbolic reality'. Their 'character drama' was supposed to stand in the tradition of Shakespeare. Proof of the ongoing debates until the very end of the war are demands that theatres should avoid 'cheap, shallow and kitsch entertainment fare' in 1943 (see Schrade, Hans Erich. 'Deutsches Theater im 5. Kriegsjahr.' *Bühnenjahrbuch 1944*. Präsident der Reichstheaterkammer, ed. Berlin: Günther, 1943. p. 3) and suggestions that the best be made of the bombed out cities as they offered new opportunities in terms of scene design (see Billerbeck-Gentz, Friedrich. 'Die Bedeutung der Kunst im Kriege.' *Deutsche Dramaturgeie* 3 (1944): p. 7. Similarly, Karsten Pagel (ibid., pp. 15–16) and Karl Künkler (ibid., pp. 65–6)).

35   The group of nationalistic and *völkisch* plays divides roughly into three sub-groups. Apart from the First World War play there is the 'Blood and Soil' and the 'Drama of Ideology'. 'Blood and Soil' plays idealised the peasant life and the unspoiled countryside especially in contrast to the 'decadent jungle' of the cities. The 'Drama of Ideology' aimed at the creation of abstract ideas of 'timeless quality' in the 'tradition' of Eckart and Ernst.

36   Already at the end of the 1932–3 season – after the take-over – the rising number of closed performances at many theatres is remarkable.

37   In Münster the number of productions in 1933–4 was lower than during the previous year. Classics and modern classics together received only five productions (four fewer than during the preceding season), while the contemporary comedies reached double that figure. Only with respect to *völkisch* drama did Liebscher seem to succeed. The number of seven productions was nearly double the figure of 1932–3. The number of performances, however, was disappointing. Although *völkisch* plays reached a share of 35 per cent in all the dramatic productions their share in the performances stood only at 23 per cent (see Fig 4.3).

38   Between 1933 and 1938, 42 per cent of all premieres were plays dramatising historical topics (see Gadberry, Glen. 'The History Plays in the Third Reich.' London, John, ed. *Theatre Under the Nazis*. Manchester: Manchester University Press, 2000. pp. 99–100). Goebbels' ban on dealing with contemporary subject matter on stage certainly endorsed this trend. For many playwrights, however, this ban also seems to have been convenient as dealing with the immediate past posed many potential problems. In that sense it seems fair to claim that the popularity of the history plays also offered dramatists a chance to 'flee' into the safety of the past. In any case, the fact that so many plays appeared which in some way corresponded to a format endorsed by Goebbels, does not automatically mean that these dramatists actively supported the Nazi cause, as Gadberry implies (ibid., pp. 100–1). Among the most popular historical characters were medieval emperors or Prussian kings. Other topics included England (for example *Rebell in England* by Hans Schwarz, *Oliver Cromwell* by Mirko Jelusich), 'exemplary' Germans (for example *Jakob Leisler* by Hans Friedrich Blunck and *Schlageter* by Hanns

Johst), and France as the Nazi paradigm of decadence (especially *Richelieu* by Paul Joseph Cremers). The fact that so many playwrights turned away from contemporary subjects, however, also provoked criticism. Commentators condemned the fact that the same topics constantly recurred, and claimed that yet another portrayal of Hermann's victorious battle against the Romans or the Nibelung saga would not exactly pull the crowds any longer (see Naso, Eckart. 'Dramaturgie.' Kaun, Axel, ed. *Berliner Theater-Almanach 1942.* Berlin: Neff, 1942. p. 169).

39   For a detailed account see Fischli, *Deutschendämmerung.* See also Ketelsen, Uwe-Karsten. *Literatur und Drittes Reich.* 2nd rev. ed. Schernfeld: SH, 1994, especially pp. 218–22, and Ketelsen, Uwe-Karsten. *Völkisch-nationale und nationalsozialistische Literatur in Deutschland 1890–1945.* Stuttgart: Metzler, 1976.

40   Despite these obvious 'shortcomings' commentators were anxious not only to propagate the *völkisch* repertoire as something radically new but also to stress the importance of its 'proper' reading (see articles on Ernst's *Yorck* (*Blätter des Stadttheaters Münster* 10 (1933/34): programme no. 1), Förster's *All Against One, One for All* (ibid., programme no. 3), Kolbenheyer's *Your Inner Law* (no. 8), Graff's *Homecoming of Matthias Bruck* (no. 11), and Kyser's *Rembrandt in Court* (no. 12).

41   The other *völkisch* plays were only performed between four to seven times. Even *Yorck*, after all one of the most important plays by Paul Ernst, the Nazi model dramatist, which was also presented as a premiere, only reached four performances. Still, even the number of fourteen performances achieved by Förster's drama seems little in comparison to the most successful comedy of the season. August Hinrichs' *When the Rooster Crows* reached twenty-three performances. Förster's *All Against One, One for All* was one of the most ardently promoted early *völkisch* plays as the 'German Stage' literally forced theatre managers to produce it. In a letter to the Prussian Theatre Council from November 1933 Osnabrück's manager Storz complained about the head of the 'German Stage', Walter Stang, and asked whether Stang now fulfilled the function of a general theatre manager who could compel theatres to produce certain plays (see BArch, R56 I/54, pp. 229–33). This episode does not only illustrate the rude methods of certain Nazi organisations, but it is also interesting with respect to the struggles for power within the system. Storz' letter of complaint came in handy for the Prussian Theatre Council and for Goebbels who wanted to curtail the influence of the 'German Stage', Walter Stang and, ultimately, the powerful figure in the background, Alfred Rosenberg.

42   See *WNN*, 27 April 1935.

43   See StdAHA, Ha1/9327, 9272.

44   The Nazis attributed these 'organised disruptions' from early 1935 to catholic youths. The protests aroused considerable interest and disturbance in the Nazi administration in Hagen and beyond. Despite being a prestigious

first production manager Bender duly took the play off. His subsequent application for reimbursement of 'lost revenue' was successful and the Propaganda Ministry paid him RM 8,000 (see StdAHA, Ha 1/9285).

45 The opera was dominated by the classical repertoire and featured only two contemporary pieces, Paul Graener's *Friedemann Bach* and Richard Strauß' *Arabella*. Although both composers were celebrated during the Third Reich and accepted official posts, these works did not contain any political messages. Graener's opera was first produced in 1931 and regularly performed after 1933 although the libretto was written by a 'non-Aryan' (see Drewniak, Boguslaw. *Das Theater im NS-Staat. Szenarium deutscher Zeitgeschichte 1933–1945*. Düsseldorf: Droste, 1983. pp. 313–14). Richard Strauß was the best-known living German composer and clearly supportive of the regime in its early years. Goebbels made him president of the Reich Music Chamber in 1933. The opera *Arabella* (1933), however, featured a libretto by a Jewish writer, too: Hugo von Hofmannsthal, whose works were immediately banned after the take-over. In the end it was this collaboration with a 'non-Aryan' writer which cost Strauß his prestigious post.

46 The one Münster production in 1932–3 which in some way corresponded to left-wing ideas, the set of one-act plays under the title *Gaukler – Mimen – Literaten*, only reached a share of four per cent in all the dramatic productions and a share of two per cent in all the dramatic performances. The loss of this genre during the next season was probably not even recognised by patrons (see Figs 4.2 and 4.3).

47 The number of Jewish dramatists was especially high in the comedy genre, whereas the highest number of Jewish composers was within operetta. Some of the most successful artists were immediately banned. The comedies by Arnold/Bach, Blumenthal/Kadelburg, Wilhelm Meyer-Förster, Ferenc Molnar, Rudolf Bernauer, and Rudolf Österreicher, as well as the operettas by Paul Abraham, Emmerich Kálmán, Oscar Straus and Heinrich Berté, for example, had been hugely popular during the Weimar years (see Schmid, Adolf, ed. *Judentum und Musik. Liste der jüdischen Komponisten als Unterlage für die Säuberungsaktionen auf dem Gebiete der Musik*. Straßburg: Abt. Volksaufklärung und Propaganda beim Chef der Zivilverwaltung im Elsaß, 1941).

48 Already during the Weimar years Nazi commentators had left no doubt regarding their radical plans. The *Völkischer Beobachter*, for example, published a 'black list' of authors belonging to the 'decadent period of decay' in 1932, which featured Brecht, Feuchtwanger, Hofmannsthal, Hasenclever, Sternheim, Toller, Unruh, Wedekind, Werfel, Wolf, Zuckmeyer, Zweig and many others (quoted in Reinhardt, Stephan, ed. *Die Schriftsteller und die Weimarer Republik. Ein Lesebuch*. Berlin: Wagenbach, 1992. pp. 84 and 241).

49 In a widely publicised speech held at the Reich Theatre Festival in Hamburg in 1935 Goebbels criticised theatre managers for their choice of programme as repertories had become too pedestrian. At the beginning 'too much

emphasis had been placed on National Socialism; now the pendulum had swung too much in the opposite direction and nobody seemed to want to mention the subject'. He criticised that putting 'on only the classics and harmless trivialities was unworthy of the epoch, as was an excessive reliance on foreign pieces'. Goebbels added that 'it is not as though the ideals of our time are incapable of being translated into art. All that they demand are artists big enough to do the translating' (quoted in Balfour, Michael. *Propaganda in War. 1939–1945. Organisations, Policies and Publics in Britain and Germany.* London: Routledge, 1979. p. 46).

50 See Schlösser, *Das Volk und seine Bühne*, pp. 27–9.

51 It is interesting to note that Hanke was reluctant to produce *völkisch* plays even if they were written by highly regarded authors – quite obviously because of their poor quality. In October 1936 Schlösser wrote to Friedrich Wilhelm Hymnen, one of the most prolific young Nazi dramatists, and mentioned that he had met Münster's manager Hanke at the Grabbe Festival in Detmold. Schlösser assured Hymnen that Hanke would premiere his latest play *The Vassal* during the current season. At this point several other stages had already declined to produce the play. Two months later Hymnen complained to Schlösser about Hanke's evasive tactics who quite obviously did not want to commit himself. Regarding the question of total control of the arts (still claimed by some historians and implied throughout in Rischbieter's *Theater im Dritten Reich*), it is interesting to note that at no point did anyone suggest to put Hanke under pressure. On the contrary, Hymnen wanted to refrain from such measures, which might result in Hanke producing the play without much enthusiasm. In January 1937 Schlösser replied that after another 'intervention' Hanke had hinted at producing the piece in April. With this time scale in mind Schlösser proposed to have the first production in Bochum instead (see BArch, R55/20231a, pp. 449, 452 and 454). As it turned out *The Vassal* was first produced in Bochum in March 1937, and during the following season received further productions at four minor theatres. Despite Schlösser's intervention, however, the play was never performed in Münster. We can note, therefore, that even with a play by a celebrated Nazi dramatist, who enjoyed support on the highest level, the regime could neither ensure that it was produced at a certain theatre nor that it received more than just a few productions and was completely forgotten afterwards.

A similar case was Felix Dühnen's *völkisch* drama *Uta von Naumburg* which Schlösser, Goebbels and even Heinrich Himmler wanted to see produced all over Germany in summer 1939. Schlösser noted that the theatres received a circular which made it clear that they were expected to produce the play. The circular went out to twenty-four theatres in July 1939 and asked the managers for specific performance dates in the not too distant future. The result was meagre. After four weeks seventeen theatres had not even bothered to answer, and by mid-September nine theatres had already indicated that they would not produce the play at all (see BArch, R55/20258, pp. 64–89).

52 See reports written for the Propaganda Ministry (BArch, R55/20349, pp. 169–175 for 1934–5, pp. 193–4 for 1935–6, pp. 245–7 for 1936–7, pp. 299–300 for 1937–8, as well as pp. 367–88).

53 BArch, R55/20349, pp. 193–4.

54 See BArch, R55/20314, pp. 15–17, 52–81, 95, 113–27, 163 and 175–9.

55 The drama *Rebaptism 1535* by the Münster playwright Prosper Heyl, for example, was produced in 1934–5 amidst massive propaganda and announced as a 'world premiere'. The drama dealt with the time of the Anabaptists in Münster and had an obvious nationalistic undertone. As part of the publicity campaign civil servants were urged to buy tickets. The official circular, however, had little effect, and only five staff reserved tickets (see StdAMS Stadtregistratur Z.B. Nr.135, Bd. IV, Fach 13, Nr.70, p. 326). The production only received eleven performances – not bad in comparison to other plays but clearly disappointing in view of a possible propaganda coup.

56 Kuropka is wrong when assuming that the highest level of politicisation of the theatre programmes was reached during the Hanke era (see Kuropka, Joachim. 'Aspekte des kulturellen Lebens in Münster während der NS-Zeit. Theater – Büchereien – Schulen'. Jakobi, Franz-Josef and Sternberg, Thomas, eds. *Kulturpolitik in Münster während der nationalsozialistischen Zeit. Referate und Diskussionsbeiträge der Tagung am 8. und 9. Juni 1990 im Franz-Hitze- Haus Münster.* Münster: Regensberg, 1990. pp. 104 and 119). From what we have seen it was the 1933–4 season which could claim this 'privilege'.

57 Friedrich Schiller was interpreted by many Nazi theorists as an archetypal German nationalist and anti-Semite. Hans Fabricius called him 'Hitler's fighting comrade' and Goebbels claimed that Schiller was one of the ideological forefathers of the 1933 'national revolution'. Others asserted that *Wilhelm Tell* clearly corresponded with the Nazi idea of national community (*Volksgemeinschaft*), and Hermann Burte established a direct line between Schiller's unfinished *Demetrius* and the war in the East (see Ruppelt, Georg. *Schiller im nationalsozialistischen Deutschland. Der Versuch einer Gleichschaltung.* Stuttgart: Metzler, 1979. pp. 13 and 26). The confusion, however, also becomes obvious in the case of Schiller. In 1941 *Wilhelm Tell* was banned because of its alleged call of tyrannicide (see ibid. pp. 41–5).

58 Westphalian theatres regularly took part in the festival in remembrance of Grabbe held annually in Detmold. This prestigious festival received national press coverage and so did the theatres taking part. As has been seen Münster's Hanke was no stranger to promoting himself, and the fact that he organised the 1936 Grabbe festival was certainly useful with future applications (for more information on the festival see BArch, R55/20451, R55/20451a, R55/20452 and R55/20452a).

59 In an internal report to Goebbels the National Dramaturge Schlösser praised Hanke's project and the Münster production (Schlösser's letter is based on a

report of Referent Scherler, which was sent to him on 15 September 1936.
See BArch, R55/20451, p. 148).

60   The 1935–6 production of Eckart's *Peer Gynt* adaptation had a successful run
of seventeen performances. The new 'quality' of this adaptation was the
presentation of the protagonist not as a 'weakling' but as a 'Scandinavian
Faust' who was 'true to his better self' (Eckart, Dietrich. 'Peer Gynt.' *Blätter
des Stadttheaters Münster* 12 (1935/36): programme no. 1). The importance of
Münster's production was further underlined by Schlösser's presence who, in
his speech at the theatre, asserted that Faust and Peer Gynt were 'foremost
authorities for the intentions and objectives of everything National Socialism
currently undertakes in Germany' (ibid., programme no. 4).

61   See *Blätter des Stadttheaters Münster* 12 (1935/36): programme no. 1.
Commentators were anxious to justify the choice of Wilde's popular play and
asserted that it was a criticism of Britain's class system and portrayed a
decaying society with low morals (see *MZ*, 18 September 1935). To support
such a reading, the question of translation became crucial. Lerbs, himself an
ardent Nazi supporter, was praised by the press because he had brought 'in a
pious but decisive manner … the text into line with the current state of
Germany's theatre through a faithful continuation, extension and discharge'
(*MA*, 19 September 1935).

62   German translations of Shakespeare have a considerable tradition. Questions
of translation, therefore, have always met with great interest. After 1933,
however, translations did not only need to have literary but also political
merit. During the 1920s the traditional Schlegel/Tieck translations had been
successfully challenged by Hans Rothe who translated Shakespeare into
modern German. He was condemned by traditionalists, whose criticism was
soon taken over by Nazi critics who accused Rothe of being *antivölkisch* (see
a letter by Schlösser to Goebbels in February 1936 at BArch R55/20218, p.
43) and a typical exponent of Weimar decadence (see articles by Werner
Kurz, Karl Künkler and Wolf Braumüller in a special issue of *Bausteine zum
deutschen Nationaltheater* from February 1936). In May 1936 Goebbels banned
Rothe's translations altogether. It is interesting to note that in his circular to
theatre managers Goebbels intended to give his order additional weight by
stressing that they should refrain from any further experiments with new
translations in view of the high subsidies paid to them from public funds (see
BArch, R55/20218, p. 35). This hidden threat hints at the fact that even at
this stage Rothe's translations still enjoyed considerable popularity in
Germany (see ibid., pp. 3–22).

63   Numerous suggestions for 'improvements' of the Schlegel/Tieck translation
of *The Merchant of Venice* reached the Propaganda Ministry. One
commentator wanted to change the script in view of the 1935 Race Laws
which made the relationship between Lorenzo and Jessica no longer
'desirable' (see BArch, R55/20218, pp. 74–7, 88–93). Another adaptation,
which made Jessica Shylock's foster child and eliminated all positive remarks

about Jews in the play, was produced in Berlin in 1942 (see BArch, R55/20194, pp. 283, 285, 287 and 291–2).

64 My translation of Rube, Wolrad. 'Agnes Bernauer. Ein deutsches Trauerspiel in fünf Akten von Friedrich Hebbel.' *Blätter des Stadttheaters Münster* 11 (1934/35): programme no. 9.

65 My translation of Hattesen, Benno. 'Stützen der Gesellschaft.' *Blätter des Stadttheaters Münster* 11 (1934/35): programme no. 11 (similarly 'Henrik Ibsen und der Norden. Zu Erich Pabst's Inszenierung der *Frau im Meere*.' *Stadttheater und Kammerspiele Münster* 16 (1939/40): programme no. 6). This reading stands in clear contrast to earlier interpretations which described Ibsen as the 'classic social critic of his time' (Richards-Ruzicka, Kurt. 'Henrik Ibsen.' *Blätter des Theaters der Stadt Münster* 6 (1929/30): p. 23).

66 My translation of Kaehler, Wolfgang. 'Alois Johannes Lippl und seine Pfingstorgel.' *Blätter des Stadttheaters Münster* 12 (1935/36): programme no. 3.

67 During the mid-1930s August Hinrichs fulfilled these requirements perfectly. He was one of the best-known dramatists during the Third Reich and wrote two of the most popular comedies of the 1930s (*When the Rooster Crows* and *Trouble with Jolanthe*). At the same time Hinrichs was politically 'safe'. He had written the *völkisch* 'folk drama' *Steding's Honour*, and his unexceptionable comedies of rural life could be easily subsumed under the 'Blood and Soil' ideology.

68 This was the conclusion the organisers drew from a series of 'model performances' in Berlin in 1934–5. The fact that audiences of comedies did not expect any propaganda but consumed these plays in a rather uncritical manner made them perfect for subtle indoctrination (see Brenner, Hildegard. *Die Kunstpolitik des Nationalsozialismus*. Hamburg: Rowohlt, 1963. pp. 93–4).

69 During the early 1920s many Westphalian theatres produced around 40 plays each season. Bochum actress Liselotte Schneider found herself performing in eight different plays over a four week span in 1932 (see Ketelsen, *Geschichte des Bochumer Schauspielhauses*, p. 141) and a weekly workload of 60 hours was nothing unusual. By comparison, during the 2005–06 season Münster's theatre presented ten plays and Dortmund in 2006–07 presented 15 plays.

70 Already during the Weimar years – and especially under Niedecken-Gebhardt – high artistic aims could rarely be put into practice. During the 1924–5 and 1925–6 seasons, for example, Niedecken-Gebhardt divided the whole programme into the headings *Feier* and *Spiel*, and had commentators discussing the importance of the current opera renaissance, along with aesthetic questions regarding recent artistic developments, modern stage design and the role of the 'new' actor (see Niedecken-Gebhardt. *Feierspiele Münster Pfingsten 1925*. StdAMS, DS 378 Spielpläne Städtische Bühnen. Folder 1923–9). These aims, however, were hardly reflected in the actual repertoire as audience demand for amusement had to be catered for.

71 Especially radical critics associated with the Rosenberg circle, like the above-

mentioned Walter Stang, quickly seized opportunities like these to criticise the repertoire policy of theatres.

72   The 'Militant League for German Culture' claimed that the theatre as a moral institution would from now on rank as one of the strongest means for popular education (see their own exposé on the 'causes and consequences of the German theatre crisis and suggestions to its rectification', published on 22 March 1933. Quoted in Ruppelt, *Schiller*, p. 104).

73   Some statistical data may suffice to illustrate the extent of state support. In 1933, for example, 147 publicly subsidised theatres employed some 22,000 people. Only seven years later these numbers had risen to 248 theatres with 44,000 employees (see Daiber, Hans. *Schaufenster der Diktatur. Theater im Machtbereich Hitlers*. Stuttgart: Neske, 1995. p. 11). The official support seems to have been successful judging from the rapidly increasing audience figures, which tripled within four years from 520,000 in 1932 to 1.6m in 1936. On top of municipal subsidies some theatres also received special payments awarded directly from the Propaganda Ministry. These special subsidies amounted to RM 9.7m in 1934. By 1942 they had risen to RM 45m (see Drewniak, *Theater im NS-Staat*, p. 39). Special emphasis was given to the international reputation of the Third Reich as a regime supporting the arts. Festivals like the Reich Theatre Festival and the annual 'Day of the Theatre' were organised on a massive scale in the presence of leading politicians. After the war Hitler planned to build a number of playhouses all over Germany with seating capacities of 2,000 or more (see Drewniak, *Theater im NS-Staat*, pp. 66–7).

74   See Goebbels, Joseph. 'Schiller und unsere Zeit.' *Stadttheater und Kammerspiele Münster* 16 (1938/39): programme no. 10. For a general overview see Albert, Claudia, ed. *Deutsche Klassiker im Nationalsozialismus. Schiller – Kleist – Hölderlin*. Stuttgart: Metzler, 1994.

75   See, for example, Immermann, Karl. '*Prinz Friedrich von Homburg*, Brief über die Düsseldorfer Aufführung (1833).' *Stadttheater und Kammerspiele Münster* 17 (1939/40): programme no. 10. See also *Stadttheater und Kammerspiele Münster* 18 (1940/41): programmes no. 2, 5, 8, 10, 12, 21; as well as *Stadttheater und Kammerspiele Münster* 19 (1943/44): programme no. 11.

76   It is interesting to note, however, that his origin was far from undisputed. Commentators from Lower Saxony, for example, claimed Grabbe for their region (see Schultze, Hermann. 'Grabbe, Dramatik aus Niedersachsentum.' *Bausteine zum deutschen Nationaltheater* 4 (1936): pp. 260–7).

77   See Schlösser, Rainer. 'Grabbes Vermächtnis.' *Stadttheater und Kammerspiele Münster* 16 (1938/39): programme no. 2. In 1936, for example, the theatres from Bochum, Münster and Bielefeld all took part.

78   *MA*, 17 October 1938. The regional press covered the festival widely. See also Broer, Werner and Kopp, Detlev eds. *Grabbe im Dritten Reich. Zum nationalsozialistischen Grabbe-Kult*. Bielefeld: Aisthesis Verlag, 1986.

79   A directive by the 'National Journal Service' from 23 October 1939 also asked

the press to avoid any mention of Schiller's 'cosmopolitanism' and idealism (see Ruppelt, *Schiller*, pp. 38–9).

80 See Pfister, Manfred. 'Hamlet und der deutsche Geist: Die Geschichte einer politischen Interpretation.' *Deutsche Shakespeare-Gesellschaft West. Jahrbuch* (1992): 13–38. Until today Shakespeare is the principal dramatist on German stages and more often produced there than in Britain. During 1999–2000, for example, 24 Shakespearean plays received 147 productions and 2,163 performances (see www.buehnenverein.de).

81 Commentators claimed that Shakespeare was not only Germanic but also expressing *völkisch* ideas in his plays (see Schlösser, Rainer. 'Der deutsche Shakespeare.' *Shakespeare-Jahrbuch* 74 (1938): pp. 23–4). Some even asserted that British audiences harboured similar sympathies (see von Trotta, Thilo. 'Rasse und Bühne.' *Deutsche Bühnenkorrespondenz* 3. no. 31, 21 April 1934). Hamlet in particular was seen as a hero in the National Socialist sense (see Türck, Hermann. 'Hamlet, eine eminent tatkräftige Natur!' *Stadttheater und Kammerspiele Münster* 14 (1937/38): programme no. 12), and his end was interpreted as a victory of the race/nation over the interests of the individual (Fischer, Friedrich Theodor. 'Shakespeares *Hamlet*.' Ibid.: programme no. 14).

82 After the outbreak of the war the Propaganda Ministry made it clear that despite the fact that some regional party officials had banned Shakespeare performances, Shakespearean drama had to remain in the repertoire (see BArch, R55/20258, pp. 41–4). The role Shakespeare was meant to play after 1939 was similar to demands made on him during the First World War. Gerhart Hauptmann, for example, claimed in 1915 that 'there is no nation – not even England – which has acquired a similar claim to Shakespeare than Germany. Shakespeare's characters are part of our world, his soul has become one with ours: and although he was born and buried in England it is Germany where he truly lives' (Hauptmann, Gerhard. 'Deutschland und Shakespeare.' *Jahrbuch der Deutschen Shakespeare-Gesellschaft* 51 (1915): p. xii).

83 The German federal archives hold several lists compiled on a regular basis by the Propaganda Ministry of theatres who applied for the permission to stage Shakespeare (see BArch, R55/20218, pp. 177–88). All the surviving lists are from the second half of 1942. Depending on how many theatres applied Goebbels was presented with lists of about ten theatres every fortnight. There is not a single case in which permission was not granted. Only if theatres wanted to produce more than one Shakespearean play within a given period the Ministry asked to choose one of them. We should note, however, that the average provincial theatre did not produce more than one Shakespeare play each season anyway. And as late as 1943 the *Völkischer Beobachter* asserted that Shakespeare, Kleist and Schiller were integral parts of German repertoires (quoted in Ruppelt, *Schiller*, p. 31).

84 The success of the play, however, had been closely linked to Mendelssohn's famous music and despite many attempts equally popular music could never

be found. It is interesting to note that even Nazi publications questioned the decision to ban Mendelssohn's stage music. In 1937 Christoph von dem Ritter, who worked on the editorial board of the SS journal *The Black Corps*, asked Schlösser 'to finally end the pathetic attempts to produce *A Midsummer Night's Dream* without Mendelssohn's music. In my opinion nothing, which has so far been offered as a substitute, is able compete with Mendelssohn' (see BArch, R55/20618, p. 98).

85 There are examples of Shakespeare productions which were used as a vehicle for critical ideas. Most of these productions, however, took place at the famous Berlin theatres where Gustav Gründgens and Heinz Hilpert had more freedom of manoeuvre than provincial theatre managers. One example is Jürgen Fehling's 1937 production of *Richard III*, which had Richard limping in a way strikingly similar to Goebbels (see Rühle, Günther. 'Ich bin Fehling. Shakespeares *Richard III.*, eine Inszenierung in der Diktatur – Jürgen Fehlings nicht geheures Theater.' *Theater heute* October 2002: pp. 34–41).

86 Note by Schlösser to Frenzel dated 12 January 1942. BArch, R55/20235, p. 41. As to the celebrations in Germany, the Propaganda Ministry wanted to concentrate the events in Breslau, which was not only Hauptmann's home town but also had the considerable advantage of being far away from Berlin. Apart from that, the Ministry allowed 'virtually every German theatre' to produce a Hauptmann play to mark the occasion. It was made clear though that the National Dramaturge would not speak at the central event in Breslau, and the press was 'told that they should not make great play' of the jubilee (note by Johansson to Haegert in the Propaganda Ministry dated 6 October 1942. Ibid., p. 184). Only the press in the occupied territories were given more freedom to mark the event as 'relating to abroad Hauptmann is a heavyweight about which we can boast' (note by Schlösser to Goebbels dated 27 October 1942. Ibid., p. 192).

87 Walter Kordt distinguished between Hauptmann's 'early works' and his 'mature oeuvre' during the Third Reich, a progress which he compared to Goethe. Kordt even tried to alienate Hauptmann from Naturalism and linked his late success to the rise of National Socialism (see Kordt, Walter. 'Gerhart Hauptmann im achten Lebensjahrzehnt. Aus einer Ansprache, gehalten in den Kammerspielen am 14. Februar 1943.' *Stadttheater und Kammerspiele Münster* 19 (1942/43): programme nos. 17, 21, 24).

88 Braumüller, Wolf. 'Von den Aufgaben nationalsozialistischer Theaterkritik.' *Die Deutsche Bühne* 7 (1936): pp. 3–4.

89 See Johst, Hanns. 'Das Theater im neuen Reich.' *Der Autor*. May 1933: p. 8.

90 See Wardetzky, Jutta. *Theaterpolitik im faschistischen Deutschland. Studien und Dokumente*. Berlin (East): Henschel, 1983. p. 79.

91 See dossier on the programmes of Berlin theatres between April and October 1938, written by Schlösser and sent to Müller in Goebbels' office, dated 9 November 1938. BArch, R55/20258, pp. 155–62.

92 Among others, complaints were filed by the Secret Police and by official

journals such as *Der SA-Mann*. Still Goebbels insisted that Shaw's plays should continue to be produced (see BArch, R 55/20217, pp. 3, 8, 11–13, 24–5 and 30–1).

93 In typical correspondence between a theatre and the National Dramaturge's office from 1935 concerning Shaw's *The Simpleton of the Unexpected Isles*, the Leipzig theatre enquired about a possible production. Leipzig regarded the play as 'in agreement with the demands of the new times', and, indeed, Sigmund Graff had no objections to its production (see BArch, R55/20174, pp. 119–20).

94 The discussions about Shaw's continuing presence in the programmes became increasingly heated, and by the end of 1937 Schlösser wanted to reach a final decision with Goebbels on the matter. In a note to his colleague Graff he claimed that 'today Shaw is already a semi-classical dramatist of the Third Reich and neither with regard to cultural politics nor concerning foreign policy does it lead anywhere to have an argument about this' (see BArch, R55/20217, p. 3). Two years later, when Schlösser demanded increased attempts to ban foreign works, he added that, of course, 'due to his Irish nationality Shaw remains out of consideration' (letter to Goebbels dated 5 September 1939, BArch, R55/20258, p. 224). As late as 1941 Goebbels claimed that Shaw's plays could be used in the regime's anti-English propaganda to such an extent that a ban would be a disaster (quoted in Wardetzky, *Theaterpolitik*, p. 81).

95 'According to reports public opinion again and again regards Shaw as being English' ('Meldungen aus dem Reich' no.169, 10 March 1941, BArch, R58/158, p. 63).

96 Hitler even ordered the press to refrain from polemic remarks concerning Shaw (see BArch, R55/20217, pp. 47–8 and 50).

97 See letter from Hoenselaars to Schlösser, BArch, R55/20349, p. 400. Frenzel replied that both plays would be possible but asked Dortmund to produce only one of them (see ibid., p. 402).

98 After a short discussion within the Propaganda Ministry regarding the application by Shaw's German publisher (Fischer) to raise the monthly payments from RM 2,000 to RM 3,000, Schlösser decided to give the increase the go-ahead. These payments, however, seem to have ceased in the course of the war although in August 1942 the Propaganda Ministry in an internal report realised that the confiscation of Shaw's funds had not been justified because as an Irishman he was a national of a neutral country. The report was quick to add, however, that the transfer of any payments to a Swiss bank account would not be feasible either because of the lack of foreign currency (see BArch, R55/703, pp. 16–17, 20–1, 23 and 24–7).

99 Wilde's *An Ideal Husband* received nine performances, Shaw's *You Never Can Tell* as many as seventeen – and was one of the most successful comedies during that season. At the same time, we have to be aware that the ban on certain foreign works affected some genres more than others. In the operetta

repertoire, for example, foreign composers had traditionally only played a marginal role. The works of Gilbert and Sullivan, for example, had failed to make a significant impact on German stages. *The Mikado* was performed a few times in the late 1920s, and Sidney Jones' *Geisha* received productions in Bielefeld and Münster during the mid-1930s, but these performances were the exception. The whole genre of musical comedy hardly left any marks in Germany, and even West End hits such as *No, No, Nanette* only had marginal successes on the continent (see Dussel, *Heroisches Theater*, p. 267).

100 See circular from the Propaganda Ministry dated 9 November 1939 (BArch, R55/20111, p. 121). See also Schlösser's letter to Goebbels two months earlier regarding the foreign repertoire on German stages (see BArch, R55/20258, pp. 224–6). Bizet's presence in the programmes was not even questioned after plausible rumours emerged that he might have been of Jewish descent (see Wulf, *Theater im Dritten Reich*, pp. 114–15). In Münster *Carmen* was the most successful opera in 1935–6 with twenty-one performances.

101 Hanke's decision to stage Huxley's comedy *General Housecleaning* was criticised by Münster's press who called the play a cheap farce with no plot and filthy humour. The commentator thought it was a shame that such a play would have to be imported, a fact which should encourage young German playwrights to do better (see *MZ*, 23 September 1935).

102 The ensemble performed Shaw's *Candida* in 1936. In early 1938 Stirling's 'Permanent Continental English Theatre' wanted to perform Shaw's *Arms and the Man* in Münster and was assured of the theatre's special interest (see StdAMS, Vernekohl bequest, folder 107). Stirling performed in Paris for about five months a year before touring the continent (see *Theatre World* August 1939: pp. 58–9).

103 See BArch, R55/20258, pp. 224–7.

104 In the first circular from August 1940 Schlösser asked the theatres to send him the relevant information no later than three weeks before the scheduled production date. This, however, seemed to have proved impossible to carry out. In any case Schlösser had to send out a new circular only seven weeks later, in which he reduced the number of productions he wanted to be informed about to special performances and first productions. It seems as if a number of theatres had complained about the additional workload or had simply not complied with the directive (see BArch, R55/20111, p. 257 [circular from 5 August 1940], p. 269 [circular from 19 September 1940]).

105 See BArch, R55/20258, pp. 172–4.

106 Münster's theatre had initially planned to premiere this play in 1942 but had to forego this right to the prestigious Berlin *Volksbühne*. This decision shows how much importance the 'Italian connection' was accorded (see Kordt, Walter. 'Zu Gherardo Gherardis *Feuer im Herbst*. Anläßlich der Inszenierung in den Kammerspielen.' *Stadttheater und Kammerspiele Münster* 19 (1942/43): programme no. 25. See also BArch, R55/20231, p. 28).

107 In Münster the play was first performed on 16 January 1943 – shortly before

the capitulation of the German 6th Army at Stalingrad. The production received a glowing review by Wilhelm Vernekohl who presented it as a fight between two ideologies, 'one, in which everything has its order and even death makes sense, the other, in which blind chaos reigns' (see *MA*, 18 January 1943). It is worth noting that Vernekohl, who was one of the central figures in Münster's post-war cultural politics, appears as an ardent Nazi supporter, not only in this particular review but generally in his work as a journalist. The case of the play's author, Herbert Reinecker, is equally interesting not least because he became a successful script writer for post-war German television. Reinecker was a leading figure in the HJ and an SS war correspondent. In a personal letter to the author Schlösser praised the play because 'the underlying idea is clearly based on National-Socialist principles'. The play is set in a Ukrainian village days before the German occupation in summer 1941, presenting the corruption and tyranny of the Soviet system and the desire of the village people for change. An added 'topical' interest was the presence of a German minority – honest, brave, 'Aryan' – who could not wait to see their homeland 'freed' by the *Wehrmacht*. *The Village near Odessa* was played all over Germany and received sixty-one productions in 1942–3 and thirteen in 1943–4 (see BArch, R55/21230 [the file has no continuous pagination], letter by Schlösser to Johansson in the Propaganda Ministry dated 4 November 1942; letter from Schlösser to Reinecker, same date; circular by Schlösser to theatre managers dated 14 November 1942; letter from Schlösser to Eugen Klöpfer dated 21 December 1942). Then, however, the problems started. In a letter from Schlösser to Johansson from December 1942 he asked him to tell the theatres and the publishers to remove the character of the party commissar Iljitsch from the play because he did not want any audience members to feel sympathy for him. Another more serious problem occurred three months later when Johansson wrote to Schlösser and expressed concerns about the play's concluding sentence 'The Germans are coming' as this assertion had caused irritation during recent productions, quite obviously because of the deteriorating situation on the Eastern front after Stalingrad. Still, Johansson's proposal 'to stop the play until the situation in the East gives cause for more optimism again' was rejected by Schlösser. Schlösser's opinion, however, was not shared by the theatres, several of which rejected the play's production (see BArch, R55/21230, letter by Billerbeck-Genz, head of the Dramaturgical office at the publishing house Eher, 16 March 1943). Later in the war the play became subject to increasing criticism and in June 1944 even the SS complained about a recent production in Bavaria (see BArch, R55/21230, letter by Roßner to Schlösser, 5 June 1944).

108 The connection between this production and the Japanese entry into the war was no secret (see Kordt, Walter. 'Über das japanische Drama und Theater.' *Stadttheater und Kammerspiele Münster* 18 (1941/42): programme no.17).

109 See BArch, R55/20235, p. 282.

110 Some of the more successful contemporary operas staged at Westphalian

theatres included Hans Pfitzner's *Der arme Heinrich*, Nikolaus von Reznicek's *Spiel oder Ernst?*, Ottmar Gerster's *Madame Liselotte*, Ermanno Wolf-Ferrari's *Die neugierigen Frauen*, Norbert Schultze's *Schwarzer Peter*, Richard Strauß' *Daphne* and Werner Egk's *Die Zaubergeige*. Pfitzner's *Der arme Heinrich* had been written in 1895 in the Wagnerian tradition. Pfitzner was never a party member, although he supported the regime. His oeuvre was fostered after the take-over and Pfitzner received many awards. The breakthrough, however, never materialised and Hitler was no fan of his music either (see Drewniak, *Theater im NS-Staat*, pp. 299–301). Although Nikolaus von Reznicek's short opera *Spiel oder Ernst?* was a conservative late romantic piece, probably written long before the take-over, the composer was favoured by the regime and presented himself as a convinced Nazi in 1933 when he wrote the nationalistic overture *Liberated Germany* (see Drewniak, *Theater im NS-Staat*, p. 162). Ottmar Gerster's *Madame Liselotte* with a text by Franz Clemens was first produced in 1933 and at least in some way corresponded to Nazi ideology. The libretto with 'its emphasis on German patriotism and sacrifice for a higher ideal' proved open to *völkisch* interpretation (see Levi, *Music in the Third Reich*, p. 186). Ermanno Wolf-Ferrari's comic opera *Die neugierigen Frauen* received its first performance in 1903 and hardly corresponded to *völkisch* ideas. The composer, however, was supported by the Nazis and in 1939 was made professor at the prestigious Salzburg Mozarteum (see Drewniak, *Theater im NS-Staat*, p. 314). Another piece failing to subscribe to *völkisch* ideas was Norbert Schultze's fairy-tale children's opera *Schwarzer Peter*, which was first performed in 1936. The Richard Strauß opera *Daphne* was set in ancient Greece. The central theme is one of peace between humanity and nature with no *völkisch* subtext whatsoever. Equally unexceptionable was Werner Egk's successful *The Miraculous Fiddle*, which was a romantic *Volksoper* set in Bavaria. Apart from Orff, Egk was one of the most important composers of a younger generation during the 1930s.

111 See Levi, *Music in the Third Reich*, p. 191.

112 See *MA*, 23 September 1935.

113 See Levi, *Music in the Third Reich*, pp. 76–7. Levi convincingly argues that Goebbels' commission can also be interpreted as directed against his arch rival Rosenberg. The archival sources show that the Rosenberg office definitely saw it that way (see BArch, NS8/243, pp. 4–5).

114 In 1936–7 Mozart's opera *Don Giovanni* was translated into German and appeared under the new title *Don Juan*. Anheisser justified his adaptation as 'the German Mozart' had been forced to compose operas in Italian against his will and only because it was *en vogue* at the time (see Anheisser, Siegfried. 'Der deutschen Bühne den deutschen Mozart.' *Blätter des Stadttheaters Münster* 13 (1936/37): programme no. 8.). The press hastened to add that the adaptation was something Mozart himself had longed for as he detested the 'obsession with everything foreign' (see *MZ*, 27 December 1937). Linked with the idea of translation was a strong anti-Semitic notion. The original

libretti for Mozart's Italian operas had been written by Lorenzo da Ponte, who had been Jewish. The most common German version was equally unacceptable for the Nazis as this had been written by Hermann Levi, another Jew. Although Anheisser had started his translation project before 1933, he quickly seized the opportunity to add an anti-Semitic notion to his work after the take-over. He promptly received the much-needed official commissions in 1935 and 1936 (see Levi, *Music in the Third Reich*, pp. 75–6).

115 In 1940–1 the theatre produced *Don Juan* (*Don Giovanni*), in 1941–2 *Così fan Tutte* and in 1943–4 *The Marriage of Figaro*, all in the new Schünemann translations.

116 For the circular see BArch, R55/20111, p. 265. For the Münster note see *Stadttheater und Kammerspiele Münster* 20 (1943/44): programme no. 11.

117 An example of one of these 'recoveries' is Nicolai's opera *Mariana*, one of his 'youth operas', with which Willi Hanke and his Nürnberg director of music were commissioned in March 1943. The Reich Office for Music Adaptations asked Hanke to revise the score according to the following points: change of setting from Scotland to Sicily, and deepening of the Enoch Arden theme, in which the self-sacrifice of the woman ends the political conflict between the rivals (see BArch, R55/20578, pp. 56–8).

118 Musical programmes in general did not change significantly after 1933. The only major change was the disappearance of the works by Gustav Mahler (see Levi, *Music in the Third Reich*, pp. 215–19).

119 The radical changes also become apparent in Dussel's study, which compares the operetta repertoire of 1919–33 with 1933–44. Between 1919 and 1933 the different shares of the different composers were as follows: Johann Strauß thirteen, Kálmán ten, Lehár nine, Benatzky six and Jean Gilbert five per cent. Of these Kálmán and Gilbert disappeared after 1933. Between 1933 and 1944 the respective shares had changed considerably: Lehár 23, Strauß 15, Walter Kollo seven, Eduard Künnecke six and Nico Dostal five per cent (see Dussel, *Heroisches Theater*, pp. 268–9). It is interesting to note in this respect that even the shares of the most successful composers changed considerably with Lehár's share rising by 14 per cent.

120 At Münster, during 1930–1 five out of ten operettas were written by Jewish composers, in 1931–2 seven out of the fourteen, and in 1932–3 still two out of eight. If we also include the works of Ralph Benatzky – who was avoided at first before some of his works returned during the late 1930s – the number of the 'outlawed' would be even higher (in 1931–2 alone the theatre featured four of his works). Additionally, we have to note that the operettas, which now disappeared, had also been some of the most successful pieces in Weimar Germany. Fall and Abraham in particular had been immensely popular.

121 It is interesting to note, however, that even the replacement composers did not meet with unequivocal approval from Rosenberg's hardliners. Nedbal, for example, was Czech and the libretto for his operetta *Polenblut* was written by Leo Rosenstein, who was Jewish. Kollo seemed equally suspect because of

rumours about non-Aryan ancestors (see Drewniak, *Theater im NS-Staat*, pp. 338–9 and 343).

122 The trend continued during the following seasons.

123 Henrichs, Helmut. 'Zur Dramaturgeie der Operette.' *Stadttheater und Kammerspiele Münster* 15 (1938/39): programme no. 1.

124 Ziems, Harry. 'Über die Operette.' Ibid.: programme no. 11.

125 Westermeyer, Karl. 'Die Operette, Stiefkind der Ästhetik.' Ibid.: programme no. 20.

12. Redlin, Fritz-Hartwig. 'Ein Wort zur Operette.' Ibid.

127 Ziems, *Operette*, ibid.: programme no. 11.

128 Henrichs, *Dramaturgeie der Operette*, ibid.: programme no. 1.

129 For the situation in Gelsenkirchen see Schmidt, *NS-Kulturpolitik*, pp. 148–50.

130 Münster's season was extended by two months in 1934–5 and by another month in 1935–6. After 208 working days during 1933–4, the 1934–5 season's 257 days rose to 291 in 1935–6. The number of performances rose accordingly from 354 in 1933–4 to 495 in 1934–5, and 559 in 1935–6. This level was retained well into the war.

131 This in turn also caused protests by commentators who criticised that theatres concentrated on comedies instead of a more demanding repertoire (for Münster see Stampfer, Oskar. 'Kammerspiele der Stadt Münster.' *Theater-Tageblatt* 7 (1935): Nr.1607).

132 At Münster, for example, the dialect plays of the 'Low German Stage' became an increasingly important factor for Hanke's repertoire policy. He offered them his directors, stage managers, costume designers and a designated rehearsal space free of charge and even guaranteed a place in the programmes for their productions of dialect plays. In 1934–5 the theatre featured two dialect comedies, in 1935–6 three, in 1936–7 four and in 1937–8 five. In 1940–1 the Low German comedy *Knubben* by Franz Mehring was the most successful play of the season with fifty-one performances. Hagen put similar emphasis on the Westphalian *Heimat*. The 1938–9 season, for example, opened with a special production entitled 'Humorous Westphalian Literature'. The theatre also produced the opera *Die Lügnerin* by the Hagen-born composer Karl Seidemann, which had been first produced in 1915 (see BArch, R55/20258, p. 173).

133 See Fischer, Kurt. 'Vom Theater der Deutschen.' *Das Innere Reich* 4 (1937/38): pp. 863–4. Others struck a similar chord and criticised 'eminent' contemporary dramatists like Bethge, Billinger, Johst, Möller and Rehberg because they had not produced any new plays recently (see Mettin, Hermann Christian. 'Vom Theater unserer Zeit.' *Das Innere Reich* 4 (1937): pp. 122–8).

134 This fact was a recurring topic even in the programme notes of Westphalia's theatres (see, for example, Hinrichs, August. 'Das Theater des Volkes.' *Blätter des Stadttheaters Münster* 13 (1936/37): programme no. 14; Klaiber, Joachim. 'Junge Dramatiker setzen sich durch.' Ibid.: programme no. 17).

135 See Wanderscheck, Hermann. *Deutsche Dramatik der Gegenwart. Eine*

Einführung mit ausgewählten Textproben. Berlin: Bong, 1938. p. 152.

136 See Ketelsen, *Heroisches Theater*, p. 71.

137 See Frels, Wilhelm. 'Die deutsche dramatische Produktion 1936.' *Die Neue Literatur* 38 (1937): pp. 613–16. Concerning the successes of contemporary comedies see also Dussel, *Heroisches Theater*, p. 304 and Drewniak, *Theater im NS-Staat*, pp. 212–15. Drewniak concentrates especially on the 1936–7 season.

138 These comedies included Otto Brues' *Old Wrangel*, Heinrich Zerkaulen's *Der Sprung aus dem Alltag*, Dietrich Eckart's *A Guy who Speculates* and Sigmund Graff's *The Graduate*. Theatre managers clearly avoided any serious pieces by Eckart (after all, a 'martyr of the movement') and Paul Ernst (equally idealised as the chief dramatic theorist and the spiritual father of the Nazi party).

139 With the outbreak of hostilities imminent in September 1939 the closure of all theatres only seemed a theoretical option. See note 184, chapter two.

140 This was a general trend in Germany. Reports regularly showed utilisations of 80 per cent and more (see BArch, R55/20259).

141 In a press release about his foundation for artists in need Goebbels urged newspapers to point out that in contrast to the generous help offered to German artists British actors suffered badly (quoted in Wulf, *Theater im Dritten Reich*, p. 94). It is interesting to note, however, that many measures the Nazis took were indeed looked at with envy from across the Channel. British commentators criticised the Reich Culture Chamber, for example, because membership was restricted to 'Aryans' and Jews had no chance to find employment. But at the same time many admired the high degree of economic and social security the chamber seemed to offer and begrudged German actors their fixed annual salaries and generous pension funds (see Johns, Eric. 'The Actor in Germany'. *Theatre World* November 1936: p. 227).

142 Ludwig Körner, president of the Reich Theatre Chamber, demanded the theatre to be a 'fortress of the German spirit' prepared to fight in the first line on the 'intellectual front' (Körner, Ludwig. 'Das deutsche Theater, eine Waffe des Geistes.' *Bühnenjahrbuch 1940*. Präsident der Reichstheaterkammer, ed. Berlin: Günther, 1939. p. 1).

143 See Schrade, Hans Erich. 'Deutsches Theater im 5. Kriegsjahr.' *Bühnenjahrbuch 1944*. Präsident der Reichstheaterkammer, ed. Berlin: Günther, 1943. p. 4.

144 The high share of classics in the programmes has led some post-war commentators to claim that theatre managements deliberately chose these plays as a way of escapism or even criticism of the regime. Theatre had been an 'island in a sea of barbarism' (see Prinz, *Geschichte des münsterschen Theaters*, pp. 64–6), and managers used the 'dominance of the classics' in their repertoire as a public statement of their opposition to the regime (see Wardetzky, *Theaterpolitik*, pp. 84–5). Although this claim may correspond to some of the leading managers at influential Berlin theatres most of the regional managements did not dare or did not want to express any critical

ideas. Admittedly, their room for manoeuvre was limited in most cities where the net of mutual control and suspicion grew increasingly tighter in the course of the war.

145 See BArch, R55/20314, pp. 52–64 for 1942–3 and pp. 67–81 for 1943–4.

146 During 1941–2 at Münster contemporary comedies reached a share of 54 per cent (see Fig 4.3). The most successful productions in Bielefeld during the same season were the operetta *Die Fledermaus* (twenty-three performances) and the fairy-tale *The Frog King* (thirty-three performances).

147 After the 1941 raid on Münster the overall number of productions was nearly halved there. To make matters worse, opera and operetta performances in the town hall were poorly attended. There were approximately 180 opera and operetta performances during 1940–1, but only 51 were registered in 1941–2.

148 See *MZ*, 18 December 1943.

149 By the late 1930s the regime was even prepared to make considerable concessions, as long as theatres performed successfully in terms of reaching a certain aesthetic quality in their productions and attracting large audiences. Bremen's municipal theatre and its manager Wiegand is a case in hand. In 1938 a leading HJ functionary wrote to the National Dramaturge complaining about Wiegand's liberal political attitudes and stating that the HJ had cancelled their booking agreement with the theatre. Instead, they would now patronise Bremen's state theatre. In his prompt reply Schlösser made it clear, however, that despite agreeing with HJ-*Obergefolgschaftsführer* Hinrichs regarding Wiegand's personality he did not want to see his position endangered 'under any circumstances'. Although Wiegand was 'liberalistic', he 'produced good theatre' and 'attracted a certain kind of audience', which, presumably, would otherwise be lost. Revealingly, Schlösser concluded that he could be generous as 'after all [Wiegand] was still under our control' (see BArch, R55/20618, p. 204 and Hinrichs' earlier letter pp. 199–202).

150 Although these findings correspond with most other regional theatres in Germany, many apologetic post-war histories (such as Prinz for Münster and Mämpel for Dortmund) claimed otherwise. It is also with respect to these questionable studies that further research in the field is highly desirable.

Conclusion

And if there's only one play on, it is almost a matter of nation credit that that play should be by Shakespeare.

Herbert Farjeon[1]

This study has not only shown that theatres in Yorkshire and Westphalia developed on parallel lines and that they increasingly presented similar repertoires, it has also proved that scholars have neglected a valuable field of research which merits extensive further investigation. The playhouses' development during the Second World War in particular shows many similarities not only regarding their repertoire but also – and perhaps even more interestingly – concerning the motivations behind this repertoire and the way they were being perceived. These points of contact are substantial and put the theatres in the two regions on a similar level. In what constitutes a radical new finding, regional theatre in Britain and Germany during the later stages of the war could be seen as all but interchangeable.

At first sight, however, the founding years of the theatres especially seem to highlight the fundamental differences between British and German theatre. The fact that York's Theatre Royal was founded by the entrepreneur Tate Wilkinson, who ran a commercial touring company, stood in clear contrast to Münster, where the theatre's foundation can hardly be imagined without the decisive influence of the enlightened prince-bishop. The fact that Maximilian Friedrich was prepared to pay for the construction as well as the running of the playhouse seems to anticipate the state-subsidised German theatre landscape. However, a closer look reveals that Münster's theatre was in fact run on similar lines to the Theatre Royal. The impresarios were responsible both in financial and artistic terms. And after the Elector had lost interest in 'his' theatre and the city declined to fund the venture, the impresarios were left to make the theatre pay. In terms of repertoire, this means that we rarely encounter Lessing or Schiller on stage but revues and farces – as in York, where Wilkinson only managed to make Shakespeare pay when he was able to offer opulent stage sets and famous stars. Until around 1900 the theatres in both regions developed on comparable lines; even their financial problems were similar. The main interest of the city authorities concentrated on two matters: a morally acceptable repertoire and a prompt payment of the lease.

Only from the turn of the century do we find significant differences in the development of regional theatre in Britain and Germany. Magistrates in Westphalian cities became increasingly prepared to pay subsidies on a regular basis, thereby acknowledging the importance of theatre for the community. Over the following years subsidies increased, and eventually Westphalia's theatres were taken over by the municipal authorities after the First World War. Such far-reaching decisions seem hardly imaginable in Yorkshire. Although councils increasingly showed an interest in theatres, and sometimes agreed to pay for renovations, it is difficult to imagine them ever having had the desire to take over playhouses entirely in order to run them as municipal theatres. Theatre and business remained related terms – in contrast to Germany where they started to be regarded as separate entities.

Although British and German regional theatres increasingly moved in different directions from the early 1920s, many similarities remained. At first sight it seems as if the economic crisis following the Wall Street Crash only affected the British theatres, whereas the German playhouses survived largely unscathed. Behind the scenes, however, the situation looks very different. At the end of the 1920s Westphalian city councils reduced their subsidies drastically and some even dropped their responsibility for the theatre to return to the lease system. Although this option was the last resort, it nevertheless illustrates that the status of theatres as municipal playhouses was far from safe. If the financial burden grew too much, councils were quite prepared to give up their civic theatre and return to a lease system similar to the one at many Yorkshire theatres.[2] This in turn also meant that despite widespread admiration in Britain for the German theatre system and the life of German actors in particular – who allegedly enjoyed an existence of social security and economic safety – the reality was very different. There was high unemployment among actors around 1930, and for those who had a job life was not much easier. Throughout the 1930s actors at Westphalian theatres performed every day of the week without a day's rest, and on Sundays they sometimes performed twice – similar to the twice-nightly shows at many Yorkshire theatres.[3]

After the economic crisis had forced many playhouses to close, British regional theatres were increasingly turned into repertory theatres with their own ensembles, strong local identities and reduced ticket prices. Some theatres were even turned from commercial concerns into non-profit ventures whose prime concern was not to make huge profits but to present drama of a decent standard to the local community.[4] This was arguably a step towards the continental theatre system. Crucially, parallels do not only relate to organisational questions and the frameworks in which theatres operated but also concerned the repertoire. German contemporary commentators, for example, criticised theatre repertoires for similar reasons as Yorkshire's critics. Instead of the latest modern comedies with 'questionable' moral standards, commentators called either for a more demanding or for a morally 'sound' repertoire – or both.[5] Linked to this criticism was a fear of modern experiments and avant-garde ideas, which was an important feature in both countries. The anti-modernism of the Nazis could build upon well-developed nationalistic and petit-bourgeois attitudes fostered during the Weimar Republic and before. Apart from some performances of Brecht's *Threepenny Opera*, for example, Westphalia's theatres produced hardly any avant-garde pieces during the Weimar years and clearly avoided controversial left-wing drama. Anti-modernist views were widespread in Britain too. Modern art, avant-garde drama and contemporary music by continental artists – which many émigrés brought with them from Nazi-occupied Europe – met with stern resentment in the British establishment. Edward Dent is on record as referring to Reger, Mahler, Bruckner and Pfitzner as 'all those dreadful composers ending in –er'.[6]

Points of contact between Britain and Germany not only concern the repertoire theatres avoided, however, but also, more importantly, the bill actually produced. Similarities are increasingly obvious after the mid-1920s as theatres fostered the drama of the other country. Although Yorkshire's theatres rarely presented the German classics,

234

they increasingly offered German comedies and musical plays adapted for the British stage. German interest in Shakespeare and Shaw as well as contemporary British comedies was equally strong. Around 1930, for example, British contemporary comedies dominated the comedy bill in Münster. Despite the fact that they had to be translated first, some of these plays even appeared simultaneously on British and German stages. Between 1928 and 1933 theatres in both countries featured plays by Maugham, Coward, Ridley and St John Ervine. Even the rising American influence had repercussions in Germany. In what research has failed to recognise until now, we can see that the British interest in plays, topics and music from Germany was substantial and stopped neither with the Nazi take-over nor with the outbreak of war.

These two dates, however, do mark notable changes for German regional theatres, although we have seen that the year 1933 was not a radical turning point. Still, performances of foreign drama became less frequent and the rich Jewish contribution to drama and music was banned. Wilde and Ibsen were presented in new adaptations, modern translations of Shakespearean drama were prohibited and the Bard's oeuvre incorporated in a *völkisch* Germanic heritage. The more radical break, however, was marked by the outbreak of the Second World War. Plays by British playwrights disappeared, and in Yorkshire pieces espousing anti-German sentiments reached the stage. But again this break is not as clear as one might expect. As late as December 1940 – during the 'Battle of Britain' – plays that transported a positive image of Germany were still produced in Yorkshire, and Westphalia's theatres continued to offer Shakespeare and Shaw.

At first sight, however, the war years especially seem to prove those scholars right who stress the differences between theatre in Britain and Germany. Corresponding to Britain's higher level of mobilisation for total war, the theatre and its audiences became accustomed to changes much earlier than German patrons. Evening performances were cancelled, the starting time of shows was changed and ticket prices were raised. Where British theatres were closed for a whole week after war was declared, German audiences were not affected until the later stages of the war. Whereas the calling up of members of Yorkshire's companies was discussed publicly and many received special honours, managements in Westphalia wanted to make changes in personnel as discreetly as possible. From the beginning of the war British regional theatres stood on the front line and fears not only of an invasion but also of air raids ran deep. In Westphalia, by contrast, municipal subsidies increased further and life continued to run smoothly. Only with Germany's changing fortunes in the war did official control become tighter and theatres were increasingly expected to contribute to the war effort. Closed performances for subdivisions of the Nazi party and the armed forces became vital parts of theatre calendars. The contrast between Yorkshire and Westphalia is perhaps best illustrated by an announcement in the *Evening Press* in 1943 that a forthcoming performance of Mozart's *The Marriage of Figaro* would be sung entirely in English.

At the same time this production highlights a development which had hugely important implications for the British stage. Although theatre continued to be regarded as a commercial affair in principle, the government realised the propaganda potential of the arts and increasingly tried to influence the culture sector. The importance of the foundation of ENSA and CEMA, the 'invention' of state subsidies on a large scale and the 'Morrison Law', which empowered the Home Secretary to interfere directly with theatre repertoires if a play was deemed 'inimical' to the war effort, can hardly be overestimated. The cabinet even decided to make theatre performances on Sundays possible for the first time in 300 years.[7] Through all this support the British state acknowledged the importance of theatre in national life and particularly during this war. In just a few years the government did more to commit itself to supporting the theatre than ever before in Britain's history.[8] Although some contemporary commentators were aware of the importance of these far-reaching decisions, research has largely ignored this 'revolution in the arts'.[9] Not only was state involvement in cultural affairs suddenly acceptable, the arts also met with vast new audiences across the country who were eager to attend concerts of classical music, Elizabethan drama and modern ballet – something many of them would not have dreamt of a few years before. Theatre came to be seen as an integral part of the war effort on the home front.[10] Particularly significant was the fact that, although Britain had to cope with the most desperate war effort in its history, no one objected to spending public money on the arts. A public opinion survey carried out in 1943 showed that 59 per cent supported continuing government support of the theatre after the war.[11] For the first time, the arts also showed real promise of voter appeal.

This result is even more astonishing in view of the history of state funding in Britain. Whereas official support for the visual arts had always been forthcoming to some degree, the theatre had not received such patronage because of its alleged purely commercial character. It seems that provincial audiences in particular mistrusted the emerging theatres not primarily aimed at making a profit during the 1910s. Barry Jackson in Birmingham, for example, met with a lack of public support as to run a theatre 'for any other reason than for profit seemed to the Midlander a frivolous occupation meriting contempt rather than admiration'. Even worse, some residents attributed a 'more sinister motive' to Jackson's activities and suspected him of trying to educate the public. Marshall asserted that 'the Englishman has nothing against education but he thinks it should be kept in its place. He resents any attempt to mix it with his amusements'.[12] This, however, was exactly one of CEMA's key aims. Dent praised CEMA for having introduced a new kind of adult education to Britain, and many other contemporary commentators expressed similar enthusiasm for the new quality of wartime repertoires, especially their return to classical drama, opera and ballet. They proudly remarked that wartime escapism had not resulted in 'farce and swing' but in Shakespeare and Elgar.[13] This means that apart from in purely financial terms, theatre was also expected to attain a new level of quality during the war. Government and population alike were not satisfied any longer with the purely entertaining fare offered to them for decades. New enlarged audiences now looked for something more demanding. Education and edification – another radical change – had lost their negative image and became the catchwords of a new theatrical era.

The most important finding in the context of this particular study is that this change also meant that the way in which theatre in Britain started being perceived was not too different from the enemy, even though subsidised theatre had clearly been seen as a continental and deeply un-British institution.[14] Although commentators during the debate about Britain's future theatre referred to either the *Comédie Française* or the Soviet theatre as models (depending on their political allegiances) and avoided any positive mention of the long-established system of state-subsidised theatre in German-speaking countries, it is obvious that they had these countries in mind, too.[15] The British Drama League's Civic Theatre Scheme from 1942, for example, in terms of local responsibility for the arts and basic ideas of organisation clearly mirrored German municipal theatres. On describing the educational role of the Old Vic in connection with his looking for models for a possible post-war theatre, Ashley Dukes called it a typical *Volksbühne* in the German sense of the word.[16] And Harold Hobson claimed that theatre in Britain had developed 'in half a century from the supremacy of the commercial to that of the subsidised'.[17] German propaganda claims regarding the 'uncivilised' life the British public were forced to lead as the country did not even possess a state theatre or a state opera seemed increasingly out of place.[18] In production procedures, too, the continental repertory system came into fashion. Commentators heaped praise on the 1944 Old Vic and Gielgud companies for offering 'true' repertory.[19] Even the plays themselves represented a bill worthy of a continental state theatre.[20] It was clearly recognised as one of the most important merits of the real repertory system that it allowed for experiments and encouraged the staging of plays which might attract only small audiences – an idea which would hardly have sounded appealing to pre-war critics and audiences.[21]

It is, therefore, not only in its role of fostering morale on the home front that we find the most important parallel between British and German regional theatres. During the First World War theatres had already been expected to fulfil this role. The novel element is the British government's perception of theatre as being educational and worth funding with taxpayers' money with an underlying motivation similar to Germany, where the propaganda importance of theatre in wartime was constantly stressed.[22] The above-mentioned tour of the Old Vic through Welsh mining villages, for example, was extensively documented and widely publicised by the Ministry of Information. Commentators asserted that Britain defended not only her island during the war but also her rich cultural heritage. The fight to keep Shakespeare alive seemed nearly as important as the opening of the second front. The theatre was, therefore, the perfect place to express this newly found awareness, and the revival of classical drama and opera alongside avant-garde ballet has to be seen in this context. The development culminated in a repertoire which became increasingly similar to the bill offered in Germany. In both countries the close attention devoted to theatre history and cultural heritage played an important part in wartime propaganda. Shakespeare and Elizabethan drama were as often quoted in support of the war effort in Britain as Goethe, Schiller and Wagner in Germany. Shakespeare's *Merchant of Venice* allegedly summed up what Britain was fighting for as much as it proved the Bard's anti-Semitic 'credentials' for Nazi Germany.[23] Such references proved useful in defending the British Isles as well as justifying the German attack on the Soviet Union. And even on the local level, historical points of reference were found in abundance. As Yorkshire increasingly looked back on Tate Wilkinson and the 'York Circuit' so did Westphalia with allusions to Grabbe.

The new perception of theatre as providing entertainment as well as education met with instant popular success. Patrons flocked to the theatres not only in the West End but also in the provinces. Yorkshire's theatres broke their attendance records on a regular basis after 1939, as did Westphalia's.[24] Secret reports stressed that although some patrons remained focused on pure entertainment, the majority of visitors became increasingly interested in the classics and other more demanding plays – as in Britain.[25] This educational aspect behind theatre in Germany, however, was nothing new and, as has been seen, many patrons went to the theatre with the expectation of learning something, of witnessing some kind of uplifting experience – in short, of being taught. By contrast, for the majority of audiences in Britain the concept of associating entertainment with education was indeed a new idea. It was also linked to a broader concept of emancipation and liberation, which emerged at the end of the war. Education was being related to ideas of social justice and equality as well as increasing calls for political change.[26] One of the results of this changed atmosphere was Labour's win in the 1945 general election.

It might prove fruitful for future research to examine in detail whether this changed attitude towards the arts found any expression in the way the British occupation forces reorganised Germany's cultural life after the war. A first glance at British occupation policy suggests that it did indeed. The British authorities did not interfere with the German theatre system. Although this had partly pragmatic reasons, it was also a sign of their admiration for the German theatre.[27] It also showed that the authorities clearly saw parallels with their own changing theatre world, in which the Arts Council of Great Britain increasingly distributed public money.[28]

After the war public demand for the arts continued to be substantial. It was so high, in fact, that neither the foundation of the Arts Council nor its need for a continual rise in funding met with criticism – on the contrary, it was widely accepted and supported.[29] Far-reaching plans for regional theatre provision included the idea that every town of over 20,000 inhabitants should have its own arts centre for drama, concerts and other events, and the repertory theatres of the larger towns would serve these centres. These theatres would in turn be subsidised by the Arts Council to enable them to feature two companies playing alternate weeks. Once the first company had finished its run it would tour the district while the second company took over at the home playhouse. The idea behind this scheme was not only to serve remote communities with quality performances but also to improve the poor production standards at the provincial theatres doing weekly rep.[30] Critics were quick to acknowledge the new quality of regional theatre productions and James Agate even claimed that Matthew Arnold, had he been alive at the end of the war, would have changed his dictum of 'organise the theatre' into 'spread the theatre'.[31]

By December 1945 the Arts Council had already taken the first steps with the foundation of the Arts Theatre in Salisbury on the above-mentioned lines and attempts for an interchange of provincial repertory companies on a large scale.[32] The Local Government Act of 1948 finally enabled local authorities to spend a certain amount of revenue on entertainment. This – in principle – opened up the possibility of building municipal theatres similar to those in Germany. Thus, the war resulted in legislation which potentially affected the arts throughout Britain and in theory could have moved Britain's theatres even closer to their continental counterparts. Given these new possibilities and the new popularity theatre had gained during the war, however, it is interesting to note that a radical change did not take place. When the Arts Council looked into the effects of the Local Government Act in 1958 they found the overall picture of local spending on the arts was discouraging. At the same time the taking over into municipal ownership and grand restoration to former glory of Hull's New Theatre, Leeds' Grand Theatre and Opera House, Sheffield's Lyceum and Bradford's Alhambra can hardly be imagined without the developments during and immediately after the war.

In conclusion I have argued that regional theatres both in Britain and in Germany not only played their part in the war effort but that they also increasingly deployed similar means. They presented classical plays, opera and dance, contemporary comedies and straight propaganda. Although many differences remain, it is interesting to see how quickly the British government changed its mind regarding the importance of theatre for the war effort and was even prepared to pay for it. We have seen that the supposition mentioned in the introduction, that the way in which official control was exerted was fundamentally different in Britain and Germany, with the Nazis' tight system of regulation in contrast to absolute freedom in Britain, needs to be clarified. Until the later stages of the war, theatre in Nazi Germany was never totally controlled and the possibility of independent decisions regarding the repertoire was greater than research has so far suggested. And in Britain the freedom of decisions was curtailed from 1942 with the 'Morrison Law', which offered the possibility of direct state intervention – powers, which commentators have so far solely attributed to Goebbels. Concerning the repertoire, too, theatres in Yorkshire and Westphalia operated an increasingly similar policy with educational concepts clearly dominating over pure entertainment. Although the British government did not fund drama on a scale anywhere near the huge subsidies paid in Germany, the basic idea that theatre was of national importance and not just a commercial affair constituted an interesting parallel. The changes in the repertoire and in the way it was perceived meant not only that theatres in Yorkshire had changed radically within a few years, but also that they had become similar to their Westphalian counterparts – cultural institutions rather than places for pure entertainment. The fundamental differences, however, have also become obvious. The similarities found do not in any way imply that theatre in Britain during the Second World War was the same as in Nazi Germany. One seemingly little event from December 1943 can perhaps best illustrate the most important of these differences. At that time Sadler's Wells performed in Yorkshire and presented, as usual, European opera classics – among them *The Marriage of Figaro*. Mozart's opera was given in a new production by Kurt Jooss – the same Kurt Jooss who had been celebrated in Weimar Germany for his avant-garde dance performances, who had helped Münster's theatre to gain nationwide recognition in the mid-1920s, and who was forced to leave Germany by the Nazis.

NOTES

1   On the choice of repertoire after 1939 (Farjeon, *Shakespearean Stage*, p. 67).

2   The ways to save money on running costs were similar, too, and especially the cost of heating the theatres was sometimes reduced, as complaints from patrons show. For the performances of the fairy tale *Das dumme Englein* in 1930 Münster's theatre was so badly heated that people feared they might catch a cold (see *Volkswille*, 19 December 1930). At about the same time York's Theatre Royal's faulty heating caused people to walk out in winter 'refusing to come again' (see Theatre Royal Sub-Committee meeting of 5 August 1933, *York City Council, Estates Committee 1931–1940*. pp. 142–4).

3   The only chance of a rest was the visit of a touring company. These visits represent another parallel between Britain and Germany. In some seasons up to five different touring companies performed at Münster's theatre, for example, some of them staying for a whole week.

4   Chisholm even claimed that the rise of the repertory movement was 'primarily ... a revolt against commercialism' (see Chisholm, *Repertory*, p. 10).

5   Commentators claimed that comedies about adultery and pure sensationalism occupied the prominent places in the repertoires (Heising, Wilhelm. 'Die Gesellschaftskultur der heutigen Zeit'. *Blätter des Theaters der Stadt Münster* 4 (1927–28): p. 126).

6   Quoted in Willett, John. 'The Emigration and the Arts.' Hirschfeld, Gerhard, ed. *Exile in Great Britain. Refugees from Hitler's Germany*. London: Berg, 1984. p. 210.

7   See *Theatre World* February 1941: pp. 27 and 46; as well as *Theatre World* March 1941: p. 51. In the end, however, Parliament voted against this bill by a small majority (see *Theatre World* April 1941: p. 75).

8   Norman Marshall concluded that 'when one recalls the hullabaloo in Parliament and the press before the war over a suggestion that a small grant should be made to finance the opera season at Covent Garden, it is remarkable how little opposition there was to CEMA being provided with some of the tax-payers' money to finance plays, opera and ballet' (Marshall, *Other Theatre*, p. 228).

9   Bernard Miles claimed that the fact that CEMA received Treasury funding 'within four months of its foundation meant that for the first time in history the State recognised the drama as one of the sinews of the national soul, and this was the most important thing that had happened to the British theatre since the birth of Shakespeare' (Miles, Bernard. *The British Theatre*. London: Collins, 1948. p. 44). Others asserted that the system of government support for the arts 'represents the most forward step in the advancement of British culture that a British Government has yet taken' (Dean, *Theatre at War*, p. 530).

10   Laurence Olivier asserted that 'no other moment has approached in splendour and achievement the glorious Restoration Period, when many

notable talents and much vitality and enthusiasm were involved in the rebirth of our theatre. That is, no other moment until now' (Olivier in his foreword to Noble, *British Theatre*, p. 3).

11 The survey was compiled by the British Institute of Public Opinion and was presented to the Ministry of Information in May 1943. Answering question five: 'Would you favour continuing, after the war, Government spending in support of music, theatre, films etc.?' a total of 59 per cent answered yes, 26 per cent said no and 17 per cent did not know. The support was highest in the age group twenty-one to twenty-nine (64 per cent) and among the higher economic classes (66 per cent) (see Public Record Office. Ministry of Information. INF 1/292 (Part 3). Home Intelligence Reports, July 1942–August 1943. pp. 105–7, quotes p. 106).

12 Marshall, *Other Theatre*, p. 164.

13 See Haskell, *Ballet Since 1939*, p. 23.

14 This view had a long tradition in Britain and had found expression before on many occasions. In the first parliamentary debate on a subsidised National Theatre in 1913 politicians warned against efforts to 'Prussianise our institutions' (quoted in Whitworth, *National Theatre*, p. 106). This sentiment resurfaced in the late 1930s when the National Theatre movement hoped to gather public support for a building on the newly acquired site in South Kensington.

15 During the first serious campaign to found a National Theatre before the First World War commentators constantly referred to the German example. Winston Churchill demanded a National Theatre so that Britain reached an artistic level already achieved by France and Germany (see *The Times*, 18 June 1906), Henry Arthur Jones remarked that Britain needed a Shakespeare memorial theatre so that people had 'the privilege of seeing as many of his plays performed in the course of a year as if they were living in a second-rate German town' (as quoted in the *Daily Chronicle*, 16 March 1908. The paper ran a daily column with comments on the Shakespeare memorial, to which German commentators were asked to contribute), and during the above-mentioned 1913 parliamentary debate Mr Mackinder MP quoted performance figures of German theatres from the *Shakespeare-Jahrbuch* and made it clear that 'we have nothing in this land of Shakespeare to show which is comparable in the least degree to the facts indicated by these figures' (quoted in Whitworth, *National Theatre*, p. 101). The handbook of the Shakespeare Memorial National Theatre Committee from 1909 even claimed that with a National Theatre 'Shakespeare, in short, would receive in his own country an assiduous homage which he now only receives in Germany' (quoted ibid., p. 84).

16 See Dukes, Ashley. 'Social Basis. The English Scene.' *Theatre Arts* 24 (1940): p. 409.

17 See Hobson, *Theatre in Britain*, p. 22. The emerging of state subsidies went hand in hand with a rise in the number of repertory companies. Before the

outbreak of the war *The Stage* listed seventy-five repertory companies in Britain. By 1946 this figure had risen to 220.

18 As quoted in *The Times*, 29 April 1941.

19 See, for example, Dukes who claimed that the 1944–5 London theatre season had been the best 'for a great many years' (see Dukes, Ashley. 'The English Scene.' *Theatre Arts* 29 (1945): p. 562). Gielgud stated that 'classical repertory has taken London by storm in the sixth year of war' (Gielgud, John. 'The Haymarket and the New. London Flocks to Repertory.' *Theatre Arts* 29 (1945): p. 166). The Old Vic produced at least three pieces each season, but kept earlier productions in the programme in order to build up a repertoire.

20 During the first season at the Old Vic the company staged *Peer Gynt, Arms and the Man, Richard III, Uncle Vanya*, two parts of *Henry IV* and *The Critic*, and Tennent Plays at the Haymarket presented *Hamlet, Love for Love* and *A Midsummer Night's Dream*.

21 Commentators praised 'true' repertory and the Old Vic's new 'repertory fashion' as a 'noteworthy feature that cannot be stressed too much' (Stephens, Frances. 'Over the Footlights.' *Theatre World* June 1944: p. 5).

22 German propagandists demanded that theatres had to be aware of their function, which 'can initiate a considerable mental and intellectual strengthening of the inner preparedness for war within the German people' (*Meldungen aus dem Reich* Nr. 263, 26 February 1942. BArch R58/169, p. 297). And British commentators repeatedly stressed how successful the theatre was in keeping up national morale (see, for example, Hobson, *Theatre in Britain*, p. 117).

23 Donald Wolfit's portrayal of Shylock and his 'terrific third act speech – "I am a Jew" – reached a high peak of intensity and brought forth a storm of applause' (*HDM*, 21 September 1943).

24 This was a general trend. A typical intelligence report from February 1942 stated that theatres experienced an unprecedented popularity and that performances regularly sold out (see *Meldungen aus dem Reich* Nr. 263, 26 February 1942. BArch R58/169, p. 297).

25 See ibid.

26 As mentioned before, the Beveridge Report, the Education Act, plans for a National Health Service as well as the general concept of a welfare state have to be seen in connection with this political change.

27 See Clemens, Gabriele. 'Die britische Kulturpolitik in Deutschland: Musik, Theater, Film und Literatur.' *Kulturpolitik im besetzten Deutschland 1945–1949*. Clemens, Gabriele, ed. Stuttgart: Steiner, 1994. p. 207.

28 British occupation policy, however, was also guided by other principles. The above-mentioned concept of a positive 'projection of Britain' played an important role, too.

29 In 1946–7 the Arts Council received £350,000, in the following year the Council already obtained more than half a million (see Minihan, *Nationalization of Culture*, p. 228).

30   CEMA's Charles Landstone was one of the driving forces behind this scheme (see Kelsall, Glyn. 'CEMA Marches On.' *Theatre World* September 1945: pp. 27–8).

31   See Agate, James. *The Contemporary Theatre. 1944 and 1945*. London: Harrap, 1946. pp. 212–13.

32   The *Theatre World* was left speechless at the speed the British theatrical landscape was transforming: 'How different the story after the last war, when the theatre in the provinces was allowed to wilt and perish … Few realised then that a country whose provincial theatres are dead (however flourishing the stage might be in the capital) is dramatically speaking like a tree without roots' (Stephens, Frances. 'Over the Footlights.' *Theatre World* December 1945: p. 5).

Bibliography

ARCHIVAL SOURCES

German Federal Archives/Bundesarchiv Berlin-Lichterfelde (BArch)

Reichskanzlei: R43 II/887b, R43 II/895, R43 II/1021

Reichsministerium für Volksaufklärung und Propaganda: R55/13, R55/72, R55/127, R55/601, R55/607, R55/647, R55/648, R55/703, R55/821, R55/849, R55/20111, R55/20174, R55/20217, R55/20218, R55/20230, R55/20230a, R55/20231, R55/20231a, R55/20235, R55/20249, R55/20258, R55/20259, R55/20261, R55/20263, R55/20314, R55/20349, R55/20451, R55/20451a, R55/20452, R55/20452a

Reichsmusikkammer: R56 II/4

Reichskulturkammer: R56 I/11, R56 I/50, R56 I/53, R56 I/54, R56 I/56, R56 I/57, R56 I/58, R56 I/59, R56 I/60, R56 I/61, R56 I/91, R56 I/128

Reichstheaterkammer: R56 I/22, R56 I/24, R56 I/45, R56 I/46, R56 I/49, R56 I/64, R56 I/65, R56 I/93, R56 II/4, R56 III/2a, R56 III/16, R56 V/153

Reichssicherheitshauptamt: R58/158, R58/159, R58/169

Amt Rosenberg, Abteilung Theater/NSKG: NS 15/81, NS 15/82, NS 15/131, NS 15/142, NS 15/149

Kanzlei Rosenberg, Stellen Musik, Bildende Kunst und Theater: NS 8/124, NS 8/150, NS 8/152, NS 8/162, NS 8/202, NS 8/243

Theatre Collection of the University of Cologne

Städtische Bühnen Münster programme notes 1921–44

Bibliography

City Archives Münster (StdAMS):

Vernekohl bequest, folders 63, 97–113, 144, 146, 148 and 150
Edith Lippold collection
Eugen Müller collection
budget plans 1926–47
Städtische Bühnen DS 378
Stadtregistratur Zentralbüro (central office) 135, 208, 232, 266, 285 and 369
statistical reports 1928–30, 1933 and 1938–48
statistical year books 1935–8
Verwaltungsbericht (administrative report) 1926–45
theatre programme notes

State Archives Münster (StAMS)

Oberpräsidium nos. 5501, 5525, 5636 and 5596

City Archives Bielefeld (StdABI)

Fritz Brinkmann. *45 Jahre Theaterbeleuchter. Erfahrungen und Erinnerungen eines*
Lebens im Theater und für das Theater. 1958/1960 [unpublished manuscript]
Anny-Marie Hinney. *Die Geschichte des Theaters der Stadt Bielefeld.* 1938 [unpublished manuscript]
Jochen Seydel. *Das Stadttheater Bielefeld. Kriegsjahre und Neubeginn 1939–1947.* 1947 [unpublished manuscript]
Theatergesellschaft (theatre association), Prot 0064, minute book 1926–33
Beirat (advisory board) theatre and orchestra, Prot 0065, minute book 1936–8 theatre and music committee, Prot 0067, minute book 1901–33
Städtische Bühnen und Orchester (theatre and orchestra) 1458, 1462, 1515, 1538, 1672, 1678, 1702, 1703, 1706, 1731, 1742, 1776 and 1778
theatre programme notes

City Archives Dortmund (StdADO)

Mämpel bequest

Theatre Archives Dortmund

theatre programme notes

City Archives Hagen (StdAHA)

theatre report 1933–6: Ha1 8890
theatre licences: Ha1 9230
appointments and contracts theatre managers: Ha1 9300, Ha1 9297
season ticket: Ha1 9224
municipal theatre committee: Ha1 10846, Ha1 10847, Ha1 9223, Ha1 9271
production of *Wittekind* in 1935: Ha1 9285
municipal theatre subsidies: Ha1 9275, Ha1 9277, Ha1 9278, Ha1 9341, Ha1 9280, Ha1 9342, Ha1 9326, Ha1 10850, Ha1 9328, Ha1 9272, Ha1 9327
theatre programme notes

City Archives Bochum (StdABO)

municipal theatre matters: D St 13, 1 BO 20/234, OB Pi 10
theatre business plans 1919–25: D St 10, 1
Prussian Theatre Council, theatre law, titles and awards, contracts: D St 15
Metzger, Hans-Ulrich. *25 Jahre Stadttheater Bochum.* 1943 [unpublished manuscript]
theatre programme notes

Public Record Office (PRO)/The National Archives

Ministry of Information: INF 1/44, INF 1/188, INF 1/260, INF 1/282, INF 1/292, INF 1/543, INF 1/760, INF 1/930, INF 2, INF 3/316, INF 4, INF 5, INF 6/1018, INF 13
Foreign Office: FO 371, FO 898, FO 930
Prime Minister's Office: PREM 1/388, PREM 1/391, PREM 1/441,

PREM 3, PREM 4
Treasury: T 161/1083, T 231
Ministry of Education and Science: ED 10
Home Office: HO 45, HO 144, HO 199, HO 262, HO 186, HO 192
Board of Trade: BT 31/33529/290285
Supreme Court of Judicative: J 13

Theatre Museum, London

Walter Hudd Archive: THM/129
Charles Landstone Archive: THM/201
Geoffrey Whitworth and *The Times*
Geoffrey Whitworth (1883–1951). Three Centenary Tributes.
British Drama League
Wartime Entertainment
ENSA

Victoria and Albert Museum, London

CEMA: EL 1/1, EL 1/3, EL 1/6, EL 1/7, EL 1/9, EL 2/2, EL 2/9, EL 2/11, EL 2/76, EL 3/1, EL 3/2, EL 3/3, EL 3/10, EL 3/11, EL 3/12, EL 3/19, EL 3/20, EL 3/21
Arts Council: ACGB/34/76, ACGB/34/165, ACGB/41/90, ACGB/41/82, ACGB/43/40
Regional Programmes: Leeds Grand Theatre 1930–49, York Theatre Royal to 1976

Imperial War Museum, London

Ministry of Information Second World War Official Collection
Eph. C 39 Theatre. L.B.S.
Bulletins from Britain, 1940–2
Germany and You, 1938–41
Joy and Work

York Theatre Royal Archives

Bill Books 1936–7, 1940–4, 1944–8

York City Archives

City of York Council, Council Minutes 1899–1947

Corporation of York, Education Committee, 1908–10

Corporation of York, Estates Committee, 1894–1949

Corporation of York, Special Musical Entertainment Committee, 1912–29

City of York Council, Entertainments Committee, 1944–6

City of York Council, Civic Committee, 1942–5

City of York Council, Cultural Development Sub-Committee, 1942–4

City of York Council, Social Life Sub-Committee, 1942–3

City of York Council, Holidays-at-Home Scheme, 1942 and 1944

Nellie Woodhouse Collection

York Empire Theatre scrap books

York Oral History Project, interviews

Borthwick Institute of Historical Research, York

Rowntree Papers: LTE/52, LEC/24, PP/21

York Reference Library

programme notes Theatre Royal and Empire Theatre

West Yorkshire Archive Service, Bradford

Alhambra records: 11D82

Bradford theatres newspaper cuttings, 1939–46: 20D99/5/19, 20D99/2/3

Bradford theatre programmes: 22D84, 47D76

Peter Holdsworth Collection: 12D93

Alhambra records: 42D91

notebooks 1916–42: 20D99/2/2

press cuttings: 20D99/5/19

theatre programme notes

West Yorkshire Archives, Huddersfield

Theatre Royal Records 1901–36: B/HTR/a/I, B/HTR/as/10–11,

B/HTR/g/1–5, B/HTR/af/1–17, B/HTR/ac/1–5, B/HTR/al/1–5,
B/HTR/m/1–2, B/HTR/z/1–3, B/HTR/p
Theatre Royal Dewsbury: KC 1052, B/DTR
Huddersfield Thespians: S/HT/m/1, S/HT/z/1–2, S/HT/z/6–9

West Yorkshire Archives, Leeds

John Beaumont, *History of the Theatre* (type written manuscript, n.d.)
Collection Grand Theatre and Opera House: WYL 762

Sheffield City Archives

Sheffield Repertory Company: LD 1552/1, LD 1553/3, LD 2342/6,
LD 2342/8

Hull City Archives

Documents Relating to the Little and New Theatres: DFBN
Santangelo, Peppino. *Historical Souvenir Booklet Commemorating Twenty-one Years of Management with the 'Little' and 'New' Theatres in the City of Kingston upon Hull.* Hull: John Hartley, n.d. [1954]

Hull Local Studies Library

theatre collection: L792
Little Theatre, Hull. Scrapbook of Newscuttings etc. 1924–1930.
Heritage Information Centre. *Theatres and Cinemas in Hull* [unpublished manuscript]
Bloomfield, Jack. *The Theatre in the Square. Celebrating Sixty Years of History: Listing all the Shows at Hull New Theatre 1939–1999.* [unpublished manuscript]

LITERATURE

Contemporary Literature

Agate, James. *The Contemporary Theatre. 1944 and 1945.* London: Harrap, 1946.
Bähr, Hans. *Britische Propaganda.* Berlin: Eher, 1940.

Bernau, Alfred, ed. *Theater der Stadt Münster. Spielzeit 1929/30. Vorteile und Bedingungen der Platzmiete*. Münster: n.p., n.d.

— ed. *Das Theater der Stadt Münster in der Spielzeit 1930–31. Verzeichnis der Mitglieder – Spielpläne – Stammsitzbedingungen*. Münster: Krick, 1930.

— *Theater der Stadt Münster. Zur kommenden Spielzeit 1930/31*. Münster: n.p., n.d.

— *Theater der Stadt Münster. Spielzeit 1931/32*. Münster: Krick, 1931.

Best, Werner. *Völkische Dramaturgie*. Würzburg: Triltsch, 1940.

Bethge, Friedrich. 'Rede bei der Theatertagung der H.J. in Bochum.' *Das Innere Reich* 4 (1937): pp. 335–54.

Biedrzynski, Richard. *Schauspieler – Regisseure – Intendanten*. Heidelberg: Hüthig, 1944.

Billerbeck-Gentz, Friedrich. 'Die Bedeutung der Kunst im Kriege.' *Deutsche Dramaturgie* 3 (1944): pp. 5–8.

Braumüller, Wolf. 'Der Kampf um Shakespeare. Eine Entgegnung auf Hans Rothes Bericht.' *Bausteine zum deutschen Nationaltheater* 4 (1936): pp. 51–62.

British Drama League. *Twenty-Five Years of the British Drama League 1919–1944*. Oxford: Alden, 1944.

Budde, Fritz. 'Entwurf zu einem Theater.' *Das Innere Reich* 3 (1936/37): pp. 1181–92.

CEMA. *The Fifth Year. The End of the Beginning. Report on the Work of CEMA for 1944*. London: Council for the Encouragement of Music and the Arts, 1945.

— *The Arts in War Time. A Report on the Work of C.E.M.A. 1942 and 1943*. London: Council for the Encouragement of Music and the Arts, n.d. [1944].

Chisholm, Cecil. *Repertory. An Outline of the Modern Theatre Movement. Production, Plays, Management*. London: Davies, 1934.

City of Hull Development Committee, eds. *The City and Port of Hull*. Hull: Brown, 1940.

Cohen, Fritz Alexander, ed. *Festschrift Feierspiele Münster Pfingsten 1925*. Dortmund: Krüger, 1925.

Coope, John, comp. *Hull. Marketing Facts and Figures 1938*. London: Northcliffe Newspapers, n.d. [1938].

Dent, Edward J. *A Theatre for Everybody. The Story of the Old Vic and Sadler's Wells*. London: Boardman, 1945.

Dent, H.C. *Education in Transition. A Sociological Study of the Impact of*

War on English Education 1939–1943. London: Kegan Paul, 1944.

Dyas, Aubrey. *Adventure in Repertory. Northampton Repertory Theatre 1927–48.* Northampton: Northampton Repertory Players, 1948.

Elster, Hanns Martin. *Die Erneuerung des deutschen Theaters.* Regensburg: Habbel, 1922.

Emmel, Felix. *Theater aus deutschem Wesen.* Berlin: Stilke, 1937.

Ernst, Paul. 'Das Drama in der Zeitenwende.' *Das Innere Reich* 2 (1935): pp. 522–33.

Euringer, Richard. *Chronik einer deutschen Wandlung 1925–1935.* Hamburg: Hanseatische Verlagsanstalt, 1936.

Fischer, Kurt E. 'Vom Theater der Deutschen.' *Das Innere Reich* 4 (1937/38): pp. 862–6.

Geisberg, Max, ed. *Die Stadt Münster. Vierter Teil. Die Profanen Bauwerke seit dem Jahre 1701.* Münster: Aschendorff, 1935.

Gerlach-Bernau, Kurt. *Drama und Nation. Ein Beitrag zur Wegbereitung des nationalsozialistischen Dramas.* Breslau: Hirt, 1934.

Goebbels, Joseph. *Die Tagebücher von Joseph Goebbels. Teil 2. Diktate 1941–1945.* Fröhlich, Elke, ed. München: Saur, 1993–6.

— *Die Tagebücher von Joseph Goebbels. Sämtliche Fragmente. Teil 1. Aufzeichnungen 1924–1941.* Fröhlich, Elke, ed. München: Saur, 1987.

Günther, Margarete. *Der englische Kriegsroman und das englische Kriegsdrama 1919–1930.* Berlin: Juncker & Dünnhaupt, 1936.

Haskell, Arnold L., Powell, Dilys, Myers, Rollo and Ironside, Robin. *Since 1939. Ballet – Films – Music – Painting.* London: Readers Union, 1948.

Henderson, Neville. *Failure of a Mission. Berlin 1937–1939.* London: Readers Union, 1941.

Hitler, Adolf. *Mein Kampf.* 434th–443rd ed. München: Eher, 1939.

Hoffmann, Heinrich. *Theaterrecht. Bühne und Artistik. Zusammenfassende Darstellung des gesamten Theaterrechts unter Berücksichtigung der Anordnungen der Reichskulturkammer und Reichstheaterkammer sowie der Bestimmungen der Reichsgewerbeordnung nebst Text mit Anmerkungen.* Berlin: Vahlen, 1936.

Hutchison, Percy. *Masquerade.* London: George Harrap, 1936.

Hymnen, Friedrich Wilhelm. 'Um ein neues Drama.' *Das Innere Reich* 6 (1939): pp. 463–70.

Kaun, Axel, ed. *Berliner Theater-Almanach 1942.* Berlin: Neff, 1942.

Kemp, Thomas C. *Birmingham Repertory Theatre. The Playhouse and the*

Man. With a Foreword by Sir Barry Jackson. 2nd. rev. ed. Birmingham: Cornish, 1948.

Knight, Charles Brunton. *A History of the City of York.* York: Herald, 1944.

Koehler, Hansjürgen. *Inside Information.* London: Pallas, 1940.

Kries, Wilhelm von. *Strategy and Tactics of the British War Propaganda.* Berlin: Zander, 1941.

Künkler, Karl. 'Es sind immer dieselben!' *Deutsche Dramaturgie* 3 (1944): pp. 65–6.

Kurz, Werner. 'Verbrechen an Shakespeare.' *Bausteine zum deutschen Nationaltheater* 4 (1936): pp. 33–42.

— 'Hans Rothe und das Theater.' *Ibid.* (1936): pp. 43–7.

Langenbeck, Curt. 'Wiedergeburt des Dramas aus dem Geist der Zeit.' *Das Innere Reich* 6 (1939/40): pp. 923–57.

— 'Dürfen wir uns bei dem jetzigen hohen Stand der Schauspielbühne beruhigen?' *Das Innere Reich* 3 (1936): pp. 764–70.

Leeper, Janet. *English Ballet.* 2nd rev. ed. London: Penguin, 1945.

Manchester, P.W. *Vic-Wells: A Ballet in Progress.* London: Gollancz, 1946.

Marshall, Norman. *The Other Theatre.* London: John Lehmann, 1947.

Maugham, William Somerset. *Theatre. A Novel.* London: Heinemann, 1937.

Medefind, Heinz. *Das war London. Glanz und Elend der größten Stadt der Erde.* Berlin: Stalling, 1942.

Mettin, Hermann Christian. *Die Situation des Theaters.* Wien: Sexl, 1942.

— 'Vom Theater unserer Zeit.' *Das Innere Reich* 4 (1937): pp. 122–28.

Meyer, Walther. *Die Entwicklung des Theaterabonnements in Deutschland.* Emsdetten: Lechte, 1939.

Miles, Bernard. *The British Theatre.* London: Collins, 1948.

Morrell, J.B. *The City of Our Dreams.* London. Fountain Press, 1940.

Müller, Eugen. 'Das Theater in Münster 1534–1927'. *Almanach 1927. Theater der Stadt Münster.* Intendanz des Theaters, ed. Münster: n.p., 1927.

Nedden, Otto zur. *Drama und Dramaturgie im 20. Jahrhundert. Abhandlungen zum Theater und zur Theaterwissenschaft der Gegenwart.* 2nd rev. ed. Würzburg: Triltsch, 1943.

Nicoll, Allardyce. *British Drama. An Historical Survey from the*

Beginnings to the Present Time. 4th rev. ed. London: Harrap, 1949.

Noble, Peter. *British Theatre.* London: Knapp & Drewett, 1946.

Ockert, Otto. *Rückblick auf die erste Spielzeit 1918/19 des wiedereröffneten Stadttheaters Münster unter der Direktion von Otto Ockert.* Münster: n.p., n.d.

Pabst, Erich, ed. *Jahrbuch 1940–41 der Städtischen Bühnen Münster (Westf.).* Münster: n.p., 1940.

— *Vorschau auf die Spielzeit 1939–40. Städtische Bühnen/Münster-Westf.* Münster: Städtische Bühnen, 1939.

Pagel, Karsten. 'Gegenwart als Dramenstoff.' *Deutsche Dramaturgie* 3 (1944): pp. 15–16.

Pilger, Else. 'George Bernard Shaw in Deutschland.' Diss.: University of Münster, 1942.

Poensgen, Wolfgang. *Der deutsche Bühnen-Spielplan im Weltkriege.* Berlin: Gesellschaft für Theatergeschichte, 1934.

Priestley, J.B. *Theatre Outlook.* London: Nicholson and Watson, 1947.

Rosenberg, Alfred. *Der Mythus des 20. Jahrhunderts. Eine Wertung der seelisch-geistigen Gestaltenkämpfe unserer Zeit.* 53rd– 54th ed. München: Eher, 1935.

Rowntree, Seebohm B. *Poverty and Progress. A Second Social Survey of York.* London: Longman, 1942.

Schäfer, Wilhelm. 'Warum der Deutsche seinen Schiller liebt.' *Das Innere Reich* 6 (1939/40): pp. 876–87.

Schlösser, Rainer. *Das Volk und seine Bühne. Bemerkungen zum Aufbau des deutschen Theaters.* Berlin: Langen/Müller, 1935.

Schmid, Adolf, ed. *Judentum und Musik. Liste der jüdischen Komponisten als Unterlage für die Säuberungsaktionen auf dem Gebiete der Musik.* Straßburg: Abt. Volksaufklärung und Propaganda beim Chef der Zivilverwaltung im Elsaß, 1941.

Shirer, William L. *Berlin Diary. The Journal of a Foreign Correspondent 1934–1941.* London: Hamilton, 1942.

Short, Ernest. *Theatrical Cavalcade.* London: Eyre and Spottiswoode, 1942.

Speaight, Robert. 'Drama Since 1939.' Hayward, John, Reed, Henry, Speaight, Robert and Spender, Stephen. *Since 1939.* London: Phoenix, 1949. pp. 9–60.

Stampfer, Oskar H., ed. *Münster 165%.* Münster: n.p., n.d

— *Künstler schaffen für Dich!* Münster: n.p., n.d.

Stumpfl, Robert. 'Vom neuen deutschen Drama.' *Das Innere Reich* 4

(1937/38): pp. 951–6.

Theaterverlag Albert Langen/Georg Müller, eds. *Junges Drama. Almanach 1937*. Berlin: Langen/Müller, 1937.

Theilkuhl, Wolfgang. *Deutsches Land und deutsches Leben*. 5th ed. London: Methuen, 1944.

Trewin, J.C. *The Theatre Since 1900*. London: Dakers, 1951.

Viehoff, Helmuth, ed. *Gaukulturwoche 1939 Westfalen-Nord*. Münster: Buschmann, 1939.

Wanderscheck, Hermann. *Deutsche Dramatik der Gegenwart. Eine Einführung mit ausgewählten Textproben*. Berlin: Bong, 1938.

Watson, A.G., comp. and ed. *York City Year Book and Business Directory*. York: Yorkshire Gazette, 1939.

Wehner, Josef Magnus. *Vom Glanz und Leben deutscher Bühne. Eine Münchner Dramaturgie. Aufsätze und Kritiken 1933–1941*. Hamburg: Hanseatische Verlagsanstalt, 1944.

Whitworth, Geoffrey. *The Making of a National Theatre*. London: Faber & Faber, 1951.

Williams, Harcourt. *Old Vic Saga*. London: Winchester, n.d. [1949].

Williamson, Audrey. *Old Vic Drama. A Twelve Years' Study of Plays and Players*. 2nd ed. London: Rockliff, 1953.

— *Theatre of two Decades*. London: Rockliff, 1951.

Wilson Knight, G. *This Sceptred Isle. Shakespeare's Message for England at War*. Oxford: Blackwell, 1940.

Wyndham Goldie, Grace. *The Liverpool Repertory Theatre 1911–1934*. Liverpool: Liverpool University Press, 1935.

Zickel von Jan, Reinhold. 'Wir brauchen Shakespeare!' *Bausteine zum deutschen Nationaltheater* 4 (1936): pp. 47–51.

Research Literature

Adam, Peter. *The Arts of the Third Reich*. London: Thames & Hudson, 1992.

Albert, Claudia, ed. *Deutsche Klassiker im Nationalsozialismus. Schiller – Kleist – Hölderlin*. Stuttgart: Metzler, 1994.

Ardagh, John. *Germany and the Germans*. 3rd ed. London: Penguin, 1995.

Balfour, Michael, ed. *Theatre and War 1933–1945. Performance in Extremis*. Oxford: Berghahn, 2001.

— *Propaganda in War. 1939–1945. Organisations, Policies and Publics in*

Britain and Germany. London: Routledge & Kegan Paul, 1979.

Barker, Clive and Gale, Maggie B. eds. *The British Theatre between the Wars 1918–1939*. Cambridge: Cambridge University Press, 2000.

Barker, Kathleen. 'Thirty Years of Struggle. Entertainment in Provincial Towns Between 1840 and 1870.' *Theatre Notebook* 39 (1985): pp. 25–31, 68–75 and 140–9.

Beach, Abigail and Weight, Richard, eds. *The Right to Belong. Citizenship and National Identity in Britain, 1930–1960*. London: I.B. Tauris, 1998.

Berghaus, Günter, ed. *Fascism and Theatre. Comparative Studies on the Aesthetics and Politics of Performance in Europe, 1925–1945*. Oxford: Berghahn, 1996.

— *Theatre and Film in Exile: German Artists in Britain, 1933–1945*. Oxford: Berg, 1989.

Bratton, Jacky. *New Readings in Theatre History*. Cambridge: Cambridge University Press, 2003.

Brenner, Hildegard. *Die Kunstpolitik des Nationalsozialismus*. Hamburg: Rowohlt, 1963.

Briggs, Asa. *Victorian Cities*. London: Penguin, 1990.

Bühnen der Stadt Bielefeld, Hg. *75 Jahre Stadttheater Bielefeld 1904–1979*. Bielefeld: Kramer, 1979.

Burleigh, Michael. *The Third Reich. A New History*. London: Pan Macmillan, 2001.

Calder, Angus. *The People's War. Britain 1939–1945*. London: Pimlico, 1999.

Chapman, James. *The British at War. Cinema, State and Propaganda, 1939–1945*. London: I.B. Tauris, 1998.

Chothia, Jean. *English Drama of the Early Modern Period, 1890–1940*. London: Longman, 1996.

Clarke, Peter. *Hope and Glory. Britain 1900–1990*. London: Allen Lane/Penguin, 1996.

Clemens, Gabriele, ed. *Kulturpolitik im besetzten Deutschland 1945–1949*. Stuttgart: Steiner, 1994.

Collins, L. J. *Theatre at War, 1914–18*. London: Macmillan, 1998.

Davies, Cecil. *The Volksbühne Movement. A History*. Amsterdam: Harwood, 2000.

Davis, Tracy C. *The Economics of the British Stage 1800–1914*. Cambridge: Cambridge University Press, 2000.

Dean, Basil. *The Theatre at War*. London: George Harrap, 1956.

Ditt, Karl. *Raum und Volkstum. Die Kulturpolitik des Provinzialverbandes Westfalen 1923–1945.* Münster: Aschendorff, 1988.

Dörnemann, Kurt. *Theater im Krieg. Bochum 1939–1944.* Bochum: Stadt Bochum, 1990.

Drewniak, Boguslaw. *Das Theater im NS-Staat. Szenarium deutscher Zeitgeschichte 1933–1945.* Düsseldorf: Droste, 1983.

Dussel, Konrad. 'Zwischen Partei und Publikum. Das Stadttheater im NS-Staat.' *Stadt und Theater.* Kirchgässner, Bernhard and Becht, Hans-Peter, eds. Stuttgart: Thorbecke, 1999: pp. 129–142.

— 'Provinztheater in der NS-Zeit.' *Vierteljahreshefte für Zeitgeschichte* 38 (1990): pp. 75–111.

— *Ein neues, ein heroisches Theater? Nationalsozialistische Theaterpolitik und ihre Auswirkungen in der Provinz.* Bonn: Bouvier, 1988.

— 'Theatergeschichte der NS-Zeit unter sozialgeschichtlichem Aspekt. Ergebnisse und Perspektiven der Forschung'. *Neue politische Literatur* 32 (1987): pp. 233–45.

Earl, John and Sell, Michael. *The Theatres Trust Guide to British Theatres 1750–1950. A Gazetteer.* London: A&C Black, 2000.

Evans, Richard J. *The Third Reich in Power 1933–1939.* London: Allen Lane, 2005.

Feinstein, Charles, ed. *York 1831–1981. 150 Years of Scientific Endeavour and Social Change.* York: Sessions, 1981.

Fieldhouse, Joseph. *Bradford.* 3rd rev. ed. Bradford: Watmoughs, 1987.

Firth, Gary. *J.B. Priestley's Bradford.* Stroud: Tempus, 2006.

Fischli, Bruno. *Die Deutschendämmerung. Zur Genealogie des völkisch-faschistischen Dramas (1897–1933).* Bonn: Bouvier, 1976.

Fitzsimmons, Linda. 'The Theatre Royal, York, in the 1840s.' *Nineteenth Century Theatre and Film* 31/1 (2004): pp. 18–25.

— 'The Theatre Royal, York.' *York History* 4 (1981): pp. 169–92.

Foulkes, Richard, ed. *Scenes from Provincial Stages. Essays in Honour of Kathleen Barker.* London: The Society for Theatre Research, 1994.

— *Repertory at the Royal. Sixty-Five Years of Theatre in Northampton 1927–92.* Northampton: Northampton Repertory Players Ltd., 1992.

Gadberry, Glen W., ed. *Theatre in the Third Reich, the Prewar Years. Essays on Theatre in Nazi Germany.* Westport: Greenwood, 1995.

Gale, Maggie and Gardner, Vivien, eds. *Women, Theatre and Performance: New Histories, New Historiographies.* Manchester: Manchester University Press, 2000.

Gardiner, Juliet. *Wartime. Britain 1939–1945*. London: Headline, 2004.

Gay, Peter. *Weimar Culture. The Outsider as Insider*. London: Penguin, 1992.

Gillett, Edward and MacMahon, Kenneth A. *A History of Hull*. 2nd ext. ed. Hull: Hull University Press, 1990.

Grange, William. *Comedy in the Weimar Republic. A Chronicle of Incongruous Laughter*. Westport: Greenwood, 1996.

Haupt, Heinz-Gerhart and Kocka, Jürgen, eds. *Geschichte und Vergleich: Ansätze und Ergebnisse international vergleichender Geschichts-schreibung*. Frankfurt: Campus, 1996.

Hayes, Nick. 'Municipal Subsidy and Tory Minimalism: Building the Nottingham Playhouse, 1942–1963.' *Midland History* 19 (1994): pp. 128–46.

Hayman, Ronald, ed. *The German Theatre. A Symposium*. London: Wolff, 1975.

Heinrich, Anselm. 'Erbauung und Unterhaltung. Das Dortmunder Stadttheater zwischen 1933 und 1945.' *Beiträge zur Geschichte Dortmunds und der Grafschaft Mark* 96/97 (2007): pp. 293–322.

— 'Shakespeare and Kolbenheyer. Regional Theatre During the Third Reich – a Case Study.' *Theatre Research International* 31.3 (2006): pp. 221–34.

— 'The Making of the Civic Theatre. The History of the Theatre Royal Between 1744 and 1945.' *York Historian* 19 (2002): pp. 74–99.

Hermand, Jost and Trommler, Frank. *Die Kultur der Weimarer Republik*. Frankfurt: Fischer, 1988.

Hewison, Robert. *Under Siege. Literary Life in London 1939–1945*. Newton Abbot: Readers Union, 1978.

Hey, David. *A History of Sheffield*. Lancaster: Carnegie, 2005.

Hildebrand, Klaus. *Das Dritte Reich*. 6th rev. ed. München: Oldenbourg, 2003.

Hillerby, Bryen. *The Lost Theatres of Sheffield*. Barnsley: Wharncliffe, 1999.

Hirt, Alexander. 'Die deutsche Truppenbetreuung im Zweiten Weltkrieg: Konzeption, Organisation und Wirkung.' *Militärgeschichtliche Zeitschrift* 59 (2000): pp. 407–34.

Hobson, Harold. *Theatre in Britain. A Personal View*. Oxford: Phaidon, 1984.

Högl, Günther, et al. *Geschichte der Stadt Dortmund*. Dortmund: Harenberg, 1994.

Holdsworth, Peter. *Domes of Delight. The History of Bradford Alhambra*. Bradford: Bradford Libraries and Information Service, 1989.

Hortmann, Wilhelm. *Shakespeare und das deutsche Theater im 20. Jahrhundert. Mit einem Kapitel über Shakespeare auf den Bühnen der DDR von Maik Hamburger*. Berlin: Henschel, 2001.

Hüpping, Stefan. *Das nationalsozialistische Theater in der Provinz – Antizipation und Anpassung am Beispiel des Deutschen Nationaltheaters Osnabrück*. Unpubl. MA thesis, University of Osnabrück, 2005.

Innes, C.D. *Modern German Drama. A Study in Form*. Cambridge: Cambridge University Press, 1979.

Jakobi, Franz-Josef, ed. *'Theater tut not'. Zum kulturellen Neubeginn in Münster 1945–1956*. Münster: Münstersche Zeitung, 1996.

— ed. *Geschichte der Stadt Münster*. 3rd ed. 3 vols. Münster: Aschendorff, 1994.

— and Sternberg, Thomas, eds. *Kulturpolitik in Münster während der national-sozialistischen Zeit. Referate und Diskussionsbeiträge der Tagung am 8. und 9. Juni 1990 im Franz-Hitze-Haus Münster*. Münster: Regensberg, 1990.

Johnson, Paul, ed. *Twentieth Century Britain. Economic, Social and Cultural Change*. London: Longman, 1994.

Joy, David and Lennon, Patricia. *Grand Memories. The Life and Times of the Grand Theatre and Opera House, Leeds*. Ilkley: Great Northern, 2006.

Kater, Michael H. *The Twisted Muse. Musicians and their Music in the Third Reich*. Oxford: Oxford University Press, 1999.

Kershaw, Baz, ed. *The Cambridge History of British Theatre. Vol. 3. Since 1895*. Cambridge: Cambridge University Press, 2004.

Kessler, Leo and Taylor, Eric. *The York Blitz 1942. The Baedeker Raid on York, April 29th, 1942*. York: n.p., 1986.

Ketelsen, Uwe-Karsten. *Ein Theater und seine Stadt. Die Geschichte des Bochumer Schauspielhauses*. Köln: SH-Verlag, 1999.

— *Literatur und Drittes Reich*. 2nd rev. ed. Schernfeld: SH-Verlag, 1994.

— *Von heroischem Sein und völkischem Tod. Zur Dramatik des Dritten Reiches*. Bonn: Bouvier, 1970.

— *Heroisches Theater. Untersuchungen zur Dramentheorie des Dritten*

Reichs. Bonn: Bouvier, 1968.

Klee, Ernst. *Das Kulturlexikon zum Dritten Reich. Wer war was vor und nach 1945*. Frankfurt: Fischer, 2007.

Kolb, Eberhard. *Die Weimarer Republik*. 4ᵗʰ rev. ed. München: Oldenbourg, 1998.

Kuhn, Ortwin, ed. *Großbritannien und Deutschland. Europäische Aspekte der politisch-kulturellen Beziehungen beider Länder in Geschichte und Gegenwart. Festschrift für John W.P. Bourke*. Munich: Goldmann, 1974.

Kuropka, Joachim, comp. *Meldungen aus Münster 1924–1944. Geheime und vertrauliche Berichte von Polizei, Gestapo, NSDAP und ihren Gliederungen, staatlicher Verwaltung, Gerichtsbarkeit und Wehrmacht über die politische und gesellschaftliche Situation in Münster*. Münster: Regensberg, 1992.

— 'Auf dem Weg in die Diktatur. Zu Politik und Gesellschaft in der Provinzial hauptstadt Münster 1929–1934.' *Westfälische Zeitschrift* 134 (1984): pp. 157–99.

— 'Die Machtergreifung der Nationalsozialisten. Dokumente, Fragen, Erläuterungen, Darstellung.' *Geschichte original – am Beispiel der Stadt Münster*. Vol. 2. Galen, Hans, Kuropka, Joachim and Lahrkamp, Helmut, eds. 4th rev. ed. Münster: Aschendorff, 1981.

Lacquer, Walter. *Weimar. A Cultural History 1918–1933*. London: Weidenfeld & Nicolson, 1974.

Landstone, Charles. *Off-Stage. A Personal Record of the First Twelve Years of State Sponsored Drama in Great Britain*. London: Elek, 1953.

Levi, Erik. *Music in the Third Reich*. London: Macmillan, 1994.

Lloyd, T. O. *Empire, Welfare State, Europe. English History 1906–1992*. 4th ed. Oxford: Oxford University Press, 1993.

London, John, ed. *Theatre under the Nazis*. Manchester: Manchester University Press, 2000.

Mander, Raymond and Mitchenson, Joe. *Musical Comedy. A Story in Pictures*. London: Davies, 1969.

Markham, John. *The Book of Hull. The Evolution of a Great Northern City*. Buckingham: Barracuda, 1989.

Marwick, Arthur. *War and Social Change in the Twentieth Century. A Comparative Study of Britain, France, Germany, Russia and the United States*. London: Macmillan, 1979.

— *The Home Front. The British and the Second World War.* London: Thames and Hudson, 1976.

McLaine, Ian. *Ministry of Morale. Home Front Morale and the Ministry of Information in World War II.* London: George Allan, 1979.

Minihan, Janet. *The Nationalization of Culture. The Development of State Subsidies to the Arts in Great Britain.* London: Hamish Hamilton, 1977.

Möller, Horst, Wirsching, Andreas and Ziegler, Walter, eds. *Nationalsozialismus in der Region.* München: Oldenbourg, 1996.

Nicholson, Steve. *The Censorship of British Drama 1900–1968.* Vols. I and II. Exeter: University of Exeter Press, 2003 and 2005.

— *British Theatre and the Red Peril. The Portrayal of Communism 1917–1945.* Exeter: University of Exeter Press, 1999.

Nuttgens, Patrick, ed. *The History of York Yorkshire. From Earliest Times to the Year 2000.* Pickering: Blackthorn, 2001.

Patterson, Michael. *The Revolution in German Theatre 1900–1933.* London: Routledge, 1981.

Peacock, Alf J. *York in the Great War: 1914–1918.* York: York Settlement Trust, 1993.

— *York 1900–1914.* York: York Settlement Trust, 1992.

Reichel, Peter. *Der schöne Schein des Dritten Reiches. Faszination und Gewalt des Faschismus.* Frankfurt: Fischer, 1994.

Reid, Gannon Franklin. *The British Press and Germany 1936–1939.* Oxford: Clarendon, 1971.

Rischbieter, Henning, ed. *Theater im 'Dritten Reich'. Theaterpolitik, Spielplanstruktur, NS-Dramatik.* Seelze: Kallmeyer, 2000.

Ritchie, James MacPherson. *German Literature Under National Socialism.* London: Croom Helm, 1983.

Ritter, Gerhard A. 'Probleme des deutsch-englischen Vergleichs'. Kocka, Jürgen, ed. *Arbeiter und Bürger im 19. Jahrhundert. Varianten ihres Verhältnisses im europäischen Vergleich.* Munich: Oldenbourg, 1986. pp. 319–24.

Rosenfeld, Sybil. *The York Theatre.* London: The Society for Theatre Research, 2001.

Rowell, George and Jackson, Anthony. *The Repertory Movement. A History of Regional Theatre in Britain.* Cambridge: Cambridge University Press, 1984.

Roy, Donald. 'Theatre Royal, Hull; or, The Vanishing Circuit.' Richards, Kenneth and Thomson, Peter, eds. *Nineteenth Century*

British Theatre. London: Methuen, 1971.

Rühle, Günther. *Theater in Deutschland 1887–1945. Seine Ereignisse – seine Menschen.* Frankfurt: Fischer, 2007.

— *Theater für die Republik im Spiegel der Kritik. 1917–1933.* 2 vols. Berlin: Henschel, 1988.

— ed. *Zeit und Theater.* 6 vols. Frankfurt: Ullstein, 1973–1980.

Ruppelt, Georg. *Schiller im nationalsozialistischen Deutschland. Der Versuch einer Gleichschaltung.* Stuttgart: Metzler, 1979.

Sarkowicz, Hans, ed. *Hitlers Künstler. Die Kultur im Dienst des Nationalsozialismus.* Frankfurt: Insel, 2004.

Schauspielhaus und Stadtarchiv Bochum, eds. *Saladin Schmitt der Theatergründer. Zum 100. Geburtstag 18. September 1983. Dokumentation zur Ausstellung.* Bochum: n.p., 1983.

Schmidt, Christoph. *Nationalsozialistische Kulturpolitik im Gau Westfalen-Nord. Regionale Strukturen und lokale Milieus (1933–1945).* Paderborn: Schöningh, 2006.

Schoeps, Karl-Heinz. *Literature and Film in the Third Reich.* Transl. Dell'Orto, Kathleen M. Woodbridge: Camden House, 2004.

Schrage, Hermann Dieter. 'Saladin Schmitt am Stadttheater Bochum (1919–1949).' Diss., University of Vienna, 1967.

Schulze, Hagen. Weimar. *Deutschland 1917–1933.* Berlin: Siedler, 1994.

Schwarz, Angela. *Die Reise ins Dritte Reich. Britische Augenzeugenberichte im nationalsozialistischen Deutschland (1933–1939).* Göttingen: Vandenhoeck & Ruprecht, 1993.

Seed, T. Alec. *The Sheffield Repertory Theatre. A History.* Sheffield: Sheffield Repertory Company, 1959.

Sheffield Theatre History Research Group, ed. *Georgian Theatre in Sheffield.* Sheffield: Pickard, 2003.

Shellard, Dominic. *Harold Hobson: Witness and Judge. The Theatre Criticism of Harold Hobson.* Keele: Keele University Press, 1995.

Smart, Nick. *The National Government, 1931–40.* London: Macmillan, 1999.

Sösemann, Bernd, ed. *Der Nationalsozialismus und die deutsche Gesellschaft. Einführung und Überblick.* Darmstadt: Wissenschaftliche Buchgesellschaft, 2002.

Stacpoole, Alberic, ed. *The Noble City of York.* York: Cerialis, 1972.

Städtische Bühnen Bielefeld, ed. *Theaterstadt Bielefeld. Bild und Bericht.* Darmstadt: Mykenae Verlag, 1958.

Städtische Bühnen Bielefeld. *50 Jahre Stadttheater Bielefeld.* Bielefeld: Sievert & Sieveking, 1954. *100 Jahre Stadttheater Bielefeld.* Ravensberger Blätter. Organ des Historischen Vereins für die Grafschaft Ravensberg e.V. Heft 1, 2004.

Steinweis, Alan E. *Art, Ideology and Economics in Nazi Germany. The Reich Chambers of Music, Theater and the Visual Arts.* Chapel Hill: University of North Carolina Press, 1993.

Strobl, Gerwin. 'Staging the Nazi Assault on Reason: Hanns Johst's Schlageter and the "Theatre of Inner Experience".' *New Theatre Quarterly* 21 (2005): pp. 307–16.

— *The Germanic Isle.* Cambridge: Cambridge University Press, 2000.

— 'The Bard of Eugenics: Shakespeare and Racial Activism in the Third Reich.' *Journal of Contemporary History* 34 (1999): pp. 323–36.

Taylor, A.J.P. *English History 1914–1945.* Rev. ed. Oxford: Oxford University Press, 1987.

Taylor, Coral. *Right Royal. Wakefield Theatre 1776–1994.* Wakefield: Wakefield Historical Publications, 1995.

Taylor, Eric. *Showbiz Goes to War.* London: Hale, 1992.

Taylor, Philip M., ed. *Britain and the Cinema in the Second World War.* London: Macmillan, 1988.

Thamer, Hans-Ulrich. *Verführung und Gewalt. Deutschland 1933–1945.* Berlin: Siedler, 1994.

Theater Bielefeld, ed. *100 Jahre Theater Bielefeld.* Bielefeld: Kerber, 2004.

Theater Dortmund, ed. *100 Jahre Theater Dortmund:* Harenberg, 2004.

Thornton, David. *Leeds. The Story of a City.* Ayr: Fort, 2002.

Tillott, P.M., ed. *A History of Yorkshire. The City of York.* Oxford: Oxford University Press, 1961.

Trewin, J.C. *The Birmingham Repertory Theatre 1913–1963.* London: Barrie and Rockliff, 1963.

Vernekohl, Wilhelm, ed. *Das neue Theater in Münster. Festschrift zur Eröffnung des Hauses.* Münster: Werbe-und Verkehrsamt, 1956.

— ed. *Die niederdeutsche Bühne am Theater der Stadt Münster.* Münster: Westfälische Vereinsdruckerei, 1965.

Vogelsang, Reinhard. *Geschichte der Stadt Bielefeld.* 3 vols. Bielefeld: Gieselmann, 1988–2005.

Wardetzky, Jutta. *Theaterpolitik im faschistischen Deutschland. Studien und Dokumente.* Berlin (East): Henschel, 1983.

Wehler, Hans Ulrich. *Deutsche Gesellschaftsgeschichte. Dritter Band. Von der „Deutschen Doppelrevolution" bis zum Beginn des Ersten Weltkrieges 1849–1914.* München: Beck, 1995.

— *Deutsche Gesellschaftsgeschichte. Vierter Band. Vom Beginn des Ersten Weltkriegs bis zur Gründung der beiden deutschen Staaten 1914–1949.* München: Beck, 2003.

Weingärtner, Jörn. *The Arts as a Weapon of War. Britain and the Shaping of National Morale in the Second World War.* London: I.B. Tauris, 2006.

Wilkinson, Ronald. *The Grand Theatre and Opera House Leeds 1878–1978. The First Hundred Years.* Leeds: n.p., 1977.

Wilson, Van, comp. *York Voices.* Stroud: Tempus, 1999.

Wistrich, Robert. *Weekend in Munich. Art, Propaganda and Terror in the Third Reich.* London: Pavilion, 1995.

Wolf, Tana. *York Theatre Royal. 1744–1994: 250 Years at the Heart of York.* York: Theatre Royal, 1994.

Wulf, Joseph. *Theater und Film im Dritten Reich. Eine Dokumentation.* Frankfurt: Ullstein, 1983.

York Oral History Project. *Through the Storm: York Memories of the Second World War 1939–1945.* York: York Oral History Project, 1993.

— *York Memories of Stage and Screen. Personal Accounts of York's Theatres and Cinemas 1900–1960.* York: York Oral History Project, 1988.

Yorkshire Observer, ed. *Bradford 1847–1947. The Centenary Book of Bradford.* Bradford: Yorkshire Observer, n.d. [1947].

CONTEMPORARY PERIODICALS, JOURNALS AND NEWSPAPERS

Amateur Theatre
Bausteine zum deutschen Nationaltheater
CEMA Bulletin
Das Innere Reich
Das schöne Münster
Deutsche Dramaturgie
Deutsches Bühnenjahrbuch
Die Deutsche Bühne
Die Neue Literatur
Dortmunder Zeitung

Hull Daily Mail
Leeds Mercury
Malton Gazette
Münsterischer Anzeiger
Münstersche Wochenschau
Münstersche Zeitung
Nationalzeitung
North Leeds News
Play Pictorial
Shakespeare-Jahrbuch
The News
The Stage
The Telegraph and Argus (Bradford)
Theatre Arts
Theatre World
Theatrecraft
Theater-Tageblatt
Völkischer Beobachter
Volkswille
Westfälische Landeszeitung
Westfälische Nachrichten
Westfälische Neueste Nachrichten
Westfälische Zeitung
Westfälischer Kurier
Westfälisches Tageblatt
Yorkshire Evening News
Yorkshire Evening Press
Yorkshire Gazette
Yorkshire Herald
Yorkshire Observer
York Star

Index